My Friend, Ellie,
Fear not!
Don't let fear rule your life.
There's victory over fear.

Moreta

Morēta
my story

MORĒTA REID CHAPIN FOSNER

Copyright © 2008 Good Catch Publishing, Beaverton, OR.

All rights reserved. Written permission must be secured from the publisher to use or reproduce any part of this book, except for brief quotations in critical reviews or articles.

All Bible verses used in this book were taken from the King James Version.

The cover photo of Moreta Fosner was taken when she was 14 years old.

Published in Beaverton, Oregon, by Good Catch Publishing.
www.goodcatchpublishing.com
V1.1

Printed in the United States of America

TABLE OF CONTENTS

CHAPTER 1	11
CHAPTER 2	16
CHAPTER 3	21
CHAPTER 4	27
CHAPTER 5	37
CHAPTER 6	48
CHAPTER 7	58
CHAPTER 8	69
CHAPTER 9	78
CHAPTER 10	90
CHAPTER 11	101
CHAPTER 12	125
CHAPTER 13	136
CHAPTER 14	178
CHAPTER 15	190
CHAPTER 16	209
CHAPTER 17	232
CHAPTER 18	260

This

book is

dedicated to

my dear children

my grand children

all my great grand children

and

every one to follow

CHAPTER 1

In the Beginning

Did people in the 1800s ever laugh — or even smile? Not according to the pictures I've seen. Grandpa Dolph Reid lived with us for a while when I was 14. I don't remember ever seeing him smile. I never saw my Grandma Reid. She died many years before, and Dolph never remarried. My dad, Johnie (John or J.T.), came into this world in 1882. There were four boys and one girl. We enjoyed visiting with each of the four boys and their wives and families. There was lots of laughter in those homes. We all remember one son's wife, Aunt Lizzie. She made fried red potatoes — in lard — the best potatoes you ever ate. She was short and "not thin." Those 'taters will do it to you every time.

My mother, Cuba (everyone called her Cuby), found her way into this family in 1891. Her parents, Cicero and Lou Isham, were nice people, but I can't recall them ever smiling. Grandpa was from a family of nine boys and three girls. He was tall, stately and a businessman in the town. He still had all his teeth, his full head of hair, no glasses and could bend over and touch his toes till the time of his death in his 90s. His daddy (my great-grandpa) was a circuit-riding preacher — on a mule. I have a picture of my great-grandma with a corncob pipe in her mouth. In our denomination today, many of our wives go with their husbands and are a big part of their ministry. Do you suppose Greatie-Grandma rode with her circuit-riding preacher on the back of the mule with her corncob pipe?

Grandma Isham was tiny and outlived her husband by several years. I never saw much activity or much exuberance in her life. They had five girls and one boy. My mother, Cuba, was the youngest. Aunt Bertha and Uncle Harvey were the only ones of Mama's family that we kids couldn't wait to see when we went to visit the grandparents on special occasions. Their children were our age, and we could play table games and eat goodies with them.

My dad, Johnie Reid, and Cuba Isham were married August 22, 1909. The word "honeymoon" had not yet been invented. The

MORETA: MY STORY

day after they were married, Mama's brother, Uncle Hillary, took her new husband away for the whole day. Mother didn't even know where they were. There were no phones in those days, either, and she spent a miserable "day after" alone. They may have been off gambling. My dad was addicted until the Lord delivered him some years later. Uncle got the blame, and he was not one of Mama's favorite people. However, she named her first son after him (Orion Austin Hillary Reid), so she must have had a forgiving heart.

All the Reid boys (and this girl, too) have had a love for cars, but when our parents were born, there was not a car to be seen. All they knew — and all their courting days — were with the horse and buggy. Automobiles were so rare in the United States by 1896, the Barnum and Bailey circus displayed an automobile as its main oddity. I'm sure as soon as cars became available, my dad was dreaming big.

My sister, Lorene, was born nearly 10 months after they were married, then my brother, Orion, came along about six years later on March 9, 1916. The third child, Melbra, made his appearance on November 12, 1917. Then I finally got my turn.

The place had been warm and tight but expanding when I first got my start. (I'm sure you realize that I don't remember that part.) The more I grew, the noisier it got. And I kicked real hard about it a lot. I don't think my folks realized that I was listening to them. They talked about me every day and night. It sounded as if they liked me alright, and they hadn't even seen me.

That place became uncomfortable, and I left it on February 20, 1922. I first saw the light of day in Harjo, Oklahoma, in Pottawatomie County, near Shawnee, on a Sunday morning. My dad delivered me just as the midwife, Ruth Jennings, walked in. She and my mother were dear friends. Mama had delivered many babies, too.

There were three other children in the family, but none of them had awakened when I was born and knew nothing of my arrival until they were called for breakfast shortly after.

Alma Lorene, Orion Austin Hillary, Melbra John, then me, Nellie Moreta. Earl Admiral weighed in at 11 pounds seven years later. I always thought he was great — well, nearly always. Lorene was 12 when I was born. Orion and Melbra were only a year and a half apart and became typical loving, fighting, quarreling, playing, helping, hindering, noisy, hungry brothers as young kids.

CHAPTER 1

However, Papa and Mama knew how to calm them down when they got too rowdy. Both parents practiced raising children the Bible way: "Train up a child in the way they should go." And when we got older, we never departed from the right way.

When I was 3 or 4 years of age, Papa built a motor home. The six of us traveled to New Mexico, where we lived in a logging camp. Papa became foreman of a group of Mexican men in the primitive work of falling trees, moving logs about and all that must have taken place in those woods. Having been married to a logger with more modern equipment, powerful log trucks and "donkeys" and "cats" (that didn't mean donkeys or cats), I can't imagine what kind of logging operations my dad was foreman over in those very early years of the 1920s. It must have been awfully small logs and not these huge trees we have here in Oregon that descend from the mountaintops to the valley in extremely treacherous paths.

My mother had heard of Aimee Semple McPherson and Los Angeles Temple, where great things were happening — miracles, people leaving sickbeds, walking out of wheelchairs, leaving crutches and large crowds. Mama felt a call to preach and wanted to go to Bible school there in Los Angeles Temple. I guess they had been working their way through by way of New Mexico and the logging camp.

When I was 4 or 5 years old, we were in Los Angeles. Papa had found work. The boys, Orion and Melbra, were in school. They could tell scary stories of big bullies and city roughnecks in the larger schools. My brothers were both big and stuck together. They kept themselves alive, but I think I remember times they outran the mean rascals. Mama was in Bible school. My big sweet, wonderful sister, Lorene, (probably 16 years old at that time) took good care of me.

From Los Angeles, we went back to my mother's hometown of Blair, Oklahoma, where her parents, Cicero and Lou (Louisiana) Isham, lived. Also, four sisters and one brother resided in the same area. I'm sure Mama's prayer was to see her family saved and ready to meet God. My daddy could do anything. In Blair, he began building two houses to sell.

Another preacher lady, Ethel Music, and Mama started a tent revival. It was well attended, and there were many healings, miracles and lives changed in that small town. Lots of people in those early days of the 20s hated the old-fashioned Pentecostal services and would throw rocks, rotten eggs and tomatoes at the meetings. They would cut the tent ropes and do lots of things to run you out of town. However, the more bad things they did, it seemed a greater number of people came to see what was going on. New folk would be saved, healed and changed until the whole countryside knew about it. The tent revival kept going until my parents rented a small storefront building right in the middle of Main Street. They scrubbed, cleaned, painted and decorated, and I'm sure they and the new converts had a Jericho march and sanctified the place. Blair had its first Assembly of God church. I remember my folks talking of how so many of the townsfolk hated the church and wished it would blow away. Well, it did!

The Cyclone

As a small child of 5 or 6 years old, we were living in a rented house with a nice yard and big trees all around. My parents and my sister had gone to town a few blocks away, perhaps for groceries, or maybe to tidy up the church, or even to pray.

My two brothers and I were at home alone when the winds hit. Just then, my folks were driving into the driveway, and the two boys ran out of the house to meet them. As I tried to follow them, the door slammed shut. The suction held it, and I couldn't get it open. Finally, when the vacuum was released and I was able to get out, I ran out and I didn't yell. I didn't scream. But in my life-long learned Southern drawl, I hollered, "Y'all better come on in here, all the winder-lights is a breakin' out."

As I ran out, the winds were still raging. Boards, sheetrock, metal roofing, windows and parts of buildings were flying everywhere. My dad was yelling at my older brother to "Come back here." He was so scared and was running down the road with all those things flying around him. We were finally all inside the house safely. Many of the big shade trees around our place were uprooted, with their root systems nearly as tall as the house. Many homes were totally destroyed. I have a picture of me sitting on top of a roof only. The roof was on the ground, every shingle stripped off.

My parents thought, *The Lord took our little storefront church and wiped out the whole town.* Not one trace of the piano, chairs, pulpit or nothing was ever found but one little part of a

CHAPTER 1

songbook. However, Papa had put insurance on the place, and there was enough pay off to build a very nice church in a great location. Papa built the church and Mama pastored it.

My mother was a powerhouse of a preacher. She was fiery and anointed. She preached the Word, and she could make you believe it. I still remember some of her sermons, especially this one: "Be sure, your sins will find you out." A young fellow had broken into the new church and stole the Sunday morning offering. After the Sunday night preaching when she had held the thief over hell, he brought the money back, confessed and repented.

Another of her sermons that I remember was: "God deals with us first in love, then in mercy, then in judgment. Turn to Him when He first deals in love. If you wait until He has to deal with you in judgment, life gets too rough. Don't wait. *Today is the day of salvation.*"

CHAPTER 2

A Big Brother

When I was 6 or 7 years old, we moved to a small town north of Blair called Lonewolf, Oklahoma. There, 11-pound Earl Admiral was born. Again, Papa built two new houses. We lived in one while he built the other. This must have been where we lived when this next story happened, because we had neighbors across the street. In the many moves we made later, we had no close neighbors across the street.

Hot Biscuits, Gravy and Prayer

Every morning, we had hot biscuits and gravy for breakfast. We all got up early and at the same time. We ate together, and we prayed together. Papa would build a hot fire in the big black kitchen stove to get the oven as hot as it could be made, at least to 450 degrees. There was no thermometer, but it had to be hot enough so the biscuits would cook just right.

When Mama put the biscuits in the oven, we all knelt and went to prayer. All praying vocally, together. We prayed until the biscuits were done. Mama always knelt by the oven. When she thought the biscuits should be about ready, she would open the oven door and peek in. If the biscuits were not quite brown enough, we prayed on.

We always had biscuits and gravy, plus sausage, or ham, or bacon, or steak, or fish and eggs, plus plenty of milk to drink and homemade jams or jellies. I don't think we had heard of peanut butter. But we had lots of fresh churned butter to go on those wonderful hot biscuits.

My two older brothers were eating so much that Mama told them one morning, "If you boys don't quit eating so much, I'll have to start making gravy in a washtub." A few days later, she sent Melbra across the street to the neighbor to borrow her washtub.

She asked, "What's your mother gonna do today?"

He drawled, "Oh, she's gonna make some gravy."

CHAPTER 2

The neighbor had to "help" him carry the tub home to see what was happening.

That same brother, Melbra, (we called him "Melbry," some called him "Bubby") many years later, after he had grown kids of his own and was living in Pueblo, Colorado, came to Bend, Oregon, to visit Mama and Papa. Mama's milk-white gravy would always thicken and jell when it got cold. I stepped into the kitchen in the middle of the afternoon, and Melbra was sitting at the counter with a bowl of cold gravy from the refrigerator. He was slicing it and eating it on crackers. I asked, "What in this wide world are you doing?"

He looked up with a contented grin and said, "Ummm, that's gooood!" He still liked his gravy!

There was no electricity or refrigeration in those earlier days, so, of course, everything was always fresh. We churned our own butter, and I think I was the main churning person. The churn was about a 2-gallon narrow crock container with a wooden lid and a hole in the middle of the lid with a long broomstick that held a wooden paddle on the bottom of the stick. You methodically pushed up and down with the stick until the cream turned to butter. It was a long, tiring ordeal. I'm sure we took turns at it until the butter was made.

During those young years, I didn't know we were poor. I do remember once when there was very little money (I found out later), we had water biscuits and water gravy. The biscuits were dark brown, quite flat and hard. The gravy was real pale, but Mama put lots of salt and black pepper in it, and I loved it! I still like salty, crispy foods, chips and dips, burritos and such things, plus brown, crusty biscuits. I can never make biscuits and gravy as well as my mother did. I still love them, though, and if they weren't so unhealthy and fattening, I'd have hot biscuits and gravy every morning.

We Moved to the Country

When I was 7, we moved to a small farm a few miles west of Tribbey, Oklahoma, into a very little house for the seven of us. The house was really old, with wide cracks in the walls and floor.

My mother could take a shack and make a little mansion of it — well, sorta. We began by stripping all the many years of old

MORETA: MY STORY

newspapers off the walls. My family would take time to read the papers and laugh at the difference in the writings of the 1800s and now (1920s), the more modern times.

Papa bought a "new" product for the walls and ceilings. It was a wide felt-like underlayment of heavy paper that helped as insulation, and the wallpaper could adhere to it. It was near impossible to make the paper stick to those old, rough bare walls. He put boards on the two "sawhorses" (those were a framework that held the boards) to stand on so they could reach the ceiling. We would brush wallpaper paste on the ceiling boards and the wide felt paper, then hold the gooey stuff to the ceiling until it stuck. Once, they had to hold it so long the moisture came through the paper and it came apart, draping over their heads and shoulders. They stood there, laughing, with the soggy stuff in their hair, face, clothes and on the floor. I was too young to have a camera to capture the fun and frustration, but they never gave up. The ceiling and walls were finished with felt and pretty wallpaper.

The old rugs were ripped out, cracks in the floor fixed and new floor coverings put in to keep out the cold. During the cold, cold winter, we would wrap the old "sad iron" in heavy paper and towels or strips of blankets to put in the bed to keep us warm at night. The old-fashioned irons were a heavy, solid flatiron pointed at both ends (that's what the dictionary says.) They were about eight inches long. You put the bottom part of the iron on the cook stove until it got hot, then there was a top covering of metal with a handle that you used to lift it off the stove and do the ironing until the iron got too cold to do its work. I'm sure the reason it was called the "sad iron" was because it made you sad to have to use it so long. This type of iron was what I had to use to do the ironing.

In the summertime, Mama and Papa would put a bed under a tree and sleep out there at night. I think the two brothers slept out there, too. My sister, Lorene, the baby, and I slept in the house. One night, as the rest of the family was in bed, Lorene and I were eating parched field corn. My dad called out, "Sis, go chase the cows out of the corn patch." It wasn't the cows he heard, it was us. I think parched corn is called "corn nuts" now, and I still like them.

Tribbey was where I started first grade. I loved school, especially spelling and recess. I played first base with the young boys. No team, we just played ball. If there was a softball or hardball in

CHAPTER 2

those days, I didn't know about it.

Playing jacks was my game. Onesies, twosies, pigs in the pen, eggs in the basket, upsies, downsies, Flying Dutchman. Then we'd play doubles of each one. If you touched a jack you weren't reaching for, you were out, and the next player took over.

In the little town of Tribbey, there was a service station, the school and a general store, which was about a block from the school. Occasionally, I would take a penny to the store and buy a piece of candy, gum or something. One night after school while we were eating supper, my brother said, "Today I went to the store, and Moreta was in line behind a big fat lady. The owner, Mr. Stufflebean, saw Moreta and asked if he could help her. She said, 'When you get through with her, I wanna sucker.'"

Of course, I was quick to say, "I did not." There was always lots of teasing and laughter at our house.

That Dirty Old Man

There were a couple of rolling hills, maybe a half mile or less from the bus stop to our house that I had to walk after school at times. I wish my older brothers were alive so I could ask why I walked those few days by myself. I don't remember walking to the bus, but I remember walking from the bus.

When I left the school bus to walk home alone, I had to cross over a small bridge. An old man who lived not too far away was under the bridge and called out, "Come down here, I want to show you a little bird." I knew the old man and his family well, and as a trusting 7 year old, I went down.

He was sitting on a rock, or stump, pointing up to a crack in the bridge. He told me that I'd have to sit on his knee to see it. As I sat down, he took my hand and placed it where he had planned from the beginning. I let go, jerked away and was up the bank of that creek, running all the way home. He never tried to follow me, and I didn't look back.

Actually, he never touched me in any private place. He just violated my hand. He never walked past our house, but probably walked down the dry creek bed to another trail through the woods. He knew every inch of the countryside. That man was a wicked old coot who had his whiskey-still, and I heard that he would get the older girls drunk.

MORETA: MY STORY

Of course, I never told anyone about this. I never told it until a couple of years ago, when I told it to my two brothers and family. This all happened before I got my "behind the barn" sex education. Really, it wasn't so much behind the barn, but in the back of the school bus as we congregated to tell dirty jokes. I still remember some of those jokes but have never told any of them since I reached the age of accountability. And don't ask!

Parents, teach your girls and boys to come to you with any such problem so they won't have to go through anything like this. You can know that the very youngest are being exposed to such treatment.

CHAPTER 3

We Moved Up the Road Apiece

We weren't in the tiny house long. We moved to a larger, nicer place on the rock, just across a small creek and up a little hill. It had large catalpa trees with extra big leaves and clusters of fragrant white flowers. It was on the edge of the woods. Next to the house there was a well drilled through the rock, and we didn't have to draw water from a cistern with a bucket on a rope anymore. I think they called the modern thing a "pitcher pump." Nice. We still had to walk on a path from the other side of the house to the privy. It was a two-holer with a Sears catalog nearby.

The Age of Accountability

My mother and sister would talk quietly, and when I came to listen, they'd stop talking. I was sure they were talking about "the birds and the bees." And, with all my recently acquired worldly wisdom, I would ask questions. Mama would tell me very little. I couldn't break into their friendly chitchats.

When I asked, "What is the age of accountability?" I couldn't pin her down to a definite age. Though day after day, I tried.

She explained, "With some children, it could be at one age and an earlier or later age with others."

Knowing that I must be getting to a dangerous age — and I sure didn't want to go to hell — I asked, "Could that age be 10 years old?"

She obliged with, "Well, yes, it could be at 10 years."

You can guess — I was a real Pharisee!

Now I knew how far I could go. I was a sinful little country girl who had tried just about everything. And soon, I would be 10.

In those days, I'd watch the smoking men "roll their own." So, I would cut the right size paper out of the Sears catalog from the privy. I'd use dried cotton leaves, crush them and roll my own. That stuff sure didn't burn good and tasted awful. One day, though, I found the stub of a "cool brand" cigarette. I took it behind the barn and wow! That was different. But that was the end of my smoking. I'd had enough. (Probably, it was just too close to the age of accountability.)

Hearing of sheep shaurel wine (However, I see in the dictionary that it's called "sheep laurel" and it's poisonous to sheep and other animals.), I got a pint jar and filled it with water and green leaves (they looked like clover and grew wild). I sealed the jar and buried it at the base of an apple tree for a few weeks. When I went out to check my wine, someone had dug around the tree, and my jar was broken — no wine! I reckon I was spared being poisoned. I never did taste anyone's wine or liquors, and I still haven't.

Oh and I was a thief. I took another little girl's big, long, yellow pencil with the eraser on the end. But perhaps the next day or so, my mother, though not knowing about it, prayed me over hell, and I decided I didn't want that pencil and took it back. However, I had emphatically told the teacher that I did not take the pencil. Man — *the way of the transgressor is hard!* That was so embarrassing having to admit the truth to the teacher.

I had a beautiful little friend, Roberta. She lived further back in the hills than I did. There was a trail that wound over the hill and through the woods from my house to hers. We spent lots of time together. We rode the same school bus and had many days and nights at each other's house. We shared our greatest secrets and things that never happened. I hope she has forgotten some of those things. I remember telling her that I had had a baby and that brown line from my belly button on down was the place the doctor took the baby out and sewed me up. I don't think I ever had to answer about where the baby could be now. Do you suppose she knew that I was lying? She was pretty worldly wise.

Roberta's older sister, Joyce, and my cousin, June, two beautiful girls (a blonde and a redhead) with figures to match, were very worldly minded. They would hitchhike to Oklahoma City (about 35 miles away) to wrestling matches and flirt with the wrestlers. Then the young fellows would drive out to the country to see the girls.

Roberta's mother, Gladys, was so sweet and pretty. Her stepdad, Dean, I'm sure was a drunkard and not so desirable to be around. I heard that he kept the moonshine whiskey-stills in business. I never knew of him being abusive to the girls, but I didn't go around their place much unless he was gone. He and Gladys would

CHAPTER 3

go to Oklahoma City often for two or three days at a time. I learned that they had lived in Oklahoma City before moving to the country. That's why the girls were so knowledgeable about the city. And that's why I couldn't remember Roberta walking from the school bus with me. She was perhaps in the third grade when they moved there.

It was about that time that my brother, Orion, though only 15 or 16, began driving the school bus. At the end of the route, he parked the bus at our house. Roberta and other kids in those hills had to walk to our place to ride the bus.

This one night when her parents were gone, I spent the night with Roberta. The boys from the city that the girls had flirted with came to see them. Joyce and June had rolled back the rugs and made all the arrangements for an exciting night. I think it was until near daylight. I was 9 years old. Roberta was about my age.

The Victrola (I think that's what it was called) had a crank or handle on it that had to be turned constantly so the records could play the dance music. That became my job at first, but seeing all the dancing that looked so fun, my young friend had to take turns with me at turning the handle. I learned to waltz, two-step and foxtrot. There was a full moon outside, and between times, we would go out to the old hen house beside the house (it had been cleaned and wasn't used for chickens anymore) and lay on the straw with the different cute guys. The door was open, and we'd watch the moon through the cracks in the wall. Each of the fellows treated me with the greatest respect. There was no hanky-panky. They weren't interested in those two little girls. I don't know what they did with the older beauties. There was no smoking, drinking, foul language or anything that I saw to be bad. Just all that great dancing. If my brothers or parents ever heard about all my activities, I never knew about it.

About this time, during morning prayer, I decided I was just going to backslide, so I didn't pray. Sinning was just too much fun. I'm guessing that my mother noticed and dangled me over "Hades" in her prayer. Then our big, white, furry cat came out from under the bed and brushed against me and scared me to pieces. I repented real fast. *The fear of the Lord is the beginning of wisdom.* I had been taught a healthy fear and wasn't about to take any chances, but you know what? When I hit that "age of accountability," my sinfulness stopped. No more experimentations. No

MORETA: MY STORY

more "wine, women and song." All I kept were the songs, but the words changed. I've written lots of good songs.

Back to Normal Living for a 10 Year Old

We had a big garden down by the creek and would have to carry buckets of water from the small stream of water to the large tomato patch. We picked the little striped-back potato bugs off the potato vines. When the fruits were ready to be harvested, they were picked, then carried up the little hill to the house, and hundreds of jars of fruit and vegetables were canned for the winter.

There were fruit trees in the backyard. We canned some of the peaches, apples and plums. Others we put on the tin roof of the barn to dry. My sister got married while we lived on the rock, and I inherited all her work. She was 22; I was 10.

There were wild persimmon trees, wild pecan trees and poke-salad greens along the creek banks to harvest and preserve. (The wild poke-salad greens were similar to spinach or Swiss chard.) We raised cows, hogs, chickens, a few turkeys and horses to pull the plow and wagon. Papa and the two boys did all the farming, milking and fence building. Mama and I did most of the gardening, canning, housework, sewing and helping out in other areas when needed. My little 3- or 4-year-old brother got by easier, though I'm sure my mother could find things for him to do. She was good at that with any age.

Sorghum Molasses

Down below the house on the north side of the road, we raised sorghum cane. It grew taller than your head. Papa built a sorghum mill on the other side of the creek, and we made sorghum molasses to sell. Each of us had our particular job to do.

The boys would bring huge loads of the cane in from the field to the grinder that gets the juice out. There was a long, sturdy pole attached to the grinder that had two big metal rollers (like the wringers on the washing machine that we put the clothes through to wring the water out). I was the one who fed the long canes into the rollers. A horse was hitched to the long pole (about 10 feet long) and went around in circles to cause the rollers to take the fluid out of the cane and into the large stainless steel container.

CHAPTER 3

This container, the cooker, was about 15 feet long and maybe 4 feet wide, with four or five center dividers from top to bottom. There were long poles with a paddle-like board on the end that were used to push the cane liquid from one compartment to the next. By the time it had gotten to the last compartment, it was wonderful, clear sorghum and went into new gallon buckets to be sold.

Underneath this large cooking utensil was the fire. Lots of long poles and small tree limbs were used to keep the fire going at the right heat. Our sorghum was never black, never burnt, not bitter and not overcooked. My dear dad built the whole sorghum mill. And I think you can see that every available hand was used, and we worked together. The gallons of molasses were stacked on the flat-bed truck, taken to market and sold for $1 per gallon. Now, when I can find it, I buy it in a pint jar and pay $5.50 for each pint. That's $44 a gallon! Plus, it's difficult to find good, clear sorghum.

I'm sure we made sorghum only that one summer. It was too much work and not enough hands, but there had been a big demand for the Reid sorghum molasses.

My two brothers, after eating their biscuits and gravy, would sop their plates clean. Then they'd put a large dob of butter on their plate and a generous amount of the sorghum. They'd take their knife and stir it vigorously until the mixture was white. The whole table shook with their stirring. With a big bite of that mix on a crispy hot biscuit, they would grin and drawl, "Ummm, that's gooood."

I Was an Old Cotton Picker

For several years, we would go to West Texas in the fall and winter to live in the cotton shacks with a mixture of blacks and whites. We picked cotton from daylight to dark. Often, we weighed up by flashlight.

My two brothers played a guitar and a mandolin. After supper, we would sit out in front of our shack, and the boys would play their instruments. Sometimes others would bring their music and play, too. Families came to enjoy those times. Two or three young black boys would dance a jig and seemed to be loose jointed. We loved it and looked forward to it again and again. It was a bright spot in that "cotton-pickin'" place. We didn't know we weren't supposed to like those great black people.

MORETA: MY STORY

My mother picked right along with the rest of us. When I was too small to pull a sack, I would put little piles of cotton on the ground for her to place in her sack. But as soon as I was strong enough to pull my own canvas bag and fill it with cotton, then throw it over my shoulder and carry it down those long rows to the scales to be weighed, I was on my own and making (big) money!

One morning, as we picked, we met four large black ladies picking toward us. My mother asked, "Do you ladies love Jesus today?"

One replied, "Yes, ma'am, I does."

Another said, "Oh, yes, I does."

The next one responded, "Yes, I really does."

The fourth lady drawled with vibrancy, "Oh, yes, we all does."

We loved those sweet people.

As I grew stronger, my cotton sacks grew longer and heavier but never as long and heavy as my dad's and brothers' were. They could carry up to 100 pounds (I think). It was hard, backbreaking work. The worst cuss word I ever thought or ever used was "cotton pickin'"!

Our parents always let us keep all the money we earned, but they helped us make right choices and taught us to spend wisely. I always feel bad when I hear of some parents who take the money their children earn. They miss a great opportunity to encourage their child to work and to spend money with care. We bought our own clothes and would have enough money to buy Christmas gifts — after we paid our 10 percent tithe.

I earned my first nickel in the cotton patch and learned to manage it early. I still enjoy finding ways to save. I know some of my siblings have given double tithe, plus many other offerings. Most of us have been blessed with great abundance. All of us and our children are serving God. What a wonderful payoff. Most of my kids and grandkids are in ministry, preaching, teaching or in music.

CHAPTER 4

Revival Meetings

There were times we were in revival meetings every night. My mother was the preacher. She had her own quartet and musicians right with her. The services would be in brush arbors, schoolhouses or old churches. Papa hooked the team of horses to the flatbed wagon, and we went sometimes for several miles through the country roads, picking up families along the way. When the wagon was filled with adults and smaller children, the older kids ran alongside laughing and teasing. We sang, prayed and blessed each other as we happily went along. In later years, we went on the flatbed truck.

The church would fill with great country folk. Many men who were moonshiners and unsaved had no use for God but liked the Christians. They wouldn't come inside but didn't want to miss the show, so they hung close around within hearing distance, in the shadows or near an open window. They heard the gospel night after night. Over a period of time, many of them turned to God and what a thrill to see their changed lives. There were many healings, salvations, miracles and testimonies of deliverance from sin and habits.

Most of those times were in the hot summer. My two brothers and my dad always wore white starched shirts when they sang. Of course, they had to have a clean shirt every night. There were no Saturday or Monday nights off. It was every night and at times, for several weeks. Somebody had to iron those shirts, and by the time I was 11 and 12, that somebody was me.

Each Tuesday morning was ironing day. We made homemade starch for the shirts. They were dried, then sprinkled and kept overnight to dampen evenly. Each week there were no less than 21 to 23 shirts. I timed myself, experimenting until I found the best and fastest way with less wrinkles.

I started with the back first, then across the shoulder, collar, sleeves and fronts last. We starched only the shoulder part, collar, cuffs and one front. They were nice and stiff. Mama made sure we

MORETA: MY STORY

didn't starch the tails of the shirt — didn't want to scratch the boys' tender behinds.

Monday Was Always Wash Day

Monday was a day to remember. Papa and the boys would build a hot fire around the big black boiler pot outside, carry the several gallons of water to fill the pot and then get the three big tubs set side by side. Two of the tubs were filled with cold water, and one was filled with hot water.

When all was ready, the white clothes were first with the old rub board (washboard) and each article scrubbed by hand, one by one. Special care was taken with the white shirts — then into the first tub of rinse water and another tub of rinse with the bluing in it.

Each of us took our turn. The boys always scrubbed their overalls. Most of the overalls were hung on the fence to dry. The clotheslines were filled with the more delicate things.

We Moved From the Rock

When I was 11, we moved a couple of miles away. It was too far for me to walk through the trails in the woods to my past way of life. I still rode the bus to the same school. My older brother, Orion, was the school bus driver, and I didn't have to walk to catch the bus. I began making friends with kids who lived closer. When I turned 12, I grew up overnight.

At Christmas time, we drove to Blair, Oklahoma, to be with relatives. They thought I was Orion's wife. We only saw my grandparents once a year, or less.

There was still no electricity, no indoor plumbing and very little of the finer things of life. We still had to study at night with the kerosene lamps. We had to trim the wicks, fill the lamps with oil and wash the black globes, and there were plenty of other chores to do.

The kerosene lanterns were for the outside when there was work to do at night. We would fill a washtub with water, set it in the hot summer sun to heat for our Saturday night bath ... and that wasn't always a joke.

CHAPTER 4

The Opossum Hunt

The boys let me go with some other friends on this hunt. We left after midnight and were out for several hours. My brothers liked our big greyhound. He was a great hunting dog for rabbits, squirrels and 'possums (that's what we called them). The dog would tree the 'possum, then the hunters had to find a way to get him out of the tree as some of us held the lantern. Actually, I didn't pay a lot of attention to details since my young boyfriend came along and a girlfriend or two.

My dad cooked the 'possum with sweet 'taters the next day. The 'possum hunt was fun, but the eating was unbearable! We were taught to eat everything. However, one taste of that was enough. It was so greasy, you couldn't stand it. Don't ever try it. Hopefully, you will never have the occasion to taste such ungodly, greasy stuff. The old greyhound probably got most of it. He'd eat anything.

We Moved to Noble

Noble was a very small town about 10 miles south of Norman. I was in the eighth grade. We moved into a gas station with one or two rooms in the back. I believe we had a few groceries to sell there.

I slept on a cot behind the counter and sometimes on the table in back. Sometimes, I'd sleep in the bathtub. Wow — we had an indoor toilet and a bathtub even! Plus, we lived on the main highway from north to south with blacktop roads. Some evenings, I worked in a small restaurant across from where we lived.

A few times, I was a babysitter. One of the dads, a businessman, hugged me up one night when he drove me home. I jerked away, ran in the house and wouldn't babysit for them anymore. I never told anyone.

We didn't live in the gas station long. We moved into a nicer home a couple of blocks north at the other end of town. I guess you've noticed, we never lived very long any place. I think my parents liked adventure. They always paid their bills. Mama was a good housekeeper, so we didn't have to move because the house got dirty.

MORETA: MY STORY

Back to the Country

Not far out of Noble, a few miles east on a dirt road, we had a few cows, pigs, chickens, ducks and a couple of turkeys to have for Thanksgiving and Christmas. We had one team of horses and one acre of garden — that's a lot of garden to have to plant and replant two or three times after a sandstorm, wind, hail or whatever came to destroy the new plants. Down by the pond, we also raised just enough grain to feed the animals.

By the time I was 14 and living east of Noble, we had a washing machine. It wasn't electric. I really don't know how to explain it. They had to crank it like a model-T Ford. They pulled a rope over and over until the motor started. I guess it was a gas motor, and it had a clothes wringer. That was nice. It got the water out of the wet clothes real good. They still had to heat the water in the old black boiler, though, and carry all the water to the tubs. Also, by then, we weren't traveling in a wagon to church every night, so I didn't have to iron so many shirts.

There was a little Baptist church about a mile from us. We'd go to that some. We also drove in to the church in Norman when we could. In our community, there was a real nice country boy who was coming to see me, sitting with me in church and showing very serious interest, but I was also seeing other interesting young men from the city church in Norman.

One boy, Earl Rogers, tried to drive out to see me from Norman. We had a big rain, and the ruts in the dirt road were so deep, he kept having to leave his car and walk to farmhouses to get the farmers to pull him out. He finally had to give up and head back to town and write me a letter instead.

Then I met "Mr. Tall, Dark and Handsome" and fell madly in love. I was 14. He was in his early 20s. His mother was a preacher, so she and my mother had a close, instant connection, and it was only natural for me to meet her son. I don't remember where they had lived, but we were inseparable. He was a Romeo and knew how to tell me how wonderful I was. No more 16- or 18-year-old teens for me. I liked those more adult city boys.

We became engaged. Shortly after, though, his mother began to hear how wonderful Oregon was with all its beauties and wealth. He promised that as soon as he got a good job and could provide a place for us, he would come for me. He'd hold me close and sing

CHAPTER 4

"Mexicali Rose" and other songs. We were brokenhearted to be apart, but he was excited about making a better life for us. We wrote every day. I'd play the piano and cry. I missed him so.

He found a good job at the C.D. Johnson Lumber Mill in Toledo, Oregon. He wrote that he had picked out a ring for me. A $90 ring. I wrote him back immediately: "No Way." I couldn't think of me wearing a $90 ring. I suggested that we needed to date others and give ourselves time. Though I was positive that he was the only one for me.

I quit school in the ninth grade. I would be getting married soon, and my parents didn't care about me staying in school. There were constant challenges with my Christian standards, so I quit. But I've wished many times that I had an education and could have gone to college and Bible school. Going to college wasn't even in the thinking in those days, with my family, or any of my friends.

We Moved to Norman

Norman was about 18 miles south of Oklahoma City. I was 14. The church was a lively, growing church with lots of young people. I soon became the church pianist. Orion and Melbra played their instruments in the large orchestra. Papa played the fiddle, but I don't think he played in the orchestra in Norman. Before he was saved, he played his fiddle for square dances.

We always had our family quartet, and Papa sang bass. Before my sister, Lorene, married, she sang alto and played the piano. After she left home, I took her part. My two brothers and I sang trios. Orion accompanied us on his guitar. We went to jails and institutions with a group of young people and sang almost every Sunday afternoon. We also sang for church and youth rallies.

The Stamps Quartet was having singing conventions all around the country. Sometimes they had all-night sings with other quartets. Orion always had a great car and would take loads of our teens with us to these special times.

The Stamps Baxter Music School in Texas was on the radio with their quartet every day at noon. They always had the most talented, cutest young pianists I had ever heard or seen. I would wear the piano out trying to do their runs and play like they played. We always had a Hobart M. Cable piano. At night, when the family was in bed, I'd be pounding the keyboard. Occasionally, my dad would call out, "Sis, get your foot off the loud pedal." It just sounded better and felt better to bang it at full speed.

Our parents always encouraged us in our music. My dad was the musician, Mama the preacher. Papa had a small booklet called *The Rudiments of Music* that we learned from. As soon as I could read, I studied that little book. I'd sing, "do, re, mi, re, mi, fa, so, fa, so, la, ti, la, ti, do, re," then every combination upscale and down. I learned the shaped notes early in life. It was such a simple, uncomplicated system. All of the quartet songbooks (*Stamps, Blackwood* and *Statesmen*) were shaped notes. Lots of different men's quartet groups began to surface fast.

I lived in the pastor's home at times to help with different outreaches. I worked in Vacation Bible School, special Sunday school classes and wherever I was needed. Two summers, I traveled with evangelist Iola Wiseman to play the piano. I was 14 and 15 years old. She was in her 20s. She played the accordion and the Hawaiian guitar, and we sang together.

There were eight of us girls in the Norman church who were together a lot. We spent many nights in the home of one of the girls whose parents welcomed us. They were always there when we came. We'd date together, double date, blind date and with whoever, wherever or whenever. We'd laugh, cry, pray, tell our secrets and share our dreams and our hurts. There was Imogene, Mildred, Louise, Maudie, Jeanette, me and another one, I cannot think of her name. Oh, yes, Thelma. I would love to hear from every one of those girls and know what their lives have been like. Edna Davenport was one of the "gang" in the beginning, but my brother, Melbra, fell madly in love with her and married her eventually. I loved Edna. She was one of my dearest friends all during their married life. They are both gone now.

Orion had lots of girlfriends. He was proud, capable and dignified. I don't ever remember fussing with my brothers. They loved me, were proud of me and taught me a lot about how to act around my boyfriends. But they never tried to control my life or stop me from having fun. Melbra once told, "Moreta has 10 boyfriends and is true to every one of them." Melbra was the tease of the family. He always had us laughing. He'd play pranks on us and was creative in his antics. One Christmas, he had found the cutest old life-sized monkey with the greatest inquisitive expression on its face. When you turned the monkey's tail, he would look at you with that

CHAPTER 4

dumb look and kept us laughing for hours, even after we tried to get serious.

Not long ago, I was at my younger brother's home in Eugene. I started talking about old Elmer. Admiral slipped out of the room and came back with Elmer! I couldn't believe it. That old monkey didn't have to have batteries. It still worked as good as ever, only it's well worn — moth holes and all.

My Family

My sister, Lorene, and her husband, Frank, had four 6-foot tall boys. Lanny, Glenn, Johnie Earl and Paul. They live around Grants, New Mexico, and Flagstaff, Arizona. Four great boys with their wives and families. We just lost Glenn to cancer in 2006. We have many on the other side. It can't be long till we go to be with them forever.

My older brother, Orion, and Elnora had four wonderful girls. Carol, Marlene, Sherri and Kristi. I love them all to pieces. I get to see them often, but not often enough. They all live in Bend, Oregon. Elnora went to be with the Lord in 1991. Orion never remarried. We just lost him in June 2006. His four lovely daughters all lived near him and took good care of him. They all have had a full, interesting life to now.

My second brother, Melbra, and his wife, Edna, had three children, Deanna, Robert John and Philip. They all live in Pueblo, Colorado. Melbra had finished his work one day and had walked to his car, heading home for the Christmas holidays. He slumped down beside the car — and was gone. That was Christmas Eve, December 24, 1971. His wife, Edna, lived until December 23, 2003.

My younger brother, Admiral, and Marie live in Eugene, Oregon. He had a boy and a girl, Rick and Lori. I'll be writing more about them. I'm with them a lot, but again, not enough. I was blessed these later years with the two wonderful brothers, and now, after Orion's passing, it's just the two of us, Admiral and me.

Back to My Sweet Teens

I worked some in the cherry cannery in Noble, and I worked in the hospital in Norman. Other than "the old cotton-picking days," which were long gone and far behind, and a few babysitting jobs, my working days didn't pay too well.

My Claude, in Oregon, and I had become so totally involved with our new friends and activities that our letters had grown further apart, until by now, they were nonexistent. It had been a couple of years since we had seen each other. And I was realizing that he was living a worldly life and not interested in spiritual things, while I was growing into more holy living. Our lives were going in opposite directions, and I should not try to hold it together. I had become content to let go.

One Saturday, when a half dozen of us girls were together for the night, I got such a burden for Claude. I shared it with the girls, and we prayed long and loud about it. The next day or two, I heard from his mother that on Saturday night he had married and while driving from the wedding, a drunk hit them. The new bride was killed instantly, and Claude was mangled and not expected to live. Oh my! How horrible for Claude to have to go through such a painful experience. Actually, he was in the hospital for many months, even into years. He hadn't been living for the Lord.

Life Had to Go On

Every Saturday night, all the young people in the area would go to town, drag Main two or three times, then park the cars, sit in the car and watch all the people go by. We'd walk the sidewalks and visit with new people and friends. We'd go into the stores for a cherry coke or whatever. I usually went to town with Orion or Melbra but seldom came home with them.

There had been a cute blond, blue-eyed taxi driver who I had talked to at times. I'd sit in his cab to wait with him for a passenger. Once or twice, I rode with him to deliver his rider. I was 14. This one Saturday night, he kept driving with me. He went to a lonely spot out of town. No street lights, no house lights. It was so black, you couldn't see your hand in front of your face. He parked the car and wanted to get out and walk — he was tired of sitting all day. We didn't walk far till he circled the car, opened the door and got me in the backseat! He began to attack me, trying to rape me. I fought with all my might. It looked like I was losing. I was exhausted and knew I couldn't keep up much longer. He had on a white shirt with the cuffs rolled up a couple of turns. I got hold of that part of the sleeve, and he must have thought I'd tear his shirt.

CHAPTER 4

All of a sudden, when I just knew I had lost, he quit. He let go and leaned back in the seat with a sigh. I got out and into the front seat. I was boiling mad! He got in and drove me home. He stopped on the road in front of my house (he had apologized already) and asked if he could walk me to the door. I gritted my teeth and growled, "No way."

There were no lights in my house, and I was glad. I slipped in as easy as I could, and I could hear my mother. She was on her knees at the other end of the couch, praying. I slipped on through the room, took my new dress off that had been wrinkled unbelievably and put it in the bottom of the clothes hamper. My mother never asked me anything about that night, and I never told her. But I was sure I knew why that boy stopped at the moment when I couldn't keep fighting. Thank You, Lord, for a praying mother.

In case you think I was an easy pushover and encouraged such treatment, I was not! My only sport was hugging and kissing. No French kissing. It was just scriptural, holy kisses — dry, but with feeling. I was addicted. The hugging, too, was closely monitored, guarded and expected. About three inches above and three inches below the waistline was as far as it went. No man ever touched my breasts until after that wonderful man and I were married.

I dated some interesting, diverse, poles-apart kinds of young men. I corresponded with several. One, Jimmy Bennett, drove back from Covina, California, and came to see me. I had been writing to him for a while and enjoyed his letters. He was a real cutie, and I have pictures to prove it. He had a nice car. We just had one day together. We drove southeast to I don't remember where — to some relatives that he had come back from California to see, I think. There was an extreme electrical storm that night, scary but constant and exciting. We got home quite late. I won't tell the rest of the story, but we didn't write anymore after that. I heard years later that he was pastor of a church in Oklahoma City. His grandkids would love to hear "the rest of the story." I'm sure he became a good pastor and a good man. *The steps of a good man are ordered by the Lord.*

Another time, an oilfield worker — tall, older, with a very nice car — took me to Shawnee to an opera. I didn't know what an opera was. It was a Ballet performance, a matinee. It was totally out of my class. I'm still not sure what it was all about, but it was different and I enjoyed it, especially all the attention. He had never dated anyone like me, no make-up, my long hair and the unusual specimen that I was. But he kept telling me how pretty I was without all the extra stuff. He treated me with the highest respect, and I appreciated that. He was different, but I liked variety. He was from the southeast part of Oklahoma. I don't remember where I found him. Somebody introduced us, I guess.

Life Was About to Change

Oklahoma was a miserable, hot place with no air conditioning. At night, I would lay on my bed with a wet washcloth on my forehead and a pan of water on the floor nearby. I had a dishpan of water at the foot of the bed and would hang my legs over the side with my feet in the water. I kept busy fanning with the washrag or towel most all night. I detested those miserable nights and hot days.

CHAPTER 5

Beautiful Oregon

Anna Kirby, the mother of my former boyfriend, Claude, came from Oregon and visited us. She made Oregon sound so wonderful to my parents and to all of us. My brothers became interested. This was in August of 1939, and by September, we were on our way. I was 17.

We sold everything. Papa even sold his car. Orion and Melbra had their cars, and another couple, Frank and his wife (Dorothy, I think), came, too, in their car. We hooked a trailer to the back of one of the boy's cars and started out. It took a week to make the trip. We, or I should say, they, slept out every night on the ground. I made a bed in a car, and perhaps Mama and Papa did, too. Admiral was 10 or 11, so he slept out with the boys.

We had a small fold-up gas camp stove and cooked all our meals outside. I'm sure Mama and Frank's wife had prepared many things ahead of time to bring along to eat. I think Frank pulled a trailer behind his car, too. It was quite a procession.

It was a long, exciting but sometimes scary trip into a new world — especially when we got into Oregon. Those high, steep mountain passes with narrow roads and rocky 1,000-foot drops to the bottom with the wide Columbia River at the lowest depth were frightening.

The main highway in those early years wasn't on the river level but up on top of the Columbia River Gorge. Many years later, after it became the scenic drive, my sister-in-law, Ruby Staten, had a jelly shop right on top of that scariest point. She sold Oregon made jellies to tourists from all across the nation and many places of the world. It was a breathtaking sight.

All the large waterfalls along the way, all the huge evergreen trees with a deer among them occasionally, were super special sights to us. Then there were the long logging trucks with sometimes only one big log on it or many logs piled high. We thought we had reached the mysterious wonder world, and we were anxious to become a part of it and learn all about it.

MORETA: MY STORY

When we left Oklahoma, everything was dry, dusty, brown and hot. Breathing was difficult. We came into Oregon and could breathe the fresh, cool air. Green grass was everywhere. The farther we came, the more we discovered, and we liked it all. We came through the Portland area and the beautiful Willamette Valley, then turned west on a winding road that took us to our destination in Toledo. We were to go directly to Sister Kirby's (Claude's mother) where Claude lived.

Of course, there were no cell phones. All communication had been by letter. Claude and I had not talked, but when we arrived, Claude was there.

As we were all in the yard talking, he came over to me, took my hand and asked if I would like to walk with him and see the orchard. When we got a safe distance away from the others and out of sight, he took me in his arms, held me tight and whispered, "I hope to the devil we never part again." (That really wasn't my kind of language.)

He was still under doctor's care. I don't remember how many operations he had had. He wasn't the same man I had known. He was skin and bones, his nerves were bad, he had no car because he couldn't drive, he couldn't hold a job, he was not interested in church and we had nothing in common anymore. And we weren't together very long that day.

Our New Life

We probably camped out a night or two at that time. There were literally miles of blackberry vines everywhere around Toledo. We tried to eat them all. There were apples rolling down the steep hills to Main Street. We thought we surely had found the Land of Canaan, The Promised Land. It was heavenly! No more miserable hot, muggy weather.

We soon found a place to rent. After we picked up enough furniture and got moved into the house, we began to meet the neighbors who weren't too far away. They had a very small garden space and invited us to help ourselves to all we wanted to eat and all we wanted for canning. When we got home, we laughed at their offer. They didn't know us and how we liked to eat. Where we came from, we had an acre of garden, and it wasn't enough. But to our surprise, this small garden produced more than we could use.

CHAPTER 5

This land of plenty produced more than we could imagine. They had two or three kinds of green beans. One was the Oregon giant bean that was 12 or 14 inches long and an inch or more wide. They were hanging thick on the vines. They were pale green with purple flecks. About six of them would make a meal, even for us. The other variety of beans were plentiful, too.

We tried to can them all. There were plenty of potatoes, large onions drying, squash, oh, all kinds of vegetables, enough for three or four families.

On Sunday, of course, we found ourselves in church. A lot of the young people were our age. Actually, most of them were from one family — the Brooks family. The mother was a preacher, too, like our mama. The husbands fit well together and had a lot of the same interests. They invited our family to come home with them for dinner that first Sunday. Sister Brooks, like my mother, always had enough food for everybody.

The two preacher ladies began making plans to go to a little community up in the hills north and east of Toledo every Sunday afternoon for a preaching service. I think the place was called Summit. It might even be on the map. There was nothing there but a little grocery store, a gas station, a few homes and the little old church building. The new highway has since cut Summit off, and the gas station and grocery store is now down on the main road that leads to the valley.

Our Social Life

The Brooks family had a very beautiful daughter, Aletha. Naturally, my brother, Orion, had eyes for her right away. But Aletha was dating another good-looking boy in the church, Harold Cable. He played the guitar in the orchestra. His parents were in the church, too, and he was an only son.

We went to church and Sunday school every Sunday morning in Toledo, then to Summit in the afternoon at 3 p.m. and back to church at 7 p.m. for the night service. Former Army Sergeant Ryan and his wife were the pastors.

Our parents and the two younger brothers went together in one car to Summit. The rest of us (Orion, Aletha, Roland, Loyal and I) went in Orion's car. At times, we would take another person or two with us. It was nice having those young people to show us

MORETA: MY STORY

around the beautiful Oregon Coast — the beaches, boats, fishermen, aquariums and shops. Then, at times, we would share a foot-long hot dog or Coney Island at a little roadside eating-place. There was so much to see and do.

One day, Orion said to me, "We need to break this thing up with Harold and Aletha. You get Harold, and I'll take Aletha." He wasn't usually a schemer, but this was so necessary! It didn't take long, and that made it nice for me. Harold worked nights at the sawmill. He had a rowboat and a nice car.

Nearly every day, he came to take me in his boat up the different arms of the Yaquina Bay. Sometimes, I'd take a picnic lunch, or he'd drive me to all kinds of sights around the wonderful Pacific Ocean.

Orion got a job immediately in the lumber mill. Melbra didn't stay out here long. He had to get back to his Edna. He couldn't marry her until she was 16, but he had no intentions of staying away from her. I think he moved in with his friend Bob Sawyer. As soon as the calendar turned to the right date, Melbra and Edna were married and on their way to Oregon around the middle of the year 1940.

There was still Claude to consider. He was not able to get around very well, no car, no interest in church and no phone. I was hard to find, so it didn't last too long. At times, he walked over the thick wooded trail to see me. One Sunday, he decided he would go with us to Summit to the Sunday afternoon meeting. When the altar call was given, he went forward and prayed. I was pretty sure he just did it to get me. He knew I would never marry anyone who wasn't a Christian.

My parents never tried to stop me from seeing Claude, but I knew they were praying. We had a promise box on the table. That was a small box with a scripture verse on different colored poster board-type paper with a promise from the Bible for the day. One day, I drew one out that read, "Ask of me, and I'll give you the heathen for your inheritance." I had been earnestly praying about Claude. I had sympathy for him, and I still cared, but I knew it should never be. God used that promise box to put the scare in me. I knew that was not what I wanted for the rest of my life. I also was sure that he was addicted to all the medications he had been on for too long.

CHAPTER 5

It Was Over

It happened shortly after the promise box, perhaps that very night. Claude came over the trail for me. We walked back to town together and to his sister's apartment above one of the store buildings. His sister wasn't home. He had never tried to force me in any way. He had always fully respected me. But this was different, like he had planned it, almost wild, trying to rape me! We fought long and difficult. Finally, when I knew I couldn't keep up much longer, at that moment, he quit! He never said a word. Just leaned back against the couch, like he was too weak to speak. I jumped up, pulled myself together, slammed the door and ran down the stairs to the sidewalk, not knowing what to expect next.

It was too dark and scary to walk over the trail to go home. There was no phone to call someone to come get me, but at the bottom of the long stairs, Claude's older brother (whom he disliked) was just starting to go up. He could tell I was upset. I didn't know him too well. "Do you need a ride home?" he asked.

"I sure do," I assured him. He drove me home. He asked no questions, and I told him nothing. But I thanked him as best I could. I never saw Claude again. I was free but felt terribly hurt and dishonored. I'm sure he felt he was losing me, and this was his last chance to keep me.

The days and months that followed were great "forgetter" days of the past. It was deliverance from a future that I knew I wanted no part of. What do girls do without a good "bringing up" and a praying mother and dad?

We didn't live in the little house down around the bottom of the hill for long. We moved to a nicer, larger home on top of the hill.

A New Beginning

What a delightful time I was having, courting and being entertained by several different young men while seeing the wonderful Oregon Coast with its beaches, parks and mountain peaks. We took long trips, short trips, some all day and some nearly all night. The Newport Bridge had just been built — what beauty! We would park overlooking the bay and bridge, or on the jetty, or up by the lighthouse above the ocean and watch the fishing boats come in.

MORETA: MY STORY

We watched the seagulls and the whales, and we'd go to the fishing docks where the boats came in and see all the different kinds of fish. And with all my excitement and thrill of seeing and being involved with it all, don't you know each young man enjoyed our times together, too? I loved it. I felt as mature then as I am now. And, as I remember the thrill of those days, I feel as young now as I was then.

There was lots to write home about to my girlfriend, Imogene Harvey. She was my dearest friend. I wrote her constantly. She was so much fun to be with those years we lived next to each other in Norman.

Orion, my brother, was working every day, except Saturday and Sunday at the C.D. Johnson Lumber Mill in Toledo. We were usually with the Brooks young people as often as we could to be going, seeing and doing. Aletha and Rowland were fun to be with as they showed us the country.

My brother, Melbra, was still back in Oklahoma waiting for his Edna to grow up. His friend Bob Sawyer came out to Oregon to see "Mama" before he had to go in the Army. Mama was like a mother to him, always praying for him, trying to get him to turn to God. All the time he was out here, he was doing everything he could to get me to marry him, then he wouldn't have to be drafted. He was sure he could make me happy. But I had found too many interesting people in Oregon, so he went to war. But he came back unharmed. Praise the Lord. I just heard recently that Bob had died, but in his last days, he had turned to God, leaving a wife and children. God is so merciful!

We were still going every Sunday afternoon to the little church in Summit. Just before Easter, in May, a young man came to the church service, and when the altar call was given, he came and accepted Christ as his Savior. He was a log truck driver from Siletz — interesting! The next Sunday, he was back and made a date to come see me in Toledo.

I was still going places during the daytime with Harold. I had gone with him to Ridgefield, Washington, to visit some of his relatives for a couple of days, and we were together a lot. We were just friends, no petting, nothing serious, and I was enjoying his company. He worked nights. Harry worked days. It got really busy for the next couple of weeks. But one afternoon, Harry came unexpected, and Harold was there. Harry had injured his hand and had

CHAPTER 5

to come to town to see the doctor. His hand was bandaged big with quite a severe wound. He didn't stay long that day, but we would go out at night two or three times a week. Harold still came almost every day, but I realized things had to soon change. My time with Harry was getting serious fast. We were falling in love! I asked Harold not to come around anymore. He understood, and I don't think he or his mother felt too bad. We were always friends, though. He was a great young man, and I had enjoyed him. He had helped to make Oregon beautiful for me.

Harry was from Michigan and had come to Oregon a few months earlier. His cousin, Gladys Hines, had lived with Harry's family in her early years after her parents were both gone. She had come to Oregon some years before and married Clyde Hines. He had a large logging operation in the high mountains out of Siletz. He had about six logging trucks that hauled the logs from the woods to the Toledo lumber mill, where they were sliced and made into lumber. It had been so interesting to go into that mill and watch the whole process of the big logs being unloaded from the trucks and onto the big conveyer belts. Oh, I don't know how to explain it. It was a huge operation and unbelievable to see it all. Wish you could have been there to see it for yourself.

Then I met Harry and found out he was a driver of one of those big trucks that hauled the huge logs. Later, I saw how hazardous it all was. The mountain roads were one-lane, narrow and winding up steep hills and were muddy in rainy weather, with few turnouts for oncoming trucks. It was an extremely dangerous job, plus he was the mechanic who kept it all going. He was living with Clyde and Gladys. They went to the Siletz Assembly of God Tabernacle faithfully. They were choice people!

Harry was able to show me more of Oregon that I hadn't seen and from a different perspective. I saw the area from Siletz and the North Coast and the coastal roads to the Washington border. We would take the back roads to waterfalls, lakes and rivers. We would even eat in restaurants and unusual places. Life was more beautiful than I had ever known.

We went together from our first date, on Mother's Day in May, to August 31, 1940. We married in just three months. We hadn't been in Oregon a full year yet. About the time we started dating, my parents were checking out the rest of the state. They started going to Springfield for two or three days at a time. They

MORETA: MY STORY

bought a lot and started building a new house. I stayed in Toledo and "kept things going" for Orion as he was working. (Now that he's gone, he can't dispute that statement.) I was a pretty good cook, though, and a good housekeeper. I could take care of all that and be ready for whatever came up, to go with whoever came first.

Orion was going out most every night there in Toledo. One night, when I knew I would be out later than he would and knowing he always checked on me to make sure I was there, I fixed a dummy in my bed. I had long hair that went almost to the chair when I sat down. When I combed, brushed or washed my hair, there would be a bit of fallout of the hair. I would wrap the hair around my finger and put it in a bag in my room. This night, I put pillows under my covers, blew up a paper sack about head size and put the curls around the sack with a hairnet to hold the curls in place. Sure enough, he peeked in and it worked! He laughed when I told him the next day. He trusted me. The whole family trusted me, and well they should. I was trustworthy!

Harry was 21 years old. He was a real gentleman and always treated me with the highest respect. Being in love, really in love with a super, wonderful man is the greatest gift this world has to offer. I was blessed beyond my greatest dreams!

When Papa got the new house in Springfield far enough along so we could live in it, we moved from Toledo to the valley. Orion quit his job at the mill in Toledo and began helping Papa build in the Eugene area.

Better Than My Dreams

Just before our wedding day, Harry quit his logging truck job in Siletz and came to Springfield and got a job. We spent the rest of our courting days around Springfield and Eugene.

One Sunday after church, we were eating dinner with my family and Harry happened to quietly call me "honey." My dad was sitting close by and said, "I want you to know, young man, I'm the only honey around here." My dad didn't say too much, but when he did, everyone laughed (or cried).

Another Sunday, as we were eating, the baked potatoes were too hot. Papa took a big bite, put his chin down near the table and spit the potato back in his plate and grumbled, "Many a fool would have swallowed that."

CHAPTER 5

A lot of years after that time, I heard a comedian on the radio tell about an old fellow who did this potato thing, spit it out and said (he quoted Papa's exact words), "Many a fool would have swallowed that."

The wedding date was near. We rented a furnished apartment and went directly there after the wedding. No one but my family knew where it was. My brother, Orion, took us away and dropped us off in the middle of the Springfield Bridge. Cars couldn't turn around there, and we ran directly to our hidden car, then to our apartment nearby.

Our wedding was not the ordinary. The orchestra from the Toledo church with some from the little Springfield storefront church played. There was no "I Love You Truly" or "Because." Those songs were being sung at about every wedding at that time. The special singing were songs that included God into our marriage. And I don't remember what those songs were. I had planned it all over the ironing board.

My friend, evangelist Iola Wiseman, whom I had traveled with those two summers, came from Oklahoma City and performed the ceremony. She stayed with my parents and preached several revival meetings while she was in Oregon.

Things were not spendy in our day. My rings were beautiful, and I loved them. The center diamond of the engagement ring was the largest, and it was tiny. On either side were two smaller diamonds set in heart shapes of gold. The wedding band had three very small diamonds set in the gold band. The cost was $25 for the pair of rings. Before my parents' new house was finished, with only the outside privy and the cracks between the boards, my rings really sparkled. I'm just trying to be funny, but that was all true. I was so proud of my rings. They had sparkle and were wrapped in love. They are still beautiful, and I would wear them yet, only the band is paper-thin. They are still worth fighting for. Anybody would love to have them.

Our first grocery bill with all the staples — shortening, sugar, flour, etc. — was only $3.85. I still have the original paper of this grocery list. Recently, I put it somewhere so it wouldn't get lost. Now, I can't find it.

We probably paid $10 a month for our apartment. Of course, we got lots of beautiful wedding gifts of household things. The landlord was glad to have newlyweds in her house. She lived in the apartment next to us. It helped me a lot to have her wisdom, plus she gave me some of her favorite recipes, one of which is still one of my children's favorite delectable edibles.

Shortly after we were married, my brother, Orion, drove to Toledo and brought his friend Aletha for the day. Harry and I met them and went shopping in Eugene. Orion and Harry went looking at cars while Aletha and I shopped in women's stores. They were to meet us at a certain corner at 1:00. We waited and waited. There was a restaurant close by, and we decided we may as well go eat — I probably suggested it, and she went along. It was embarrassing standing on the street corner for so long. Just as we finished eating and were back to our street corner, the boys drove up. They were so sorry. Time had just gotten away from them. They suggested, "We may as well go in here and eat."

We agreed. There were few people in the restaurant, and the waitress hadn't taken our plates away. We slid into that same booth. I had left food on my plate, and I began to eat. Orion was totally shocked and embarrassed. Harry was saying, "Honey, stop it. What are you doing?"

I said, "I'm starved."

Aletha was bent over, laughing. The kitchen crew and waitress were standing off enjoying it all.

Back to the Coast Again

We didn't live long in Springfield. The larger wages of the logging truck were calling. We moved back to Toledo. In the summertime, we had to get up by 4 in the morning so Harry could ride the "crummy" to the logging woods. (The crummy was a large covered truck-van-like vehicle that was used to transport the logging crew from their homes to the workplace in the woods.) I always made him a good breakfast, packed his lunch, we prayed together and he was gone for 10 or 12 hours.

I never went back to bed. I was too much of a coward. I kept the wood fire going in the kitchen stove, sat with my feet on the open oven door and studied the Bible for hours every morning. I was especially acquiring knowledge of the book of Revelations about the coming of the Lord, the end times just before His coming and the things that would be happening in the world after the rapture (the return of Christ for the believers).

CHAPTER 5

The few years we lived in Toledo were in three different rented houses. We bought the fourth house. It was a white house on a hill with one bedroom and a bath downstairs and two bedrooms upstairs. It was spacious enough with lots of windows, and the view of the coastal sunsets was delightful. We paid $700 for the house, and during the war, we sold it for $2,500. Also, while we lived there, we bought a new five-passenger blue Pontiac for $1,040. Prices were a bit different at that time.

CHAPTER 6

Life is Changing

Pearl Harbor had happened, and most of the single men had been called to serve in the military, with thousands being killed every day. We began getting those friendly letters from Uncle Sam, and all too soon, my husband received his notice to enlist. We thought we couldn't live through it. He enlisted in the Navy as a mechanic — non-combatant.

We had been married now for more than three years and wanted a baby so badly. But with him having to be gone to war and leaving me alone to go through all that trauma by myself, we decided no way. But a short time before he would be leaving, I started turning green in the early mornings with the smell of coffee and other nauseating scents. Then the bringing up bile that turned me inside out as it came up from the bottomless pit.

We decided we didn't want to tell anyone about this new discovery yet. Our other young friends and relatives were having to leave, too. My brother, Orion, joined the Army, and Melbra joined the Navy. Harry's brothers and brother-in-law in Michigan were called up. Seemed about every home was torn apart by this terrible worldwide war. Orion was sent to Germany.

My parents had moved back to Oklahoma. I had to have someone local to talk to about my pregnancy. Harry's cousin, Gladys, and her husband, Clyde, had moved from Siletz to Toledo. She and I had been really close, and of course, Clyde and Harry were inseparable. We loved them. So before that horrible day where we had to say goodbye, we told them of our new discovery. I knew she could keep our secret. We all went to the same church, with lots of close friends. When I had questions about what was going on in my body, I could go to her. She had three children and was experienced in childbearing.

The day that Greyhound bus came to Toledo and took a load of our choice men was an impossible day for us. Harry sat by an open window, and I held his hand and walked alongside the bus as it slowly pulled away.

CHAPTER 6

He was sent to the Navy boot camp in Washington State for six weeks (I think). Then home for a few days. We didn't know where he would be sent next for more training. I said, "It'll probably be the farthest point of the United States." I guess I was a prophet! It was Florida.

While Harry was in boot camp, Gladys and I had an interesting time regarding my pregnancy. Two sisters were pastors of our church. One of them, Irene Cooper, lived just across the street from Gladys. We had been close friends through the years. She began trying to convince me to get pregnant when Harry came home. I guessed she thought she was pregnant and wanted me to be, too. Her husband wasn't having to go off to war. Of course, I was having all the symptoms, and I knew she wasn't. She was the kind that could get sick with anybody who was puny.

One morning, five of us ladies were going to Eugene to go shopping. Just before they drove in my driveway, I had to run to the backyard and pull up some more green bile! I was sick as a hound dog.

The Red Box Coat

Gladys knew that I was going along to find a box-style coat. I always wore fitted, bright colored clothes. I knew I would soon be showing and needed help to conceal my condition as long as possible. Eugene was a good hour's drive, and when we arrived, I got out but was just too sick to go to the stores, so I laid down in the car. In a few minutes, Irene came back to the car. She was sick, too — must be the flu that hit us. She laid in the front seat. Now we both had the flu. Gladys was enjoying it all, with much sympathy.

Later in the morning, I got to feeling better and was able to go shopping for a new spring coat. Irene was feeling better, too, and decided she needed a new coat. She began telling me that I needed to get a box coat, something completely different from what I always wore. So, I let her talk me into a box coat — a red one. She got a box-style coat, too.

Isn't it interesting how God's sense of humor makes life so laughable, even when you are lonely and hurting?

I also had been spending a lot of time during Harry's absence at Irene's sister's home, Siama Southwell. They lived just a few blocks from me. Siama insisted that I stay with them and not stay

MORETA: MY STORY

so long by myself. They had a young son, Gene, and a daughter, Elsie, who was two or three years younger than I. They were musicians, and we enjoyed our times together. I had my own bedroom there and stayed several nights off and on. During this time, I was craving ice cubes and lemons. Siama would say, "We can't get any fat on those bones with you eating like that." So she fed me well. My morning sickness had stopped by then.

While Harry was gone, I worked a few weeks in the bunkhouse at the C.D. Lumber Mill where the winos and wooly characters stayed. With so many workers gone to war, they had to bring in anyone who could work. I mostly made beds and picked up their bottles and junk. I first felt my new baby kick while I was working there. That was the only thrill I experienced while in that place.

Harry Home From Boot Camp

What fun we had with Irene and her husband, Ralph. They had us to their house to try and get us to get pregnant before Harry would have to leave again for his next training. I was now five and a half months along, so we decided to tell Siama and Irene about the good news. I just wasn't showing much at all, though Siama had decided she was getting a little fat on me.

We went to Siama's first. I called her into the bedroom and she followed, saying, "You silly kids. What are you up to now?"

We told her. She absolutely could not believe it! She began remembering the lemons and ice cubes and a few such things. I pulled off my jacket, and she could see a little pooched out belly. We told her we were going to Irene's, "... and you stay off that phone!" I made her promise.

We went into Irene's and told them we had something to tell them. I thought we would have to do something to revive her. She was speechless! Ralph was just blank. I got her to admit that she had thought earlier that she was pregnant. I think she forgave me. We were still friends until she died a few years ago. They had been married for several years without a child, but she finally became pregnant after our announcement.

Off to Florida

Sure enough, my fears were realized. My dear husband was

CHAPTER 6

sent to the southeast corner of the United States of America — Fort Pierce, Florida! We lived on the coast in northwest Oregon. He was Private first class — PFC Harry Chapin.

As long as he was in the States, he sent me gifts real often. In fact, all our married life, he was the greatest gift giver. One earlier Christmas, he gave me a wine-colored velvet dress and wine suede shoes to match. It was a total surprise, and they fit perfectly. While he was in Florida, he sent me a beautiful baby-blue satin negligee set — the perfect fit! There were many gifts, too many to list.

When he was sent to Florida, so far away, I began making plans to go to him. The friends in Toledo tried hard to talk me out of it. They warned me, "You'll get as far as Salt Lake City and not be able to go on." They would come and help me get back home. It was "What if?" and "What if?"

Gas, tires, refrigerators, sugar, about everything was in short supply and rationed. The speed limit for the whole nation was 35 miles per hour to save on fuel and tires. My car was nearly new, so I didn't worry. I managed to get gas stamps and certificates for tires if I needed them. So, with my new little Pontiac, gas stamps in hand, six and a half months pregnant, "Charlie" kicking quite often and July weather, I was on my way to Noble, Oklahoma, where my parents lived. It took a week to get there in the hot summertime with no air conditioner in the car and driving 35 miles per hour. Few cars were on the road.

I heard of a high school brother and sister who needed a ride to their home in Kansas. I stopped somewhere in Oregon and picked them up. They were sweet Christian kids, so I didn't have to travel the whole way alone (it was nearly a 2,000-mile trip). I left them at their parents' home in Kansas and went on alone to Oklahoma.

My parents lived on a little farm east of Noble. I got to their place about 4 in the afternoon and left the next morning at 7 on the train for Fort Pierce, Florida, where Harry had rented an apartment for me. I made the whole trip fine. I would come back to my parents' place to have my baby.

Those trains were something to write home about, no air conditioning, wide-open windows and the trains were powered by coal with choking black smoke coming in. We sat on the side tracks for hours. Food in the diner was too expensive, and the train was full of young men in uniform. There were very few civilians.

MORETA: MY STORY

Harry would be on duty two days and off one. I knew he wouldn't be there to meet me and that I should just go to the bulletin board and find his directions, call a cab and go to my room. He would be there the next night. Everything worked out as he had told me. I knew it was going to be one night out of three. The reunion was out of this world! It was the greatest thing I ever did. Don't you wish I'd write more details? You can't even guess how delightful it was.

When I was in Fort Pierce, I had to walk to town, two or three long blocks for all my meals at restaurants. August and September in that place were extremely hot. Around noon every day, it would rain, and I'd think, *Wonderful.* But as soon as the rain stopped, the steam would rise, and it became muggy, sticky hot and miserable!

One day, when I had walked to town to eat, I was in a 10-cent store buying thread and ribbon to work on baby gowns or embroider things. It was so steamy hot, I almost fainted. I slid down beside a wall and sat on the floor. A lady saw me and asked if she could help. She called a taxi for me, and I made it safely to my room. That made us realize it was about time to head back to my parents' home in Noble.

Several other Navy wives had rooms there in the home where I lived. One, a Lieutenant, and his wife were very nice. He gave me advise for several things we could do for Harry and I to be together. Number one was how to get Harry to go with me on the train back to my parents to have our baby. That worked, and it was all legal! I just had to get a doctor to put in writing that it was necessary. When I went to the doctor about my condition and my near fainting spell, he said, "If you are going anywhere to have that baby, you'd better get going, and you need your husband's help to get there."

When we went to the window at the Navy base with the request from the doctor, they gave us the papers we needed. We went around the corner of the building and hugged, cried, laughed, hugged some more and cried our thanks to God. We smiled and "happied" all the way to my parents' home in Noble. We had two wonderful days together. Then he had to return to base in Fort Pierce.

The second suggestion the Lieutenant gave us was how to get Harry back to see his baby when it was born. That worked, too, with the doctor's help. That was miraculous!

CHAPTER 6

My parents lived a few miles east of Noble on country roads with no phone. We heard of an older doctor who had come out to the homes of some of the neighbors when they needed help. I went to see him. He was glad to oblige us. At midnight, October 25, a full moon was shining through the window. When I got up, there was a spot of blood on the white sheets. I called my mother. She said, "This is it." Papa had to drive a ways to get to a neighbor who had a phone. I wasn't worried because I knew my mother had delivered lots of babies.

When Papa got back, I was in heavy labor. He said the doctor's wife had answered the phone. (His office was in Lexington, Oklahoma.) The doctor was in Oklahoma City at a doctors' seminar, but not to worry, he would be there as soon as he could. I cried, "Oh, no, he won't be able to get Harry to come."

My dear dad rushed about getting scissors sterilized while my mother was helping me. "Bear down; don't scream; breathe deep." Then, a louder, "Bear down, child, bear down." I knew this was an emergency, and I gave it all I had. The baby's head was out and turning blue. In my exhaustion, I had quit pushing, but in just a minute, Mama held that little bloody specimen up and said, "A big fat boy, I'd reckon."

Just then the door opened, and the doctor walked in and took over. Immediately, I asked, "Oh, Doctor, did you call for my husband?"

He said, "No, Mrs. Chapin, I knew I had to get here fast. But don't you worry, I'll take care of that as soon as I get back to my room." And he did!

In a few hours, we got a telegram. "Meet me at the Norman train station. I'm on my way." How wonderful!

During the bearing down and exhausting emergency time, I tore quite badly and had to have several stitches. It was during wartime, and many things were not available for civilians at home. The wounded service men came first. I had to be sewed up with catgut string and in bed for 15 days before the stitches could finally be removed. My mother and daddy were angels for me during those times. I never could thank them enough.

Ormel James was born October 25, 1944, and weighed in at 8 pounds and 4 ounces and was 21 inches long. He was two days old before his daddy got to see him. Those slow, dirty, hot trains could not be rushed. Words cannot express how happy Harry was to see

MORETA: MY STORY

and hold his baby boy. And what a comfort it was to have him hold me all night for two nights. I loved that man!

When he left the Navy base, he received his orders to return to New York instead of back to Fort Pierce. They would be shipping out for the war zone in the Pacific immediately. It was so hard to say goodbye. As I write this more than 60 years later, it's hard to hold the tears back. No one can know the pain of those times except the wives who are saying goodbye during these Iraq war times. I suffer for them and pray for them daily, that the good men whose wives are true to them and who love each other as we loved each other will return to them safely.

We had no way of knowing if or when he would be home, but his baby was 1 year and 2 months old when Daddy came home. Ormel went right to him and called him "Daddy." He would hold the 8 by 10 picture of Harry and look around behind it to see where his daddy was, so when Daddy came home, he knew him.

The third bit of help the Lieutenant gave us in Fort Pierce was a foolproof code that only my husband and I would understand, to let me know where he would be when he got into the war zone. And that worked! It was never censored or cut out. I knew when he was in Iwo Jima and in the battle of Okinawa.

There was no television in those days. We had only the radio, and we hovered around that little box night and day, especially during the horrible Iwo Jima battle when thousands were being killed every day. Whole platoons of Marines were totally mowed down.

The name of Harry's ship was the *Muliphen*. It was a Navy ship that carried the amphibians, which took the Marines onto the beaches. I found out later, as they were unloading Marines, the *Muliphen* was bombed, and Harry had to swim to shore with the Marines.

He had no weapons and had to help dig a foxhole, with Marines falling around him, but he was spared. He was in the foxhole for several hours. It was at the time that the Marines took Mount Suribachi. Harry was able to swim back to another ship and on to the next battle. He was a mechanic for the ship and amphibians.

While Harry was overseas and when I felt I could travel again, Ormel and I took the train back to Toledo, Oregon. I had gotten a power of attorney and sold our $700 house for $2,500. I sold the furniture and stored personal things.

CHAPTER 6

We wanted to live in Springfield, Oregon, when he returned. My only thought was saving and living for the time he could be with me.

Michigan

I made a trip on the train to Battle Creek, Michigan, to be with Harry's family and let them enjoy my baby. They were such a loving, caring family. They always treated me royally and still do.

After I returned to my parents in Noble, they moved to Norman, Oklahoma, where we had lived before moving to Oregon when I was 17.

My younger brother, Admiral, was still at home, and my older brother, Orion, had returned from the war in Germany.

Harry had written every day while he was gone. I had written him, too. I sent pictures continually of Ormel: sitting on his little pot, of him nursing, growing, 2 months, 3 months, etc. But his letters stopped coming during Iwo Jima and Okinawa for a whole month. I just knew he had to be a casualty. It was a sad time for all of us around there.

I began drawing plans for a small house for Ormel and me there in Norman. Orion and Papa would build it for me — if that's what would happen. Of course, nobody was rushing into anything. I was just trying to keep my sanity.

One day, a big stack of letters came that were tied together. Oh, the tears, the relief, the thanksgiving! I could live again. I wish I could have kept all the letters he had written while he was gone. Not long after that, VJ Day came. The war was over! August 14, 1945. He would be coming home, but not until December.

Together Again

Gladys and Clyde had moved to Albany. When Harry returned from the war, he came to Albany. I arrived there from Oklahoma close to the same time, and he met me at the train. It was unbelievable! It really was happening. We didn't have to do any adjusting. We were together, and that was all that mattered. It was so wonderful that his 14-month-old baby left me and went right to his daddy and called him "Daddy." It was shortly before Christmas.

MORETA: MY STORY

We stayed a few days with Clyde and Gladys, then boarded the smoky old train back to Oklahoma to pick up our pretty blue Pontiac. We stayed a few days with my parents then up to Battle Creek to be with his family. What a beautiful honeymoon!

When we finally finished visiting with family and friends, we went back to Toledo to visit and pick up a few things from storage. We returned to Springfield, where we had lived when we first married. We bought a lot to build on at 834 E Street and began drawing plans. We had saved $3,500 to build the house. And that's all it cost to build our two-bedroom and one-bath with a formal dining room. The living room was 14 by 20 feet. We had all hardwood floors with linoleum in the kitchen and bathroom. We put a 10 by 18 foot carpet in the living room, but no furniture. I had a small window put over the kitchen table so I could open it to talk with my husband while he worked in the garage. He was so much fun to be with.

When we got the new house started, Harry's sister and husband, Grace and Thaine Crandall (he had just come home from the war, too), came from Battle Creek and stayed three months with us to help build the house. Thaine was an experienced carpenter.

We had started going to an auction sale every Friday to buy furniture. We also watched the paper for items. We found a beautiful waterfall-pattern bedroom set with a big round mirror that went about 18 inches from the floor, exactly like the one we had bought at the auction for next to nothing before they came, mattress and all. All four of us stayed in the singlewide garage while we built the house. So the twin bedroom sets were not far apart. I think their baby girl, Donna, was born about eight months later. They loved Ormel and were anxious to start their family.

The weather was really hot for several days that summer — 105 degrees! On those days, we would quit working early and go to a pretty river, go swimming and play in the water, then have a picnic. We had bought an Army jeep and trailer to haul lumber and supplies. Harry had built an enclosure on the jeep, and we enjoyed times with that.

When the house was about finished and Grace and Thaine had to leave for Michigan, we were a sad lot. We hugged and kissed and held on till they finally had to drive off. In a few minutes, we jumped in the car and speeded to catch up with them. They

CHAPTER 6

stopped, got out and we hugged and cried all over again. We loved them so. They are both in heaven now.

Even now, as I write all this, I have to lean back in my rocking chair with misty eyes and say, "Thank You, Lord, for those wonderful times." What great memories.

We did without a lot of things until we could afford to pay cash. We didn't have to buy a television, computer or cell phone — there weren't any of those things. We didn't have a refrigerator, or a couch in the living room, or big chairs. We had found a beautiful waterfall dining table with six chairs and a buffet, probably for about $20. It didn't take us too long, though, to have enough furniture to be comfortable. However, we still had company, even before we had things. They could sit on the floor with us and laugh about it.

When the house was finished, it was all paid for. Harry had a good job, and we were happy. Real happy. That little boy of his loved his daddy, and that daddy loved his little boy.

CHAPTER 7

The Worst to Come

We were attending the Assembly of God Church on Seventh and B Streets in Springfield. Arthur Hyland was pastor. He lived right across the street from us. I had already become pianist, and shortly after, I became the youth pastor. It was called C.A. President in those early years (Christ Ambassadors). Ages 13 to 35, they were mostly high school and college age, also young marrieds.

When special evangelists came to the church for revival meetings, we would invite them to our house to eat. There was Paul and Violet Pipkins and their little daughter, Sylvia, who was Ormel's age. They hugged and enjoyed their chocolate milkshakes together. We enjoyed them so much.

Then there was Vernon and Anita Klemin from California. They had moved to Oregon and came to our church to preach. They have been some of our dearest friends through the years, and we see them often.

One preacher couple we invited was the Hockers. I had a candlelight dinner. We asked him to give thanks for the food. When he finished praying, he got up, turned on the lights and said, "Now we can see what we are doing." I loved him for it. We entertained lots of fun-loving preachers and have had long-lasting friendships.

Harry was only with us from December 1945 to August 25, 1947, less than two years.

After we finished building our house, Harry got a job driving a lumber truck. That day in August, when he got home from work, we picked up my mother and dad and drove 18 miles south of Eugene to pick corn for canning. A couple who came in to church regularly, the P.Z. Reeds and their daughter, Wanda (one of my high school girls), had a large garden and had invited us to come and get corn.

Brother Reed needed to go up the hill and drive his cattle down, so Harry asked if he could get the cows. "We'll ride up in the car. You and Dad can drive the car back and let me bring the cattle." There was a gate that had to be opened along the way.

CHAPTER 7

When they got to the top, Harry began to drive the cows down, just inside the tree line, parallel to the dirt road.

When Papa and P.Z. Reed (our name was Reid — not related to Reed) got back to the gate, they both got out of the car and visited by the gate to give the slower herd time to catch up. They heard a cry for help. Papa said, "That sounds like Harry." They ran in the direction of the voice.

Just as they got within hearing distance, they heard Harry say, "Snake."

By the time they got to him, he was unconscious. He only had his low-cut leather house shoes on. Papa found the snakebite and tried to draw out the poison but realized it was too late. It had hit the main artery of his foot, and the venom went to his heart. In August, the snake loses its skin over its head and is blind, so it will strike at anything. Harry was larger than Papa and our friend, and I'm sure it took them quite a while to carry him and get him into the backseat of our five-passenger coupe.

Mama, 2-year-old Ormel and I were in the corn patch about 100 yards from the house, when all of a sudden, our car came flying down the road, dirt rolling high. Wanda came running out to the car and yelled down to me, "Moreta, come quick! Harry's dead!"

"That's not what she said," Mama assured me. Then she instructed me, "Go on, child, I'll bring Ormel."

When I got to the car, blood was coming out of Harry's nose, mouth and eyes, and I knew that was it!

The Lord had been preparing me for this for several days, and I didn't realize it. When I would be washing dishes, I would begin to think, *What If Harry was taken from me? What in the world would I do?* The tears would begin to drip in my dishwater.

As I would write checks and pay bills, I'd begin to have a mental image. *What if something happened to Harry? What would I do?* Then I'd think, *What's the matter with me?* I would quit what I was doing, dry my tears and do something else for a while.

My Dedication

Always hungry for God, I was seeking Him earnestly. But I loved Harry so much, I would repent before the Lord, "Lord, I want to love You more than anything in the world. I want to please

MORETA: MY STORY

You and be more effective in Your service, but You'll have to help me, because I sure do love this man."

Awhile before all these warnings began to happen, I was at the piano during the altar service at the church. I felt that God was asking me, "Do you really love Me?"

My answer was, "Yes, Lord, I do love You."

Then His next question seemed to be, "Are you willing to give Me your most prized possession?"

As people were praying loud around the altars, I fell from the piano stool to my knees on the floor and wept almost uncontrollably for a long time. I finally could say, "Yes, I will give You my most prized possession and anything I own — I am willing to be made willing. I'm Yours."

I didn't name it, but I knew and God knew what that was. It wasn't easy, but as I look back on it all, I realize that God was asking for my permission and to let me know what He was about to do, though I didn't understand it at the time.

But let me encourage you. Live in the Word. Eternity is worth everything. Obedience to His will is the only answer. Everything is promised to the overcomer. He has told us that trials and suffering will come our way. But He has promised to be with us through the fire, through the flood, through the storms of this life. I shudder to think what could have happened in this life and in eternity to Harry, to me and to all my children and grandchildren. I still say, "Nevertheless, not my will but His will be done." I don't know what the future holds, but God has promised to be with us now and always. We can trust Him.

Let me give you the last part of the things that God had given me to prepare me for this death. I had played the piano at church that Sunday night. Harry had led the song service. We had to leave Ormel with someone else while we were on the platform. There were no nurseries in our churches those days. When the song service was over, Harry went down and got Ormel, and then I went to sit with them when my piano playing time ended.

We had to sit on the backseat with Ormel. He entertained everybody all around. When the song leader led the songs, our kid would wave his arms around, too. When the preacher preached, he hit his fists together like the preacher did. He learned to be quiet (most of the time) because he had been taken out immediately, spanked and brought right back in, so he was learning early.

CHAPTER 7

A trio of my young people (I wish I could remember who they were), just before the message, sang "Tomorrow May Mean Goodbye." I wasn't connecting all the earlier experiences of tears, etc., but while that song was being sung, I wept all the way through. Harry was holding Ormel and had his arm around me, holding me tight, saying nothing, but caressing me with all the love in the world. Ormel was still and quiet, not seeming to notice.

Tomorrow Was the Goodbye

When I saw Harry in the backseat of the car, all those things that had come to me before flashed in front of me in an instant, and I knew this was it.

We headed for town. Papa asked, "Do you want me to drive, sis?"

"No way," was my answer. I had to do it. Papa, Mama, Ormel and I were in the front seat, with Harry in the back. There were few cars on the road. I put my foot to the floorboard, put the emergency lights on and hoped a cop would stop me and get me the 18 miles to the hospital with his lights and siren on.

All the way into town, the death rattle was coming from the backseat, and I was silently praying, *Just don't let him die until I get him to the hospital.* The doctors couldn't do anything for him, though they tried. After quite a while, they got him into a private room, and I could be with him. The doctor came to me and said, "Don't worry, Mrs. Chapin. He's going to be all right." I knew that he knew it was not going to be all right.

Papa had called my brother, Orion, and his fiancée, Elnora, and they were at the hospital almost immediately. All of them were praying. Elnora was fervently praying in the Spirit. They were in the room with us for a short while, then they left to take my parents and Ormel home. They would be right back.

I was in the room alone with my dear husband. His face and lips were swollen, but he revived enough to try to smile at me. He reached both arms up to try to hug me. He breathed one big breath, fell back on the pillow and was gone!

I was able to get the nurse and they got my family stopped before they got out of the parking lot. There's no way to express the horror of those two hours, the grief of that moment and the pain of the days that followed.

MORETA: MY STORY

He Lived Less Than Two Hours

Now I had to go home without him. All the arrangements and decisions to make — calling his parents and family in Michigan. Thankfully, my parents and Orion were there to guide and help me. What funeral home; what cemetery; clothes for his burial; funeral day; more phone calls to make; preacher; obituary; all the plans for the funeral.

Relatives and friends were coming, and many were calling from everywhere. People were bringing food, and many wept with me. It helped me to tell the story over and over. All the "busyness" no doubt kept me from falling apart.

It was such a shock for everyone. Harry was 28. He was young, healthy, fun loving and dedicated to God and his family. The newspapers and radio carried the story across the nation. Snakebite deaths were not the common news of the day.

The Large Funeral

The funeral was beautiful. Flowers lined the front of the church, literally, wall to wall and across the platform. My trio sang again "Tomorrow May Mean Goodbye." My two brothers, Orion and Melbra, sat on either side of me. Mama and Papa, with Ormel, were on the same front seat with us. Ormel wasn't quite 3 years old, but he seemed to understand it all and was totally compliant during everything. He had been there from the beginning and had seen it all.

Harry's parents, with his sister and her husband, Grace and Thaine, and others of the family drove straight through from Michigan to be with us during this painful time. It was so hard for them to lose their pride and joy. He loved his family and showed his love to them continually.

Ormel went right to them and would love on them and be with them. He was amazing. He was quiet and seemed to be grieving in his own way. At home, he would softly cry at times, when he was with me. Though I tried to hold up for him, he was a comfort to *me*.

Iola Wiseman, who had married us, was holding a revival in Oregon. She and Pastor Hyland ministered at the funeral. I think it was the largest crowd ever in the lovely new church. All seats and

CHAPTER 7

the balcony were full. I don't remember what the casket was like, but Harry was handsomely beautiful with his black wavy hair and his expression of "I love you, and I care." Of course, all funerals in those days were open casket. This observance was not a celebration. It was a solemn occasion.

I had eight of the high school girls in my youth group as flower girls for after the service. Those young ladies sat behind the pallbearers during the service. When the people had walked by the casket and on to the outside of the church, and when the family had their last time at the open viewing, the funeral director gave the eight girls sprays of flowers to carry.

At the entrance of the church there were lots of long, wide steps. The girls stood on every other step, four on each side, making a passageway of flowers for the casket and the family to walk through when they came out of the church and to the hearse and the family cars.

To the Cemetery

That painful trip to the cemetery in the large family cars, following that long, black hearse carrying my dearest possession on earth was unbearable. All was quiet, and I was thinking, *There's nothing in this world harder than this.* It was a long, heartbreaking ride.

The burial place was on West 11th, through Springfield, through Eugene, *past the west side of everything.* The police were all along the way, leading the very long procession. People on the sidewalks would stop in respect. Cars would stop.

It seemed everyone came to the service at the gravesite. I had told the undertaker that I would not leave until the casket was lowered in the ground, the last clod was in the grave and every flower was in place. There were so many flowers, they covered some of the graves nearby. The waiting time wasn't difficult as most of the people came to me with their condolences and love.

And then the long trip back to my home. Death is so final! I was to discover this more as the days came and went.

In case I haven't been knowledgeable enough to clearly write so you can see how difficult those times were, the next few weeks became unbearable, too. There was more, much more.

MORETA: MY STORY

Mad at God

Not only did I lose my dear husband, but because of my grief and bitterness, I lost God, too.

All my life, I had been taught about heaven and God. I had been teaching about it for years to my young people and Sunday school classes.

Now, as I tried to imagine what Harry could be doing up there when I knew he would rather be with his wife and baby, it just wouldn't balance out. I became very bitter at God.

There wasn't a heaven!

There wasn't a hell!

The Bible wasn't true!

Harry was just dead and would turn to dust. I would never see him again.

And if it was God that took my husband, He was an unfair God and would take my son, too, and then my house. How painful that all was.

I couldn't possibly tell my family how I was thinking. I couldn't tell my pastor or my friends. They all believed the Bible to be true and would just preach to me. Oh, I wanted to believe. I wanted to have hope that I would see him again. At night, I would cry and pray, "God, if there is a God, please reveal Yourself to me. Show me. Talk to me."

Nothing!

I have discovered that when you are at your lowest point in life, Satan hounds you, lies to you and uses his most convincing schemes to destroy your faith in God and God's Word. "Don't tell anybody" is one of the devil's plots. He doesn't want to be exposed. And as long as I agreed with him, he was making headway with me.

For a whole week or more this battle with the devil was raging. And that's torment! God is a gentleman. He won't force Himself on anyone who is entertaining Satan.

But God has promised and has given us His Word that He will never leave us or forsake us. "With every temptation there is a way of escape." I was searching for an escape, grasping for a straw, grasping for anything that would give me hope again. What in this world do people do without God and without hope during times like this?

CHAPTER 7

During this time, I had lots of visitors. Lots of "Job's comforters." People with stupid remarks. One dear old maid whom I had known for many years expressed her encouragement. "Well, we never know what the future would be. Harry was so loving, and everybody loved him. He may have left you later for another woman." That, I'm sure, was the worst I received. Most of them, though, were comforting and wonderful.

Ormel was having his own quiet grieving times. One day, when I set him in his high chair and put his food there, he looked at it a while, pushed it aside and said, "I just want my daddy."

Usually, I could hold my tears for my baby's sake, but this was too much. I had to put my head on the table, my arm around him and cry, too. There were lots of lonely, rough times.

God Came Through Miraculously

One night, my brother, Melbra, and his wife, Edna, were at my house. Iola Wiseman had canceled her revival meeting and came to me. She was there that night, and they were talking about heaven. (They had no idea of what I had been going through.)

Iola began telling of a book she had read of a lady who had died and gone to heaven, then was revived to tell what she had seen. A river, flowers, animals, birds, children, angels, groups of young people laughing, singing, going about with large bouquets of flowers that they would imbed into mansions that were being prepared for people of earth as they came to heaven.

All of a sudden, I could picture Harry being busy, happy, laughing. It sounded possible. I got excited. As I was walking toward the phone, I asked, "What's the name of that book?" It was 9 p.m., but I had to get that book and would call the Open Bible School in Eugene. Surely I could find someone around who could find that book in his library.

Iola was saying, "Oh, I believe it was *Intra Muros*." I couldn't believe it! I had that book!

I called, "Come on, Melbra." We rushed to the garage and put a ladder up to the attic. There were three small books in reaching distance.

The year before, at Camp Meeting in Brooks, Oregon, Harry and I had bought that book but had never turned its pages. God had planned it for me for this very time. God came through!

MORETA: MY STORY

Can you believe what a small, insignificant thing to restore my hope and faith? To have God again and be able to live *in my thinking*, with Harry in heaven and to have deliverance from the devil's torments.

However, now that there was a God, I was still angry with Him. It was many months before I could forgive Him for taking my wonderful man and our baby's daddy. I couldn't go back to church and to my young people for several weeks. I was still their youth pastor, but I just couldn't do it.

Isn't it strange how God had been so faithful to prepare me for what was about to happen? I had even given my permission, but when it happened, I could not accept it.

Ormel and I went to Arizona for a few weeks to Aunt Esther's with June, Clinton and Githon, my fun-loving cousins. They loved Ormel. It was a healing time. They lived near Superstition Mountain. I'd sit on the cabinet counter, peel and eat fresh grapefruit from the tree in their yard. When I got home, a little time had passed, and I soon could go to church again.

My young people began coming, writing me, calling me.

"We love you."

"We miss you"

"We need you."

"Please hurry back to us."

Finally, I was ready to go back and resume my duties again. It was a start to my healing. They didn't know I was mad at God. They just thought I was sad and missing my husband whom they had loved and missed, too. I could still talk about heaven and teach the scriptures of how to live a godly life. I now believed that the Bible was true. God was loving me and helping me, day by day.

However, it took several years for the total healing to come. I couldn't bear to hear the word *snake*. Some of the scripture I wouldn't talk about. I still had fear that my son would be taken from me. And, if that happened, my house would burn down. The devil is such a hateful tormentor. He never gives up. He knows doubt destroys faith.

I fasted and prayed that day in 1951. I had to have deliverance from my fear and doubt. I couldn't allow this thinking to go on forever. At the end of the day, I wrote this poem, and I have been free from the bondage that held me captive from that day to now.

CHAPTER 7

That Little Boy, Daddy and Me

God, You gave my baby to me
Just seven years ago.
Such a tiny little bundle
And so sweet. I love him so!

His sweet Daddy wasn't with us
But in the Navy across the sea.
'Twas a long two years without him
For that little boy and me.

He knew his Daddy's picture
And when at last he did return,
Went right to him, called him "Daddy."
No readjustments hard to learn.

Our little home was really happy
Real contentment for us three.
It was so good to be together
Our little boy, Daddy and me.

One sad day, God chose our Daddy,
And with us here he'll never be.
Then all alone with all our sorrow,
Was my little boy and me.

Not quite three when Daddy left us,
Since then four years have passed.
That sad time we'll long remember,
Until we meet in heaven at last.

There no sorrows can molest us.
No more heartaches shall we see.
There we can always be together.
My little boy, Daddy and me.

God, You see how much I need this child
And how much he means to me.

MORETA: MY STORY

When he puts his arms around me,
Says, "Mommy, you're sweet as you can be."

Please don't ever take him from me.
Unless You see he'd fail to run
The race that You have set before him.
Not my will, but Yours be done.

If You can use him in Your service,
That's my prayer, my earnest plea.
Make him. Mold him. Keep him, Savior,
Close to Thee, Oh, let it be.

You see the tears I've shed today, Lord,
Wondering if You should call him away.
Or is it just a consecration
That You've asked of me today?

Though his Daddy up in heaven
Would welcome him when day is done.
I weep and make this consecration!
Not my will, but Yours be done.

Moreta Fosner

CHAPTER 8

Trying to Fit In

Before long, some of my young people were trying to court me or match me with some of the other men they knew. Now I was single and just one of them. But no way could I be interested in anybody.

Two or three weeks after the funeral, my doorbell rang. It was a tall man and a rambunctious little boy about Ormel's age. He wanted me to know that he had been in the hospital with his wife the same evening I lost my husband. His wife had died there that night, too.

His lively little guy broke away from his daddy and ran in the house. Oh, my! Now what? Of course, the dad had to come in to persuade the little rascal to come out. The man expressed his wish. "I thought, since we are both alone now, maybe we could get together." My answer was so definite, I didn't have much trouble getting him out. And I never saw him again.

Learning to Live On Less

After my husband was gone, I still had all the same expenses. The house and car were paid for. Thank the Lord! Harry used to say, "I'm building this house for you and Ormel." I'm sure he hadn't had a premonition of his coming death. That's just the way he thought. He was always wanting to do things for me. That's why our marriage was so good. We both loved to please each other. The electric bill, water, sewer, heating oil, phone, car and house insurance, property taxes, food and such had to be paid.

The only thing I could stop was the newspaper. I felt I had to have the telephone to feel safe and for any emergency. We both had life insurance. Now I had to cancel mine because of lack of finances.

When funeral, doctor, grave and all other related expenses were settled, I had $2,000. Harry's life insurance paid $1,000. A few churches and friends had given me money. There was no bank

MORETA: MY STORY

account. I just kept what little I had in the house. My youth pastor job was strictly volunteer — no wages. The social security monthly check was $47. Ormel's part was $17. And, of course, I used it all. That was all that came in each month.

The Bible says if I will give 10 cents out of every dollar to my church that the remaining 90 cents will go a lot further. It says, "Try me, prove me and see." It also says that the 10 percent is God's, and if I kept His part, I was a thief and a robber and no thief would enter heaven.

We had always paid tithes, and it really was true. Now, at our young age, everything was all paid for. All my siblings had paid tithes, plus much giving, and some of them have been able to add a few zeros to the ends of their holdings.

Let me tell you how the $2,000 and the $47 a month stretched for two years. It doesn't make sense. It's hard to believe, and it will not add up. Only one who tithes can fully understand.

All my bills were paid by me — nobody paid them for me. My dear brother, Orion, told me not to worry, that he was going to help me. He was building lots of homes in Eugene and making good money. He was also engaged to be married and was building a home for them. He was a busy man, and I knew I was not going to depend on him. But I promised him that I would let him know if I needed help.

When it was almost property tax time, he asked what my taxes were and gave me a check for the $167. I put the check in my dresser drawer with my cash and never used it. I paid the taxes with my own money. The next year, when he began getting tax bills for his several homes, he remembered and gave me a check to pay my taxes. I asked, "Do you want me to put this check with the one you gave me last year?"

"Didn't you use that?" he asked. "No wonder I couldn't balance my account." I used his check this second year.

***

Determined to make it work, I was very frugal in my spending. I always had very nice "new" clothes. I had a rich taste and liked the feel of those expensive duds. Those old, sweet, rich gals in the big formal churches only wore their fine garments one time. I could keep up with the best of them in their clothes.

CHAPTER 8

Melbra's wife, Edna, my mother and I would go to Eugene or larger cities to church rummage sales (we never heard of garage sales or yard sales at that time). I would get beautiful things for practically nothing, including shoes!

We would come home from those exciting times and try on everything to see what each one had bought. It was a fabulous style show. I came out feeling rich, happy and beautiful.

My car always had gas in it. However, Ormel and I would walk to church often to save gas. I never ran out of food and could even have friends in to eat with me. I had a garden and wasn't afraid of work.

For several weeks, I had ladies in for early morning prayer at 8 a.m. As I knelt, Ormel played at my knees. Much prayer and giving was greatly rewarded.

One of those times on a Sunday night about the end of my second year, the offering plate came by with a special need for something. I had less than one dollar in my purse and no more at home. I reasoned, *This won't even buy milk, I may as well give it.* I wasn't thinking of the widow's mite in the Bible. I hardly gave it a second thought, until years later. I had given the "widow's mite" (Mark 12:41, 44). And God saw it!

Now, Get Your Believing Cap On

In the second year, I knew my $2,000 wouldn't last forever. I had to do something to make a living. I had always been interested in pictures (photography). I discovered a photography school in Eugene. I drove over to check it out. How much? Where? What? When? I enrolled! It was $25 a month.

I started right away. It was five days a week, eight hours a day. I could take Ormel to Mama's in Eugene each day. I went for five months. After a short while of training, I had to buy my own professional camera and film. I bought a used 4 by 5 Graflex camera from the school for $200. It was black and white. There was no color in photography then.

After I had the darkroom training and was developing film and making prints, I had to buy my own darkroom supplies to use at home. I got a new professional De Jour enlarger for $200. I had all the stainless steel utensils for the chemicals made to my specifications. I had a new paper cutter, the squeegee, the chemicals, darkroom light, extra 4 by 5 film and photographic paper to make the final picture. There were also film clamps and various other things.

I became the only special wedding photographer for the school. Someone went with me the first time or two to take the pictures, then I was on my own. And they let me have part of the money for those weddings, which was very little. However, with my "little," every little bit helped. I also took pictures of babies when they were brought to the school for portraits. You surely know, I loved my new profession. This all happened in the second year of my being a widow.

Papa and my brother, Orion, built a darkroom on my house. They made the room 10 by 10 feet with a window in it. The room was large enough for an extra bedroom later. They were quite sure I wouldn't last as a widow very long.

The thing that doesn't add up is how the $47 a month and my only cash of $2,000 stretched two full years. When I married, all my bills were paid. No one paid them but me.

Big Brother Is Married

Orion and Elnora were married in December. He finally got the girl that he had fasted and prayed for. And she fit into the family perfectly. She had four sisters. Elnora was the oldest of the girls, then came Doris, Lois, Mae and Joyce.

The first night he dated Elnora, he drove up in his sporty car and came to the door for her. All four of the younger sisters came into the living room to look him over. The "chatterbox," Joyce, jumped up on Orion's knee and began to question him. He had on a shirt with the sleeves rolled up a turn or two and the front of the collar open enough to show some of his chest hair. She reached up and touched the hair on his chest and asked, "Do these go all the way down?"

All the girls disappeared from the room but the one on his knee. She looked around and seeing they were all gone, muttered, "Well, what did I do wrong this time?"

It was so great to see my 33-year-old brother married to this choice girl. He had dated lots of dear girls, but this one he had to fight hard for — and she won!

CHAPTER 8

At the End of the First Year

When I saw a woman who had lost her husband a year before, I would think, *If she has made it, I can make it. Maybe when the year is up, I will be able to live again.* But dating was still not in my thinking.

My dear friends, Mildred and Leroy Marsh, were dating. They loved Ormel and would take him with them at times. This one evening, they came for him. I had walked with them to the car and sat in the backseat visiting with them. A big, golden full moon came up over the horizon. They had been hassling me about dating again. When that moon came up, my response was, "Okay, if anybody calls me tonight, I'll go out with him." Almost immediately, my phone rang inside. I had absolutely no one in mind, but I teased, "There he is right now."

As they were driving off, they called out, "We'll bring Ormel home sometime tonight."

Well?

That's what it was! Pastor Lloyd Fosner from Drain, Oregon. He had lost his wife very recently. He had showed up at my door a month earlier, but I didn't give him any encouragement. In fact, I was a bit disgusted that he would come so soon after his wife's passing. But by now, it seemed he dared not wait any longer and tried the phone this time. He wanted to take me out to eat. Having just made that statement and with that full moon — that golden moon on that balmy night — I never even thought of saying no. He was there at the appointed time — shortly!

Not wanting any of my young people to know anything about this, we drove through Eugene, then north a ways on the old road to Corvallis to a small restaurant. No pizzazz. Just a place to eat. He had asked me where I'd like to go. My main thought was not to be seen by anyone who knew me. Surely no one would know me this far away.

However, we just got seated at a booth, and one of my young men was sitting across the way. He saw us come in and gave me an impish grin. Soon he came to our table, and I introduced him to my "uncle." I was sure he didn't believe it, and he didn't. He had fun with that later.

MORETA: MY STORY

We drove back through Eugene and Springfield and up the old highway east to the Mckenzie River for several miles to a bend in the river with that moon shining on the water. He pulled aside and parked. We sat there and just talked about our lives for a long time. He had the radio on to a popular song, "Cruising Down the River on a Sunday Afternoon." That became our song. Although this was Monday. Since he was a preacher and Sundays were always busy with the church, we would sing it "Monday Afternoon."

When he took me home that night, Mildred and Leroy were still there, and I wouldn't let him walk me to the door. They had put Ormel to bed. When I walked in, they began to ask, "Well, tell us all about it."

I said, "Oh, it was just a couple of old ladies who wanted to take me for a ride in their new car." They didn't believe me, either. I knew they didn't, but that was all they could get out of me that night. Really, part of that was true. Lloyd had just bought a new wine-red Frazier. After all, he was a pastor, and I was a youth pastor. Was that a truth stuffed with a lie? Nah, I have scripture for it. I was just being like Jesus when He was walking with a couple of His disciples on the road to Emmaus. "He made as if He was going farther."

You know, really, when people want to sin and justify their sins, they can find a Bible verse out of context to ease their conscience. That wasn't what I was doing. I knew they didn't believe me, and I wasn't deceiving them. They just had to wait for the whole story. Does that sound alright? I hope so. But kids don't do it that way.

When Harry and I lived in Toledo after we first married, Lloyd and his wife, Rena, were pastors of the Assembly of God church seven miles north in Siletz. We would see them at monthly fellowship meetings where all the Assembly churches in the section came together for services. We really didn't know that much about them.

A Difficult Year

My husband, Harry, had been gone for a year when Lloyd and I started dating. I couldn't bring myself to say yes to marriage. I had always said I would never marry a preacher. With my logger husband, I was free from becoming a preacher's wife. There had been some inconsistencies with a few preachers, and I wanted no

CHAPTER 8

part of it, though I played the piano, cherished my Bible, was a pray-er and loved people.

This was a big order. Move out of my lovely new home. Leave my wonderful group of young people and my church that I was a big part of. Marry a man with two little girls, which was a challenge already, and mixing families that I had heard about and read about. It was scary!

I prayed. I cried. I fasted. I asked for advice from about every honest-looking evangelist and camp meeting speaker around. I put out fleeces. I searched the scriptures. I begged God. I wanted Him to give me a yes or no answer. Guess what? He seemingly wasn't gonna take responsibility for this one. He evidently thought I was smart enough to figure this one out myself.

One of the fleeces should have made it easy for God to answer. He even ignored that! I had solemnly asked, "If I should marry this man, have him bring me a dozen red roses. Not 13, not 11, but one dozen." But, *If I should not marry this man, have him bring me a dozen yellow roses.*

Now it seemed like God should have appreciated my desire to know His will in something this important. I found out during our 57 years that a request like that would have been quite impossible. This man's thinking didn't dwell on things like roses, red or yellow. The interesting thing about all this, though, (you'll love this) was Lloyd had been staying with Grandma and Grandpa Hines when he came to Springfield. A short while before our wedding, my hubby-to-be brought me a little stick about 18 inches long with a few knots along the sides. He said, "Grandma Hines sent this to you."

"What in the world is it?" I asked.

"It's a yellow climbing rose for you to plant in your yard," he proudly replied.

Now please tell me. What would you do with an answer like that? There wouldn't be a rose till next year, then hundreds of them. You'll hear the rest of the story after the wedding.

More Frustration

Trying to forget him, I'd go places and do things to help me forget. Once, I asked him not to come back. Soon he was back again. I reminded him that I had asked him not to come.

MORETA: MY STORY

His answer was, "Faint heart never won fair maiden!" So he kept up his persistent pursuit passionately! And I weakened.

A trip to Michigan to visit my dear in-laws would surely help in the forgetting process. I wanted to forget he existed. He had resigned his church in Drain, Oregon, and was boarding with Grandma and Grandpa Hines. My dad had put him to work building a house.

One day, he was using the electric saw. The board split and the saw cut off the middle finger of his left hand and injured the other three fingers.

My parents had the key to my house. They moved in when this happened and invited Lloyd to stay there, too. When I got home from Michigan, they were all in my home. Lloyd was sleeping on the fold-down davenport in the living room. My parents were in the guest room.

Did my folks feel responsible for his keep since the accident happened on the job? Why didn't they move him into their house instead of mine? They lived in a lovely home in Eugene not that far away. I never thought of those questions until recently. So, I never asked them why.

The messed up hand had a big wire contraption holding his fingers in place. There was heavy bandaging, and it was very painful. It had gotten infected and stinky. The bandages had to be changed and the wounds cleansed and sterilized two and three times each day. And I had to be the nurse, had to take him to the doctor and see that all was going well. The doctor had sewn the finger back on his hand and had cut his own hand in the process. The recovery was a long, painful procedure for Lloyd. My parents were right there to chaperone and help until Lloyd was well enough to leave.

Before long, the Assembly of God church in Yoncalla, five miles south of his former church in Drain, invited him to come pastor that church. So he moved into the parsonage in Yoncalla.

It was still several months before I could say yes to marrying him. Finally, we picked out the engagement ring. It was hard for me to pull off my former rings and wear this one. I still was frustrated about it all. Still weighing. Still asking. Still praying. Did the Lord really want me to be a preacher's wife? Was it because I had said I would never marry a preacher? I was willing to do anything if I knew God wanted me in that place.

CHAPTER 8

I'm sure one of the reasons I hesitated was because Lloyd was a man of few words. He was dignified. He was not a romancer like I had known during my dating years, especially the years with Harry. But when the time was over of being his nursemaid, I had become part of the furniture of his future.

I knew if I married Lloyd, there would have to be no comparing him with Harry. And I never did! I felt qualified to be a pastor's wife. I had been involved with that life all my years. So that was no problem, or so I thought. If I could just get the Lord to say go, I would. I didn't want to do anything to miss what God might have in mind for Him, for my future, for Lloyd or anyone else.

No one except the preachers that I was counseling with (not even Lloyd) knew that I was having this humongous time of indecision. By now, I was enjoying our times together. He felt very convinced and comfortable with me.

After quite a while, we set the wedding date, and I questioned no more. We dated for one year, from August to August.

CHAPTER 9

The Wedding

August 21, 1949, at the Seventh and B Street Assembly of God church in Springfield, Oregon, we did it! I had my youth services in the large downstairs auditorium at 6 p.m. Sunday nights. The main service was at 7 p.m. upstairs in the sanctuary. I never told anyone in the church about the wedding, except the pastor. My family lived in Eugene and didn't attend my church.

Lloyd's sister, Ruby, and Elliott brought six dozen gladiolas with them from Portland. The decorations were bright and very beautiful.

Lloyd told his church in Yoncalla on Sunday morning that he was getting married that night. They were shocked. They knew he had been seeing me and that I was the youth pastor in Springfield, but they hadn't realized it had come to this.

Usually, I told my young people what would be the next Sunday service. This time, I just told them, "Don't miss next Sunday night, or you'll be sorry." I did lots of unusual things in my planning, and they trusted me. All were there Sunday night at 6!

I wore an elegant mid-calf, long sleeve, teal-blue satin dress. I didn't carry a bouquet. Instead, I wore a bright-red large rosebud spray of flowers from my shoulder halfway to my waist. Oh, I just thought of this — *I'll bet it had a dozen red roses in it!* It was so long, I had to take a few off. I told the girl to make it big. She did! And Lloyd had to pay for it!

I had the usual — *something old; something new; something borrowed; something blue* — only the something borrowed wasn't borrowed. It was stolen! *I DID IT!* The hat! My friend Mildred had just recently married and had this lovely hat. I hadn't asked her yet to use it, but I went to her house to borrow it, and she wasn't home. I tried the door, and it was locked. I tried the window in her bedroom and it opened, so I climbed in and got the hat. She hadn't discovered the loss until she saw it on my head during the wedding. It was a silvery (perhaps sequined) hat that covered a small part of my head, with a shoulder-length veil that was fancy and just

CHAPTER 9

what I needed. I think she liked it. We are still friends and have been these many years. This is the Mildred and Leroy who had taken Ormel the night of our first date.

My photography instructor came to the wedding and took our pictures for free.

It was a simple ceremony with no reception. Just a time for all to come around us and love on us. And I wanted to love on them, too. Some were crying, knowing they were losing me.

We felt since we had been married before that we wanted no big, elaborate celebration but just a pretty, uncluttered ceremony. Also, I didn't want people to bring gifts. (However, the pastor had a lovely gift there for us: a small walnut stand table and a chrome toaster that I use to this day. It's still beautiful!)

The 7 p.m. service would soon start upstairs. So no cake and no punch. We said our goodbyes and were on our way. My family would clean up the room.

The Honeymoon

We drove the first night to Vancouver, Washington, and stayed in a hotel. Next morning, we drove through Washington, and (I think) we took the ferry from Port Angeles to Victoria, B.C. We went to Butchart Gardens on Vancouver Island. We rode on the old cobble streets and saw the very interesting Parliament building and the pretty landscaping in front. I had my big 4 by 5 Graflex camera and lugged it around, taking pictures of everything.

We crossed the Strait of Juan De Fuca on a ferryboat to Neah Bay, then down the coast to La Push, Washington, to an Indian reservation and a visit with George Effman and his wife, Doris. They were friends that Lloyd had known in Bible college a few years earlier. We stayed with them a couple of nights during an Indian celebration. It was great to watch the Indians tie the big, filleted salmon on the sticks, then prop them over the large open fire pit to bake.

What a wonderful experience to taste all the primitive foods like venison, the salmon we had watched them cook and lots of specialties the women had made. Then to see all the Indian headdresses and garments at their native dances that evening. It was great! And I was taking pictures all the while.

MORETA: MY STORY

From the Honeymoon to Reality

We came from the honeymoon to the parsonage, which was about 10 feet from the back corner of the Yoncalla church, to our young triplets and a fastidious group of women. But it was a good church. They "taught" me how to be a preacher's wife, they thought. More about this rude awakening later. But, for now, other problems. Other hurts. The mixed family and the church ladies, with the beginning of a life together, had its difficulties that were almost too much for me. But I was not a quitter. It had to work.

Corrie Ten Boom, in her book, *Tramp For The Lord*, wrote, "When I left the German concentration camp, I said, 'I'll go anywhere God sends me, but I hope never to go to Germany.'" She wrote, "Now I understand that was a statement of disobedience."

The Mixed Family

I have known for years and taught in classes that God uses our hurts, our heartaches and our problems to make us into *His* image. I have cried and I've poked fun at my hurts, disappointments, misunderstandings and emotional wounds. I've forgiven, I've performed with joy and even pleasure but with grief and a lonely, broken heart inside. It was "the peace that passes all understanding" (Philippians 4:7). My smile was not fake. It wasn't a mask I wore. It was for real. I was the happiest, unhappy person in the state. "Even in laughter, the heart is sorrowful" (Proverbs 14:13). I decided many years ago that I was not going to be a cranky old lady. A verse of scripture helped: "Let no man take your joy" (John 16:22).

During times of stress, I learned to live in the Word (Bible). A lot of times, I wouldn't even think about what I was reading. I'd read it over and over. Eventually, I decided I should just keep reading. Start from the first book of the Bible, Genesis, and read it like a storybook and keep on reading. For many years, I've read the Bible through every year, plus studying to teach.

I wasn't the only one who lived with the difficulties. Mixing the family wasn't easy for any of us. It was hard for each of the children, and I knew as they grew older that they, one by one, would have to pray through, forgive, gain an understanding, give it to God and come to the realization that the rough times were times

CHAPTER 9

where God was molding them into His image, too, and equipping them for leadership in the work of God. They all four have been, and are, leaders in their respective places. More about this later.

It was hard for Lloyd, too. His way of life had not been happy, while my upbringing had been strict obedience, but total love, acceptance, singing, going, doing, friends and happiness. He was not a disciplinarian. I had to guide, teach to obey, teach rules, coach, drill, love, spank, explain, expect and command obedience with much prayer, tears and fasting. I had to be all to all three of the children if I would be able to train my own son.

I had made a promise to and with the Lord: "If You will help us know how to train Ormel, I will weigh every time I have to discipline these two girls with how I would correct my son."

I believe I have kept that vow and was fair with my two new daughters. Correcting the girls was like scolding or spanking the neighbor's kids with the neighbor looking on. I was sure God had entered into that covenant with me, and He has for certain kept His part.

My thinking was, *If these girls grow up to love God and to be girls of godly character, they will make their daddy look good. If they should turn out to be a disgrace, it will be because they had such an evil stepmother.* I decided to make him look good. So, I would have to train them in the same Bible way that I must teach mine. With God's help, their daddy was proud of his two super lovely girls. They made him look good!

Lloyd's Life

Lloyd was born to older parents in Sherwood, Oregon, on August 18, 1918 (8/18/18). (I was born 2/20/22.) His sister, Ruby, was 22 years older than he. His brothers were Harold, Edward and Shirley.

I think Shirley was the only sibling at home when Lloyd was growing up. He felt Shirley was overbearing and ornery with him. "But one day," Lloyd told me, "when Shirley met me on the sidewalk and expected me to move off so he could pass (I was larger and taller than he), I stood with my hands on my hips and never budged. Shirley stopped, glared at me, moved off the walk and went around me. I never had any more trouble with his bullying me." He soon left home, and only Lloyd was left.

MORETA: MY STORY

Lloyd's dad was a dentist. Some of his patients paid him with butter, eggs, milk and such things. If he would hear of a family in need, he'd walk a long distance to give them money. He never owned a car. He was seldom at home but out helping others. They never went anywhere as a family on trips or any pleasurable things, except to church. They were Quakers — godly people who kept lots of the special speakers.

One time, his dad took him on a train ride for a fishing trip up the Columbia River. They slept out nights in a farmer's haystack by the river. Lloyd never told me about any fish they might have caught, if any. He was just so pleased with the time he had spent with his dad. He related that story to me several times through the years.

What a shame dads don't take time to be with their children. It was a big loss for Lloyd growing up. Also, what the dad missed for training and really caring for his son.

He left it for someone else to do.

Lloyd could be gone all day on his bike, and no one seemed to know or care. When I wouldn't even think to ask my dad for a nickel, this young boy could walk into his dad's office and get a quarter from him. A cheap payoff instead of his times with his young son.

He would tell me of times he rode his bike into Portland, or when he would go to a river not far from Portland, find a group of boys and swim.

As he told me this, he would stop short and say no more. I've wondered if those groups of boys perhaps taught him the facts of life. I never tried to quiz him further.

Lloyd's dad died before I knew them. He sat down on a bench, a log or whatever and died from a heart attack. I think he was in his late 60s. Lloyd was married by then.

His mother, Isabel, was small and quiet with few words, but a faint smile was always there. I think she was in her 70s when we married. She lived not many years after that. She would stay with us at times for a few days.

Lloyd, as well as his sister, Ruby, told me a story. His mother had the one girl and three boys. She felt her childbearing years were over. But she said the Lord had asked her to have another baby, and if she was willing, it would be a boy and he would be a preacher.

CHAPTER 9

She had loved the Lord and wanted to do what He wanted in her life. After considering it a short while, she said, "Yes, Lord."

Soon she became pregnant and got her preacher son. However, he was an ordinary boy until he left home when he was near 17 years old. He started going to the large 20th and Hawthorne Calvary Tabernacle in Portland. There were lots of young people there. He was chosen for one of the leading parts in a big drama the church was doing. He never went back to the Quaker church, and that was a disappointment to his mother. They felt he was getting into a cult — Pentecostal! And he has been Pentecostal ever since.

Lloyd met Rena Armstrong at that church, and they married shortly after. He worked in a pickle cannery in Portland for about a year after they were married.

He heard about Northwest Bible College in Seattle and was interested immediately to prepare for the ministry. He sent in his application. There would be no job and no money, but he was accepted. The college had great inroads for jobs that students could get to help pay their way. That was a plus.

After a while, he learned the painting trade, and the last year of school they lived pretty good, but it was *poor living* the years before.

Rena got a job and worked for a year. Her sister, Jane, came to live with them in their one-room apartment building, sharing the kitchen with others. They all three slept in the same bed. Rena and Jane started Bible college, too, in Lloyd's second year. Rena was a month older than Lloyd. Her birthday was July 3, 1918. They married on a Sunday, two or three days before his 18th birthday! She was the only girl he ever dated.

Rena didn't get to finish her schooling there. During Lloyd's last year, she had become pregnant and had to quit. After Lloyd's graduation, they went to Newport, Oregon.

He worked for Raymond Hall's crab boat out on the ocean. He was seasick every day for the whole nine months, but he had to keep going. He was too broke to look for something else. His number one daughter, Judy Jane, was born in the Newport Hospital, June 24, 1942.

Somewhere during this time, he took the pastorate of the Assembly church in Siletz, Oregon. This is where they lived when we met them. We lived in Toledo, seven miles away. Their number

MORETA: MY STORY

two daughter, Rhonda Mae, was born to them October 15, 1944 in the Newport Hospital while they pastored in Siletz. We never crossed paths after that until about the time of Rena's death from diabetes.

A well-known healing evangelist, William Branham, was conducting a special area-wide service at the Eugene Fairgrounds. It was a Sunday afternoon in May. Lloyd was with the ministers during and after the services. His wife, Rena, was alone. I sat with her and later walked with her in the park.

She died the following Wednesday. I didn't know about it, so I didn't attend her funeral.

Lloyd told me later that she had been prayed for that day at the fairgrounds and afterwards had said if God didn't heal her, she didn't want to live and refused to take her insulin. She was such a lovely person but always seemed so sad and alone, even when I first knew her. She was petite, very pretty and played the violin beautifully.

It was hard for Lloyd to try to pastor and take care of the girls and deal with all the problems. He resigned from the church and took Judy to Rena's sister, Jane Landes, in Yoncalla and Rhonda to Rena's mother, Grandma Armstrong, in Portland. He worked for those months.

I started writing this book in February of 2007. When I get to rough places like this, I read, reread and wait for days, and sometime longer, to write, erase and write again. The following is proof of such writings.

Introspection

Today is April 5, 2007. As I look back to the time I was asking God for an answer about marrying Lloyd, I'm reflecting on all the questioning I did. The realization comes to me of my not accepting anything unless it was on my terms and my timing.

Just this morning as I was reading in Proverbs and was in prayer, searching, digging and crying for wisdom, knowledge and understanding (though only in my daily Bible reading, not thinking about this past era), I began to apply this to myself and to my book writing. And to learning this contrary, stupid new computer! And wisdom, knowledge and understanding in His service, soul winning and ministry for His glory. Plus wisdom with my

CHAPTER 9

children, neighbors and friends and piano playing. Plus-Plus! I need His wisdom, knowledge and understanding for everything.

"My daughter, if you will receive my words, and hide my commandments with you; so that you incline your ear unto wisdom, and apply your heart to understanding; if you cry after knowledge, and lift up your voice for understanding; if you seek wisdom as silver, and search for her as for hidden treasures; then you shall understand the fear of the Lord, and find the knowledge of God. For the Lord gives wisdom and out of his mouth comes knowledge and understanding. He lays up sound wisdom for the righteous. He is a protector to them that walk uprightly." (Proverbs 2:1-7)

God does not work on my schedule. I couldn't put Him in a corral and demand He do it my way with my terms, my thinking, my timing. God is creative. He works on His terms, not mine.

Is it possible? Yes, it's very possible that God was trying to show me what I should do, but I had set the only way that He could answer, and I couldn't see the few warnings that I had overlooked.

On one occasion, an obscure sweet lady, who had had a similar circumstance, was very definite. I thought about it but didn't really listen.

Only one preacher, the older Ray Marks, had asked me, "Do you love him?"

I had replied, "I'm not sure."

He warned, "You'd better wait."

I had asked advise from one camp meeting speaker. He stood up, shook a leg and said, "If I was a little younger, I'd try for you myself." He did say, though, that it wouldn't be easy. I knew that! I hardly reflected on that part. All I could remember was him shaking his leg.

And then my dear dad, a few days before the wedding. I know it was hard for him to see his little girl get into such a difficult situation. I guess, though, I thought it was too late to reconsider.

Is it possible that just because He (God) didn't see to it that I got the red or yellow roses, that I just went on dating, petting, entertaining and enjoying all the attention, I didn't clear my way in quietness and listen for what He might be saying?

I should have refused to continue dating until I had heard from God!

MORETA: MY STORY

April 9th

Was this God's perfect will? Or was it plan B? I'm not really sure about that, and as I look at all the good things God gave me because of this marriage, I have to thank Him and praise Him for all His blessings.

The first blessing is my young son that I had been so concerned for, Reverend Ormel Chapin (he kept his daddy's name). If I had married someone other than a preacher, with our entertaining all the worldwide preachers, missionaries and VIPs, Ormel might have been a politician, a farmer, banker, mortician, doctor or even president. There's nothing wrong with any of those professions, but you know what? I'd rather have my sons be preachers of the Gospel than president of the United States or any other thing in this world. And Ormel's wonderful wife, a preacher's daughter, Sandi Bedwell Chapin. And Ormel's three sons all married girls who were preacher's daughters.

All are serving the Lord in places of ministries. I could write a book of all their talents and separate ministries.

The Icing on the Cake

And what if I hadn't married *this* preacher? Last, but not least, our 6 foot, 3 inch son (14 years younger than the others), Reverend Verlon Lloyd Fosner. And his special, talented preacher's daughter wife, Melodee Davis Fosner. They have three super specialties, two girls and one boy. Both girls have graduated from Northwest University. Their young son is a junior in the same university. Already, the three of them are involved in their separate ministries. And just this week, one of the girls announced her engagement to be married to a great young man preparing for the ministry. More about this later. It's good!

And then, the two little girls that I married. When I married Lloyd, it was a package deal. The two young girls were included as a bonus. I had to take my two boys sight unseen, but the 4- and 7-year-old girls I saw face to face and chose them as my own. The oldest, Judy, married a wonderful young man she found in Santa Cruz at Bethany Bible College, Robert Harkins, a preacher. They produced two girls, who have married preachers. You'll hear more about them later, too.

CHAPTER 9

Our youngest daughter, Rhonda, is the only one of the four who didn't marry a preacher. She married an unsaved Native Alaskan, Paul Wolcoff. We called her our missionary to Alaska. Miracle of miracles, she was able to see Paul turn to the Lord, plus his four lovely sisters and their husbands. His whole family was in church. One sister became the Missionette Director for the state of Alaska. Others of the husbands became deacons and workers in Assembly of God churches. Rhonda and Paul had two boys and a girl who still live in Alaska.

We lost our sweet Rhonda to cancer in 1998.

You will hear a lot more about my four great kids and 11 grandkids and now, four great-grand ones.

In Retrospect

When I consider why we were able to stay together, when I try to put it in black and white on paper, it's difficult.

I remember a statement Billy Graham's wife, Ruth, made when someone asked her if she had ever thought of divorce. She said, "Divorce? Never! Murder? Yes."

Honestly, I wasn't as bad as that. Murder? No. Divorce? No. But leaving? Separation? Quitting? Many times.

There's a cute story I heard of an old couple who were always in each other's way. One day, she said, "Why don't we just pray that God will take one of us, and I'll go live with my sister."

I thought such thoughts and prayers like that, and some that would kink your hair, but fortunately, God didn't answer. Seriously, though — actually, I've been serious all along. Just being able to laugh after a while has helped see me through a lot of hurts.

First of all, I was not going to bring disgrace to the ministry, and I was not going to hinder, nor destroy a man's ministry. I had gone into this marriage not wanting to displease God if this was His plan. We had made vows to God and before this host of people. "Till death do us part." The Bible had taught me that *you don't break a vow to God.*

The fear of God is the beginning of wisdom. I didn't have a lot of wisdom, but I knew I didn't want to go against God's Word! We had made a commitment to each other for life, and that had to stand. It held till the end. Praise the Lord. "For better or for worse."

MORETA: MY STORY

So, Where's the Better?

All the several pages I have written of the frustrations, hurts, grievances and how the Lord brought us through could make you feel that the nearly 60 years were terrible. No way! There were lots of joys, happiness, miracles of God and His blessings as you will see during the remainder of this book.

We played together, hunted together, fished and camped together. We traveled in this nation and several countries of the world.

I was chief cook and dishwasher, gardener, bookkeeper, barber, disciplinarian, wallpaper-hanger, manicurist, chauffeur, architect, designer, butler and a few other things. But I was not a nag. Someone once said, "If you will treat your wife like a thoroughbred, she will not become an old nag." That is good advice! After seeing a few wives nag their husbands, I decided many years ago that I would not be guilty of such behavior. And I was not a nag!

So, what in the world did he do?

He was a good preacher.

He read lots of books for inspiration and knowledge — a real student of the Word.

He spent much time in study and prayer in the church office in the very early mornings.

He had an unusual faith and discernment at times when it was needed.

He took care of the church needs, board meetings, the schools he started, the hiring and firing.

He was a painter, a builder and a master at putting volunteers to work on church projects.

He was a fiery preacher, and I was his number one amen corner.

I was also his number one master at putting our kids to work!

We never carried our hurts or disappointments to the church, to our kids, or anywhere else. And we were not fakes nor hypocrites. We were genuine, true, caring and giving of ourselves to our churches.

CHAPTER 9

I Was Obedient

God didn't promise me
A life of ease, or comfort without pain.
He never said happiness
Was all there was to gain.

But in His Word it's very clear
That there would be times
I would have to lean on Him.
But He would always be there.

He suffered pain.
He had rejection,
was misunderstood
And it was undeserved.
But when I'm made in His likeness
I'd walk the path that He had trod.
Yes! I was willing to walk that path … with God.

I do believe this was His plan for me.
And I came through with joy,
Peace and even happiness
With no regrets.
I walked in obedience
With God!

Moreta Fosner

This was written August 2, 2007, at 5:00 in the morning. And I just realized … Lloyd died one year ago this day.

CHAPTER 10

Yoncalla

Lloyd was pastoring here when we first married. The church was small with only one or two high school people and one or two college age girls. Lloyd had told them nothing about me, only that I was youth pastor in the Springfield church.

When I came on the scene, I was not accepted by a group of the older women. Some of them had plans for their daughters. One lady was sure that her unsaved husband would die (though he was healthy and a hard worker), and she had "dibs" on Lloyd. The worst part, though, was they thought they had to teach me how to become a preacher's wife.

Wow! What a life. (I think I can tell this because those ladies were much older than me, and I'm sure they're all dead by now.)

One of the dear ladies (the ringleader of it all) started coming to our house at 8 a.m. every morning to make sure we were up and to line out the pastor's day for him: what all he needed to do, who he needed to call on, etc. Lloyd got tired of all that pretty quick and kindly let her know that he was quite capable of taking care of things himself.

She stopped coming, but she would go early to several of the main ladies' homes and help them paint or paper their house, clean their chickens and help them can. Anything to spend hours being helpful and to influence them.

About six of the ladies were my trainers. I had never felt rejected or unloved before, but I sure got it there from these girlies. I couldn't understand why they were being so unlovely to me.

One Sunday morning before service time, I stepped into the sanctuary at the side door by the piano. These ladies were all seated in different parts of the auditorium reading their Bibles or whatever. When I came in, they all looked up, never changed expression, never said a word and went back to their reading — real saint-like.

Happily, I said, "Good morning, I'm here." No wonder they hated me. I was just too happy. No, I'm sure they didn't hate me.

CHAPTER 10

They just didn't know how *sweet* I was! I had to teach them.

One night after service, a young high school girl wanted to talk to me. She explained, "The ladies asked me to talk to you about your dresses. They are just too short and tight."

"You tell those ladies," I responded kindly, but emphatically, "if they want to buy me some new ones, I will be most appreciative. When I came here, I weighed 104 pounds. In six months, I am up to 133 pounds. My dresses, no doubt, are tighter and shorter." I never heard anymore from that department about my dresses.

My youngest brother and his wife were newlyweds and came to see us that night. As they walked up the sidewalk and came in, I was sitting on Lloyd's lap telling him all about my dress conversation. My brother's wife said, "What in the world is going on? We heard you laughing clear out at the street."

When I told her the story, she gritted her teeth. "I would have kicked her out of the church." I had learned to laugh instead of cry.

With our three kids, there were lots of laughs. Judy had started the second grade in school. One day, she came home from school all excited. "We did this, and we did that, and we drew, and we played, and we ..."

Rhonda was sitting across the room, and when Judy stopped to get her breath, 5-year-old Rhonda drawled, "Aw, I'll bet you couldn't even give a pern-a-ment."

Another time, the three kids were playing in our little backyard behind the church. Lloyd had just gone out past them, backed the car out of the garage and down the driveway. I heard our back door slam, the bathroom door bang and the toilet lid bang loud. It was Rhonda, saying, "Well, hurry up. Hurry. Hurry up." As she was running back out the back door, I rushed to the window to see what was happening. Just as Rhonda got to Ormel and Judy, who were standing at the driveway where Lloyd had just backed out gone, Rhonda whined, "Did you kids get to go?"

A Trip to Mecca? No!

General Council of the Assemblies of God was to be in Missouri (or wherever back there) where preachers and delegates go every two years to do business nationwide. We were making plans with another young preacher couple to go. Their parents lived in that town, and we could all stay with them. They had to take their cute little 4-year-old girl or the grandparents wouldn't forgive them. We would take our car and all go together.

One morning, Lloyd came in from his early morning time at the office in the church just a few days before we were to leave. He approached the subject carefully, but definite. "I'll have to call our friends this morning and let them know we can't go to the convention with them."

"What are you talking about?" I asked.

"In prayer this morning, the Lord said no."

"We can't do that to them," I wailed. "All the arrangements are made." I'm sure I voiced a dozen different reasons why this couldn't possibly be the right thing to do.

He let me make all my statements until I ran down. Then he calmly stated, "We can't go." He went back to the church office to make the calls.

The young preachers (I don't remember their names) took their own car and went back, anyway. While they were there, the little daughter took sick and landed in the hospital with a contagious something — mumps or chicken pox or whatever. And they had to stay for a couple of weeks before they could bring her home.

We couldn't possibly have stayed that long! What a problem that would have been for all of us.

Plus, if we had been gone, we would have missed a great miracle. One of the older ladies of the church, perhaps near 80 years old, had cancer and was in terrible pain. She lived several miles out in the country with her daughter and family. They called us in the night to come pray for her.

Our kids were in bed asleep, and we went. We prayed all night till day was beginning to break. We used to pray in those days until the answer came. We walked, we knelt, we sang and we prayed more. The cancer stench was so dreadful, I would bow low with my nose to the clean linoleum and keep praying. We prayed with praise, with the scriptures, in the Spirit, with the understanding, with singing, resisting, rebuking, taking authority and with power. We prayed with all prayer and supplication and with the Spirit (Ephesians 6:18). We watched and prayed with perseverance. We wept, we laughed, all praying together at the same time. She was in a semi-coma, but in real pain.

At last, she began to relax. Her countenance changed. She looked angelic. We knew the healing had come. She could talk, she

CHAPTER 10

could praise the Lord with us and wanted something to eat.

I walked into the kitchen weeping and praising the Lord. Then I began to pray, "Lord, this isn't a happy place for her. Would You please take her home with You? She doesn't really have anything to live for here." Heaven had been looking sweet to me for several years, and I was anxious for people to go there if they were really ready to meet God.

We left them and went home to get our children up and off to school.

Later in the morning, they called us. She had gone into a peaceful coma, had seen heaven, pointed up and looked up to the ceiling, smiling. They knew she was seeing special things. The angels must have come to carry her to her heavenly home.

She was beautiful in the casket at her funeral. Her complexion, her color, her face. She looked like a 16 year old — really!

Expressing my appreciation to the mortician, I thanked him for the wonderful coloring on her face that they had done so perfectly that made her look so young.

He said, "You won't believe this, and I don't expect you to. We did absolutely nothing to her face — no coloring, nothing!"

"I believe you," I assured him and explained to him how angelic she had looked when we all prayed for her.

He believed me!

We wouldn't have missed that experience for anything and what the Lord had spared us from when He said no to our trip to Missouri.

Isn't God good?

And I was learning that God really does speak to my preacher man.

One Sunday morning after church, I brought a bouquet of flowers to our kitchen to put water in it. When I was at the sink, my knees buckled under me, and I began to cry for no seeming reason. I pulled myself to the table. With my head still on the table, crying, my husband came in. When he asked, "What's wrong?" I tried to explain that I didn't know. It just happened. (I thought I was handling the pressures just fine.) He said nothing but went back to the church, called the deacons together who were still there and told them we would be leaving for a while.

He farmed the kids out, and we went to Los Angeles for two weeks to visit my longtime girlfriend, Imogene.

MORETA: MY STORY

Face It Head-on

Sometime later, while the few women were still trying to train me to be a preacher's wife, one of the teachers quit her class, and I would have to take it. Two of the ladies thought they finally had me. Everyone else had gone after the service, and these two were twittering, almost in mockery to me as they quipped, "So, Sister Fosner finally has to teach a class."

I said, "I want to know what this is all about."

They got a bit serious, telling me, "We thought you didn't know how to do these things and that you should learn."

A few more such quotes from them and I suddenly got anointed. "Well, for goodness sake! Is that what this is all about?"

And with clarity, my *sweetness* came through, loud and clear. I declared, "I want you to know I was raised in a preacher's home. I have lived in other pastors' homes and helped with different services in the church. I have traveled with evangelists. I have been involved in every area of the church. Not only have I been a youth pastor and pianist, I have been a Sunday school teacher in every class. I have had children's church and directed daily Vacation Bible Schools. I have been a women's director. I have even been a Sunday school superintendent." (That's what the big ringleader of all this nastiness against me was.)

When I finally stopped to get a breath, the younger of the two ladies asked, "Why didn't you tell us about this?"

My answer was, "Why didn't you wait to know more about me? If I had come here taking your class or your responsibilities from you, you would have been really upset."

She very kindly suggested, "Will you tell this to the other ladies?"

"No, I sure won't!" I declared (I knew she would). I just had to make them understand what a *great* person I was!

In spite of these few ladies, most of the church people were great. We had healings, victories and a real move of God in the services, with the unsaved coming to the Lord. We had the junior age boys' class in our living room, so the house always had to be presentable.

One of the young married ladies fasted and prayed for her unsaved husband for 10 days. On the 10th day of her fast, as she and her two little boys were getting ready to walk to church, he

CHAPTER 10

said, "I'll go with you." They lived perhaps a half-mile away, and when they got to the church, he walked on past and went to the tavern. She was disappointed but still sweet and trusting.

In the middle of the service, just before the preaching, he walked in, a bit wobbly, smelling like a walking tavern. He came straight to the altar, weeping. It broke up the whole service, but no one cared. People began to gather around, praying for him. That's what it's all about! He was genuinely, instantly and totally changed! The stench of alcohol was even gone. He later became the policeman in that small town.

A Real Breaking Out!

One day, our daughter, Judy, was with me on a country road. All the bright colored leaves on the small trees caught my attention. She helped me pick lots of the long branches, and we filled the trunk of the car and the backseat with them. We unloaded them in the sanctuary of the church to decorate for Sunday, which was the next day.

As I was making them into large arrangements, my hubby stepped in. He gasped, "What in the world are you doing?"

"Aren't they beautiful?" I proudly answered.

"Beautiful nothing! That's poison oak!" he groaned. He gathered them all up, took them to the back of the church and burned them (I think).

By the time he came into the house, I was beginning to break out. It didn't bother Judy or my man. He went to the barbershop for a haircut and came home with the remedy for me — a big box of Epsom salt. He had me get into the bathtub with the water as hot as I could stand with the whole box of Epsom salt. *If a little would do good, a lot would do better.* That was one of his theories.

I told him I knew hot water would spread poison oak, but his argument was, "Well, do you want to get rid of it or not?"

By the time I got out of that deathtrap, I was broken out all over (face and everywhere). I was a mess!

For many days, I suffered. People came to see me. I tried everything they suggested. I got so bad, I couldn't stand even the sheet over me.

My sympathizers told all the sad tales they had experienced. One lady said, "My friend died with it."

MORETA: MY STORY

Some advised, "You'll have to go for shots."

I tried that only once. That was horrible! I said, "No more." They shot me in the hip, and I felt paralyzed for a while. That was scary!

You'll be happy to know I lived through it! I don't know if I became immune to poison oak or if I just haven't been around it, but I haven't had poison oak since.

Next

We had been pastors there for 18 months and were in revival meetings with a very powerful evangelist who had a healing ministry. He and his wife stayed with us. We enjoyed them. He would go without food all day, fasting and praying for the night meeting. After church, he would relax, laugh, tease and want a full meal. The services would go till late, and he would be starved. The fried chicken, mashed potatoes, gravy, vegetable, salad and dessert were most welcome and devoured, with variety every night. When he finished with the food, he went back to the church and prayed for hours. Lloyd always went with him. I went with them most of the time. They didn't turn the auditorium lights on, but the streetlights outside shone brightly through the church.

When the special meetings ended, my pastor husband felt that we should resign the church and further this man's ministry. He was just starting in his ministry and was not well known. We began to schedule meetings for him in Washington, Oregon and California.

We bought a large truck to carry the tent and equipment — chairs, lights and everything we would need for the tent meetings. When we were trying to buy the tent, truck and all the rest of the stuff, we ran into problems at every turn. We got a local pilot to fly us to Washington and California to try to find just the right tent. All the expenses connected with that were astronomical.

My husband had built a small house near his mother's home in Sherwood, Oregon. He had just sold his new house for $2,000. That was a lot of money. He spent the whole $2,000 on this project.

We were doing this unselfishly, with absolutely no thought of financial return. We were willing to give it all, knowing the Lord would supply our need as we went. We would say to each other, "I wish we knew if God was trying to stop us, or if it was the devil

CHAPTER 10

trying to hinder us." We kept barreling through — pushing every door, every struggle until we had it all together.

I don't enjoy writing these next few lines.

On the Road Again

While all this was going on, we had to take our three kids to three separate places again — Rhonda to Grandma Armstrong in Portland, Judy to Aunt Mae in Wenatchee, Washington, and Ormel to Grandma and Grandpa Reid in Oklahoma.

Before daylight when we left to take Judy to Aunt Mae's, we were surprised with a real snowstorm. Lloyd said, "Well, we are young and ready for adventure. I guess we will just go on." The blizzard lasted the whole 500 miles to Wenatchee. We had to have chains on the tires all the way. The chains were beating the fenders, and he had to stop to adjust them often. What a trip!

The three kids were in the backseat, and I was driving. Before we got to Eugene, as I rounded a small curve, the car started to slide. When we got to the edge of the ditch, I touched the brake, and the car turned around and headed straight for the ditch on the other side of the road.

At the edge of that ditch, I touched the brake again, and the car whirled around to the ditch a second time. This kept up until the car had made three complete turns, just going in a circle until at last it stopped on the right shoulder, next to the ditch and died, heading in the direction we were originally going!

When the car first started sliding, I cried, "Jesus!" Not another word was spoken during the whole spin. I could see the kids leaning against the back of the front seat, with their heads turning as my head turned. (I can still see all heads turning in unison.) Lloyd, seemingly, was unconcerned. I guess that's faith!

When the car finally stopped, we sat quietly for a few seconds. I started the car and drove on. When we got about a mile up the road, my foot began to beat the gas pedal. The car was jerking and bumping along. The kids loved it and giggled loud and long.

"Do you want me to drive?" Lloyd asked.

"No way!" was my retort. I didn't want to lose my nerve after all this. I drove on till I was calm before I turned it over to him. I'm quite sure, though, that I was happy to see him drive the rest of the way. We got Judy delivered to her destination, and we made it home safely the next day. I think we left Rhonda at her grandma's in Portland as we came through on our way to Wenatchee. We hadn't delivered Ormel yet to his grandparents in Oklahoma.

A Troubling Encounter

I'm not sure where we stored our furniture during this time. I think it was in my rental home in Springfield that had probably become vacant about that time. The parsonage was all cleaned out except the bed in our bedroom and a sofa in the living room for Ormel to sleep on. We would load the rest of the things in the rental truck the next morning.

We had had a few occasions of Satan's demonstrations during the year and a half we had been in Yoncalla. This, our last night there, the doors were locked, and we were asleep. I heard the back screen door rattle and bang, and I knew there was a strange presence in the house. Lloyd slept and didn't seem to hear the noise. I listened, wondering, and then I heard the back door close and the screen rattle loud again.

Immediately, it was like a wind along the side of the house, then a big boom three times on the oil barrels outside our bedroom window, like someone was hitting them with a metal rod. Next was a loud hissing sound as it faded into the distance toward Rice Hill.

My husband did not hear those sounds, but as soon as they ended, he immediately got up and went through the house. I was also up and going through the downstairs rooms. Neither of us was saying anything. When he found nothing, he went back to bed.

When I came back through the living room, Ormel calmly said, "It went that way." (He was pointing toward the back.)

I asked, "What did it look like?"

"It had on white britches and a black shirt, and it had long, shaggy hair," he explained. That was in the days when men didn't have long, shaggy hair.

"What did it do?" I quizzed.

"It just stood, looking at me." He showed me how he was laying on his side with his knee out from under the cover. "It slapped my knee and went hisssss. And then it went that-a-way."

"Were you afraid?" I questioned.

Very confidently, he said, "No."

CHAPTER 10

"What did you do?" I questioned further.

"I kicked at it," was his reply, "and it left."

We were both calm as we had this conversation with no fear. He never called the creature anything but *It*.

The next morning, Lloyd got up real early and went to the church to pray. When he left, Ormel came and got in bed with me. We began talking about last night. I asked him, though I knew the answer, "How could you see all of that? It was after midnight."

"But, Mama, you know those streetlights shine through the house all night."

Yes, I knew that. I also knew that Satan wanted to hit us with one last blow, but the blood of Jesus covered us from his attack. Ormel had no fear, and Satan was defeated! Praise the Lord.

We had dealt the devil some lasting blows, and he hated us. I had gained the respect of all those ladies and felt their love and honor for me. We had seen some great victories and even miracles through the areas that Satan had used for many years to hinder the church. The church was ready to move on.

Ormel to Oklahoma

It was hard for me to send the kids off to relatives again, especially Ormel, all the way to Oklahoma. I was brokenhearted but just had to grieve inwardly and bear it. I knew my parents loved Ormel enough that they wouldn't spoil him, and he loved them. But that didn't take away the mother heart in me for my son. He was only 6 years old.

Ormel was too young to send back on the train alone. I don't know if the Greyhound bus existed at that time. Our travel was always by the slow trains. But he was too small to send alone, and there was no other way.

We were in Springfield, near my home, and had stopped at a stop sign. Lloyd put his arm on the back of the car seat and said, "Why don't we just drive Ormel to Oklahoma?" So, we went back to the house, picked up a few things, drove night and day and delivered him safely there.

We had had our farewell service in Yoncalla and were ready for the next challenge.

MORETA: MY STORY

Just Like Me

There were two little girls who needed a Mother
Just like me!

I had a little boy whom God had chosen
For a special ministry that wouldn't always be easy.
He needed two sisters and a brother,
And a Daddy like no other.
He says he still needs that Mother
Just like me!

God was training a certain woman for that special little boy
And for two special little girls
And a very special young preacher man.
And they needed a helper,
A worker and a trainer.
And God chose this certain Mother
Just like me!

That preacher Daddy needed a helpmate
To train his children and bear another son.
And God said, "She'll do!"
He needed two sons and two daughters
And a woman like no other.
He really had to have someone
Just like me!

Moreta Fosner

I wrote this August 2, 2007 at 7 a.m. Lloyd has been gone one year ago this day.

CHAPTER 11

Helping the Other Preacher

We were totally moved out of the parsonage, and our final service was over in Yoncalla. We had held a few weeks of meetings in my Springfield home church, also, two or three weeks of revival in a church in beautiful Wenatchee, Washington.

Now we were ready to travel to Orange, California, with the tent. My husband and the evangelist were in the truck; I drove our car and took the preacher's wife with me.

Going down through Sacramento, I had to stop for a red light. Lloyd drove on and never waited to see where I was. I continued driving, knowing I surely must have missed him along the way. When I got to the edge of town going south, I pulled aside in front of a service station with a big open area, so if he came looking for me, I would be easy to find.

We waited there for hours. I called the police. I knew something had happened to him. The summer heat was unbearable. We waited, looked, prayed and fretted. Finally, late in the evening, with many hours yet to our destination, I called the evangelist's parents' home to see if they had heard from the boys.

"Oh, yes. They are sitting right here, drinking ice-cold lemonade. They've been here for hours!"

Should a shot that man!

California, Here We Are

That meeting in California went sour. It was a joint meeting with several churches cooperating. The services were going good, with great healings and victories. Attendance was building.

The preacher became overconfident and began to criticize the pastors. He started having "discernment" about some of them. Attendance began to drop. He fought more, and the crowds dropped more.

My husband tried to talk to him. "You just can't do that and keep the people with you."

MORETA: MY STORY

Then he started openly defying and criticizing Lloyd. I guess he needed someone to blame because the crowds were dwindling and nothing was happening.

My husband warned him, "One more night of this and the tent is coming down."

The "one more night" came that night — and the tent came down. Crowds had dwindled to almost nothing. *It was in his hometown! What a disgrace!*

We loaded up the tent, poles, lights, chairs, pulpit and songbooks and headed for Oregon. We never heard if that little red-headed preacher ever held another meeting. I don't even remember their names. It's too bad he lost it. As long as he had integrity and honesty with God and man, God was with him.

Now we could rent a house, gather up our brood and forget the pushing of another preacher.

We let another evangelist in Oregon use the tent and all the trimmings. About the second meeting, a big wind hit and tore the tent to pieces. We sold the truck for a pittance.

Lloyd had sold his new house next door to his mother for $2,000. It was all gone. We never complained about it or blamed anyone. We did it all ourselves.

We realized we had gained a university degree in knowing the will of God. Getting special schooling is costly. That $2,000 was the price it cost us. And it was worth it through our many years of ministry thereafter. Watch for it in stories to follow.

Listen, kids! When everything begins to go wrong, gets difficult, doesn't come together, gets confusing or there is no peace, whether in looking for a job, moving, deciding which church, building a home or church, making any kind of decision like dating or getting married, and God doesn't give a clear answer, the answer is to wait.

In some cases, the answer is no. Regardless of how hard it may be to do differently than you planned, don't do it at all! Please, let our education in this department teach you, okay?

As I look back on this experience, I'm glad it ended as soon as it did and only lasted a couple of months. The timing was good to get Ormel back from Oklahoma. My brother and his wife were in Oklahoma and coming back to Oregon at this time. They brought Ormel back to us. I bless them yet.

We got the girls back home and rented a two-bedroom house

CHAPTER 11

in Eugene. The kids had to sleep on bunk beds in the same bedroom. While there, the girls got the chicken pox. Ormel escaped that part.

At night, I would go into their room and pray with them. They all prayed so powerfully. This one night, I was just ready to burst into tears because of their fervency. Rhonda was praying, "Oh, God! Oh, God! I'm so glad You answer prayer — sometime!"

We didn't stay in that small place long. We found an apartment house in Springfield with a nice yard and no other children. Everything was more roomy. We had a dining room, and now we could have company.

My parents had moved back to Oregon. My brothers were here, too, and we had some special times together. Lloyd would hold a few revival meetings for two or three weeks at a time. Sometimes I went with him.

My brother, Orion, was building homes in the Eugene area. Lloyd would paint for him and other builders between meetings. So he kept busy. The kids were all happy to be home and going to school in Springfield. I was happy to live a more normal life again and have my family close with us. We had big feeds at our house often and played table games such as Pot Suey, Rook or Spooning. Ask me, I'll tell you how to play them.

To the Coast — Seaside

Atwood Foster was the district superintendent of Oregon at that time. He contacted us about taking the pastorate in Seaside. There had been a lady pastor there for some time. I think she had known Lloyd in Bible college and was requesting him for the church. I don't recall her name. He felt no drawing to go there at all and was saying no.

Two or three months later, the superintendent came to Lloyd again. "The Seaside church is still open. Would you be willing to go and preach on Sunday for them?"

Lloyd reasoned with me at home. "We haven't felt a call to any other church, and Seaside has kept open for us so long." He was embarrassed to keep saying no. We had been out of a pastorate for more than a year, and it's difficult to get back into the flow when you aren't in circulation. "Maybe this is God, and we don't know it." So, we decided to check it out to see if it was for us.

MORETA: MY STORY

We took the three kids and were there for the Sunday morning service only. Lloyd preached a fiery Pentecostal message. "Jesus is coming soon. Make sure you are ready to meet Him."

When we came out after the morning service, the two main couples of the church, who were business people, were standing on the front steps, politicking against us as the crowd came out. The two couples were nice, but very cool to us. They thanked us for coming.

We got in the car, Lloyd brushed his hands together and said, "Well, I guess that took care of that."

We drove out of town feeling totally released. "That's the last we will hear from them," Lloyd quipped. We forgot about them.

What a surprising shock! About three weeks later, we got a call that we had been voted into the Seaside church as pastors! We did some more reasoning among ourselves and tried to pray about it. Finally, we decided to go. We would see if it was God or what.

There was no parsonage. The church rented a nice three-bedroom house on the Necanicum River in downtown Seaside. We moved in. This was the first week of November.

By Christmas time, when we came into the house (we never locked our doors in those days), someone had been there and left a beautifully wrapped large gift on the couch. The pretty Christmas card gave the names of the givers. They were the two couples who had been on the front steps trying to influence others against us that first Sunday. The gift was an elegant table lamp, bright red, large and impressive. I cherished it for many years. The card read "To our pastors, with our love." They had become some of our dearest friends.

Our first night there after we moved in, a family came by with lanterns and clam shovels for both of us to teach us how to dig razor clams. How exciting! We got our boots on, and our family went with their family about a block from our house to the beach. We learned about the tides. We even got a few razor clams that first night. We loved the beach and all that went with it.

Many times, early in the morning when the tides were good for clamming, we would leave the kids in bed, go get our limit of clams, come home and get our youngins up for breakfast and off to school. Then we started our ordinary day.

Judy was in the fifth grade, and Rhonda and Ormel were in the third grade at school.

CHAPTER 11

The church was right on the main coast highway that went through Seaside. We put a neon sign on the front of the church that read "God is your answer."

A parsonage was necessary in that town, so we began to draw plans. There were rooms upstairs in the church that weren't needed, so we made those into three bedrooms, a large living room and a spacious kitchen with an eating area and a bath. We designed the living room so we could enjoy the sunsets and the Necanicum River, which was about 50 feet from the back of our church. The water in the river rose and fell with the tides. We put in a large window to the west that overlooked all that beauty. We could see seagulls, ducks, swans and birds of all kinds, plus hear the roar of that mighty ocean.

Seaside was a fairyland to us. The people treated us royally. One lady brought us a pie every Sunday. People had us to their homes to eat. At times, one of them would call and say, "Set the table just for your family. We are bringing your complete dinner." What a delight!

Another lady brought me a corsage every Sunday morning. She also decorated the church with flowers each Lord's day. They would think up great gifts and different ways to bless us.

I took a correspondence course in taxidermy. Why? I don't know. It only cost $10, and I liked to learn. During that time, a car had hit and killed a seagull. A policeman stopped his car and picked it up. He gave it to me, and I fixed it with a wingspread, and it turned out really beautiful. I about blacked out, though, at the scraping out of its brains and digging the eyeballs from their sockets to put in the artificial eyes. However, my finished product had earned me a taxidermist's license for life. I still have my card, but I don't carry it with me anymore. Things easier to stomach were my choice!

One of the couples in the church had two cute little boys about 3 and 4 years old. The parents had gotten a big box of prunes to can. Little Jimmy asked if he could have a prune. His mother gave him one. "Johnny wants one, too." She gave him one for Johnny.

This kept up several times. Finally, when he asked for a prune, she emphatically stated, "No more prunes! You'll be sick."

"But Johnny wants one," was the plea.

"No way. He has had just as many as you have."

"Huh uh," Jimmy said. "Johnny hasn't had any."

MORETA: MY STORY

Another time, when Daddy was helping this same little Johnny put his shoes on, Johnny wanted to do it himself. "No, me tie," he said, showing his independence.

His daddy explained, "You've got your shoes on the wrong feet." Johnny would look up at his daddy quizzically, then again try to tie his shoes.

This went on two or three times until finally little Johnny declared, "But dems de only feets me got."

While we were in Seaside, Judy and Rhonda went to be with their Aunt Ruby and Uncle Elliot in Troutdale for a day or two. Our three children always took turns clearing the table, washing and drying the dishes. Because of their young age, they could just stack them by the sink, and I would put them in the cabinet. We had mine and his, odds and ends of dishes and mismatched sets.

One day, as I was holding a stack of the plates in my hands, I held them up and said to my husband, "I'd just like to drop these and break every one of them." Nothing more was said. Of course, hubby knew the reason — it was so I would have to get some new ones.

When the girls were with Aunt Ruby, she asked them if they thought their mother would like to have her dishes. They said, "Oh, no. She's got so many now, she'd like to break them." Aunt Ruby's dishes were a set for 12 of Franciscan Ware Desert Rose with lots of different side dishes! Well, it wasn't their fault. I had it coming. I didn't even tell them about it for many years afterward. I could have cried!

Seaside to us was an out-of-this-world fairyland. It was just what we needed to make us feel loved by people, to restore our trust and make us want to be pastors for the rest of our lives. We were in the Seaside church one year. The Tigard church was next.

Tigard Church

We moved into the parsonage above the church during a struggling time for the Tigard Assembly when it was on Greenburg Road. The Sunday morning offerings were extremely low. One morning $11. Another $16. Then $23. My husband would drive to Eugene at times and paint for my brother who was building houses across the city. He would go to paint just often enough to keep food on our table and for the bare necessities.

CHAPTER 11

Pastor husband, during a board meeting at the church, set the board at ease with instructions that they should know and understand that our wages were low now, but the church would begin to grow and when the offerings increased, "Don't muzzle the ox." (That's a quote from the scripture.) And when things picked up, they remembered.

Our three children started school in Tigard in the middle of the year. Judy was in the sixth grade and in the same building with Rhonda and Ormel, who were in the fourth grade for the rest of that year.

When the next school term started, Judy was beginning seventh grade in Fowler Junior High. This was the same schoolhouse, and with the same principal, Thomas Fowler, that her daddy had when he was in high school. (Lloyd's birthplace had been in Sherwood, about five miles away.) Judy remembers that during that year, her principal, Mr. Fowler, had gone home to take a nap and didn't wake up. Rhonda and Ormel were in a different school building and in the fifth grade. They had separate rooms and different teachers, which was nice for them that year.

I always worked with the children and with young people in those early years. We began to dream of a large neon sign across the top of the long church roof. We took the youth and all that could help to the strawberry fields and picked strawberries all day, from early morning till late, and gave our earnings for the sign, which read ASSEMBLY OF GOD, and was easily seen from the main highway, which ran right through town and only a half block away from our church.

Lloyd had picked strawberries, beans and other crops in his early years and went along with the rest of us that day to pick. It was a backbreaking ordeal! He would have done better to donate money instead. He had to go for a back adjustment that cost more than he made in the field.

Kay Livingston was one of our first converts. His wife, Bessie, and young daughter, Virginia, were attending church, and now, her husband was saved and *full steam ahead* for God.

One Sunday morning, Pastor preached on tithing. Afterward, Kay came to him and asked more about "this giving stuff." He was convinced that it was in the Bible, but how much would it cost him? He wanted more details about it all. Should he pay any back tithe? How far back?

MORETA: MY STORY

Lloyd told him, "No, just start where you are." He did!

Kay was a large building contractor with several houses being built at one time and with quite a large crew of men. He was building in Portland, Tigard and in the Vancouver, Washington, area.

He had a new home near Tigard that had been for sale for several months. He said, "I'll pay 10 percent on what that house should sell for." The house sold that week!

The economy was bad during that winter. Lots of men were being laid off from their jobs. Many builders were shutting down completely. Kay's jobs kept going. Not one of his men had to be out of work.

Kay was convinced. Tithing worked! He not only gave 10 percent, but every time there was a need in the church, he wanted to pay it all. The parking lot needed to be paved. Kay wanted to pay it all. My husband talked to him. "Kay, you don't have to give it all. Let others share in some of it."

"But God just gives so much more back to me," was his reply.

One of the other men in the church who had learned the rewards of giving called us. "Would you please come pray for me?" His knees were so bad, he couldn't walk on them and would have to have an operation to correct the problem.

As we were praying, I heard him also praying. "Lord, Your Word says if I pay my tithe and give, You will rebuke the devourer for my sake." He was healed! There was no operation, and he was back in church. I don't remember the man's name.

We had to make some changes in the over-the-church parsonage when we moved in. The little bathroom just had a shower. Our family had always preferred a bathtub. One day, I expressed my choice of a tub instead of a shower. That week, two of Kay's men came with their tools, and a green bathtub was installed.

Hullitt Holcomb was one of the board members. He and Alice had three children near the same age as our three. They had two boys and a girl.

The girl, Patti Holcomb, grew up to be a beautiful, talented young lady. She went to Oral Roberts University and married Oral's son, Richard Roberts.

Hullitt and Kay became close friends and helped to make life interesting for everyone in the church, but especially for our family. Every church needs a pair like those two.

CHAPTER 11

Don't Trust Your Taster

We had mentioned something about bear meat. "You'll never get me to eat bear meat," Hullitt bragged. Some months later, we were having a workday at the church with a potluck meal. I made a large casserole of meat, potatoes and carrots with cream of chicken soup over it all, then biscuits on top. It was good.

Hullitt began telling everyone as he came back for seconds and thirds, "Try some of Sister Fosner's dish. It is delicious." I was delighted! But I didn't tell any of them until the meal was completely finished that the dish that Hullitt liked so much had bear meat in it. He never lived that one down, but he still loved me.

Ormel began losing a lot of weight and was too sick to go to school at times. He had an early morning paper route, but one morning, he couldn't stand up. Lloyd had to carry him to the car. Rhonda or Judy would have to go along for a few days to put the papers at the homes Ormel would point out. He was 10 years old. The doctor decided it was his tonsils, and they had to come out. A few days after the operation, the weight came back, and he was his busy, happy self again.

The three kids were out picking berries and beans in the fields during the summer. They were learning to save their money, give God's tithes first, then buy their clothes and spend wisely. Trucks and farmers' vehicles would pick up kids at close by locations and deliver them to the fields. I would go with them at times to make sure everything was alright. Judy was always the competitive one. Ormel and Rhonda just went along because it was expected of them and would eat a lot of their profit. But all three of them made pretty good wages by the close of the summer crops. Daddy would always tell them how good he had been at picking when he was their age.

Some months after the harvest season was over, Ormel had only $10 left. We had a missionary in a church service. When he finished speaking, Ormel came and asked if it would be alright if he gave that $10 to the missions' need. I could see he really wanted to give it. I explained to him that he could but, "Don't expect us to repay you." If he gave it, he wouldn't have any money for anything, but God would honor him for his giving.

"I really want to give it," he reasoned.

It was only two days later that Ormel got a letter in the mail

MORETA: MY STORY

from Grandma Reid (my mother). It was a check for $70 made out to Ormel Chapin to buy himself a guitar. When we told her later about him giving his last $10, she explained, "I told Papa that I just felt from the Lord that I should send this money to Ormel."

"Well, if you feel you should," Papa agreed, "you'd better do it."

I'm quite sure there's never been a dollar paid or given to Ormel after that time that he has not given the first 10th and even more to the Lord.

Rhonda went through a season of breaking things, not on purpose but by accident. Seemed everything was going wrong, and things would just jump out of her hand and break. She and Judy always shared a bedroom. Judy was organized and capable. Rhonda would throw her dirty clothes under the bed or wherever. They were two different natures, and it was difficult for them to learn to cope. Judy's grades were always near the top or her teachers were in trouble. Rhonda just barely made her grades with a lot of help. Ormel was enjoying people and suggested that he just makes sure he doesn't go below "C" level.

One day, I realized what was happening with Rhonda and talked with her daddy about it. "Rhonda is being put down and criticized for everything she does. We have to turn this around. We must begin to praise her, find the good that she does and enlarge on those things."

Instead of scolding, "Rhonda, not again."
"Well, Rhonda's here."
"Can't you ever do anything right?"
"She messes up everything."
"What's wrong with you?"

Accusations, accusations! Poor Rhonda would walk off with her feathers drooped and hurt to the core.

I'll admit it was hard for a while to think of things that were positive. I talked with Judy and Ormel. "We must change our comments and actions toward Rhonda." It took a while, but it finally came through. Rhonda became a sweet, lovely young woman and so loved by all who knew her. We won!

There was a Grandma Newbry in the church who brought us a home-baked pie every Sunday morning. Judy remembers times she would go home with Grandma Newbry. They made fudge, and she taught Judy to crochet.

CHAPTER 11

While we were in Tigard, Judy would babysit at times. She tells of Ormel, Rhonda and her playing school, and Judy was always the teacher.

We made a lot of improvements in the church while we were there in the parsonage and the interior of the sanctuary. We put a brick planter in the foyer, with mirrors and lighting. Plus, we improved the bathrooms and the parking lot.

One day, Lloyd's sister-in-law, Mae Craghead, and her husband, Clarence, came out from Portland to see us. She had on a beautiful three-quarter-length fur cape. I suppose it was new. I complimented it by saying, "Just pull it off and put it right here (around my shoulders); I'll take it."

She pulled it off, put it on me and said, "It's yours. I've been looking for someone to give it to. I'm tired of it." Wow! It was gorgeous. I couldn't believe what I had just heard. I wore it for years. I still love capes.

Ormel came in one day in tears. He had been across the street playing with a neighbor boy in their backyard behind the garage. He had been telling the boy about Jesus and was praying with him. The boy's mother came out and sent Ormel home. He was brokenhearted. "Now, Joey may never know Jesus and go to heaven."

We thought we would be in Tigard for a long time. The church was growing. It was close to the large city and near where Lloyd was born and raised. We found a beautiful piece of property with a full view of Mt. Hood to build a house on, and I had drawn plans for the new home.

We began to get calls from Pastor Nels Fast about the Molalla church. He hadn't resigned yet but was going to and would like us to be considered to follow him. Would we be interested? We told him no.

"Would you pray about it?" he asked.

"Well, alright, we'll pray." But we were sure the answer would be negative.

The family who owned the building lot we had picked out was sure we could close the deal immediately, but they began to hit snags. One of the family members refused to sign for the property to be sold. That bug-a-boo put us in a position to pray in earnest concerning Molalla. "Did the Lord really have other plans for us? Were the doors closing here?" We loved Tigard and the Tigard people.

MORETA: MY STORY

Pastor Nels Fast had been a good pastor in Molalla. He and his lovely wife had four or five teens who loved the Lord with all their heart. They each played instruments and were happy, heading-for-the-ministry young people.

I had recognized the need to seek advice from others who were capable of giving me help in areas I would be coming into. I had gone to Sister Fast for her knowledge that I could use in raising my three. She was a good model to follow, and I treasured her wisdom.

The pendulum, with much prayer, began to swing to Molalla. Peace came and even excitement about the move and a new ministry. We were invited to preach for a Sunday, and they voted us in as pastors. We felt assured that this was the right thing to do. We moved at the end of the school year. We had been in Tigard only a little more than two years.

With the many moves we made as a child, I would always cry. I never wanted to leave my friends.

I didn't cry in my grownup years, but I always grieved over leaving every friend. I loved people.

4 years old in Los Angeles

I'm on the left with friends

Age 18 in 1940

Me with my husband, Harry Chapin

Ormel kissing Mama

Mildred and me in Toledo

Me and my Pontiac

Harry, Ormel and me at our $700 home

My mom and dad at their 60th
Anniversary: Johnny and Cuba Reid

My three brothers with Papa: Orion, Melbra and Admiral

My sister, Lorene, Mama and me

My wedding to Lloyd Fosner 1949

Our blended family: Ormel, me, Judy, Lloyd and Rhonda

Musical me

Lloyd and me at Odell Lake

The family moved to Klamath Falls 1960

Pastor Lloyd and me

Me and Baby Verlon, one day old

My 48 lb. Chinook salmon

Our family in 1994:
Rhonda, Judy, Lloyd, me, Ormel and Verlon

Me in 2007 when I started writing this book

CHAPTER 12

The Move to Molalla

The congregation had been trained well with lots of good people willing and capable of working in the church. They had sent word for us to bring a large freezer, which they would keep full for us. They did with breads, beef, poultry and a lot of fruits, nuts and things from their gardens.

Molalla had lots of small farms and orchards. The people raised their own edibles. They loved to give, and we sure enjoyed all the goodies they shared with us, plus all the beautiful flowers.

The parsonage had three bedrooms with one bath. Two of the large bedrooms were upstairs where the kids slept. We remodeled the house while we were there with a new front entrance and a lovely breakfast nook off the kitchen in back with big corner windows. It had a nice dining room and was very livable.

The church was right in the middle of the small town with the parsonage wedged in between the main grocery store and the church. The store was perhaps 20 feet from the north side of our house, and a sidewalk separated the house from the church on the south side.

That walkway went the full length of the house, and anyone could look in our windows as he or she cut through from the front street to the alley. There were a few simple people who would do just that, fully enjoying the pastor's family view.

Judy was in the ninth and 10th grades in Molalla. She went to Canyonville Christian High School for her junior and senior years and graduated from there. Rhonda and Ormel were in the seventh and eighth grades. They graduated from junior high, then spent their freshman year and part of their sophomore year there.

All three of them practiced the piano and each took horn lessons in school. Judy and Rhonda played the clarinet, and Ormel played the trombone. Squeaks and music came through loud and clear at our house. I also taught them to sing. They were a very nice trio. Ormel played his guitar and sang for their eighth grade graduation.

MORETA: MY STORY

Ormel preached his first sermon while we were there. Pastor Marion Ravan, from Estacada, came on a Sunday evening and took him to preach in their church. One man was saved that night.

We had a nice big orchestra in the church in Molalla. People came to enjoy the music and singing.

Camp Meeting in Brooks was only a few miles from Molalla. We always liked to stay on the grounds so we could be with friends from all over the state before and after services. We got a 9 by 9-foot center-pole tent with a canvas floor. We put our bedroll on one side of the pole, the girls' on the other side and Ormel's sleeping bag on the backside of the pole with a few clothes hanging above. Most of the clothes were in the pickup.

We had a little two-burner gas stove we set on the tailgate of the pickup to do our little bit of cooking. We planned to go home every two or three days for new supplies. All was well ...

However, about the second or third night, a big rain came. And, of course, with that small area, everything had to be touching the sides of the tent. Nothing escaped the soaking we endured that night. We loaded up, went home and dried out, re-primped and drove back and forth to every meeting we could, which wasn't every daytime service. There were prayer meetings at 9 a.m., morning service at 10 a.m., afternoon service at 3 p.m. and then the night service was at 7 p.m. with thousands attending.

Our old-fashioned Oregon camp meetings were always wonderful with special speakers from all over the world. Each year, the term was for two weeks. Families were there in tents, pickups and a few homemade trailers in the early years. We were cooking out, crowded and living in places close together. In those early years, there were sawdust floors in the tabernacle, where there was shouting, dancing, healings and miracles. At times, we would hear or be a part of loud praying that lasted all night.

In later years, we began to get trailer houses and motor homes. There were cabins built on the grounds and a lodge with rooms to rent during camp. Then there were fewer tents. There was also less all-night prayer meetings.

While we were in Molalla, we bought our first trailer house. I think it was a 13-foot one, and it slept five. Our double bed was in back. The table had seats that folded down to make a double bed for the girls. A hammock-like bed above ours was for Ormel.

CHAPTER 12

The Northern Lights

One year, Lloyd and I, with Pastors Bill and June Rose of Woodburn and Marion and Margie Ravan of Estacada, took our high school and college-age young people from our three churches to the Cannon Beach conference grounds, just south of Seaside on the Oregon Coast. The young people got out of school at noon on Friday, and we brought them home late Sunday night. We were in cars and pickups loaded with food, musical instruments and kids, plus bedding, luggage, extra pots and pans, utensils and things we would need for the days in that beautiful Bible campground a few feet from the ocean. Everything was planned to the last napkin.

The three pastors and their wives had gotten together several times to make all the plans — the services, play times, beach walks and wiener roast and so on. The six of us did much fasting and prayer ahead of time. We made every decision that was ours to be involved in, then expected God to take over, and He did!

We had no extra workers to help us. We wanted to do the work ourselves and with our young people to really get to know them and allow them to know us. They were involved in helping us with everything. Each one had their work times, play times and prayer times. It was one of the most efficient, smooth running projects ever. There was no friction and no misunderstandings or surprises, except the surprising things God did.

There was morning training or teaching sessions, and each night was a powerfully anointed celebration of praise, true worship and the Word. Those were heavenly times, with repentance, fillings of the Holy Spirit and re-fillings. We witnessed healings, miracles and deliverance in every life.

On Sunday evening, we started the meeting early so we could be on the road to our separate towns before it was too late at night. The service began at 4 p.m. and lasted until almost midnight! Power and glory came down. It was glorious!

We had encouraged each one who played musical instruments to bring them. Before the evening service began, we had everything loaded in the rigs (except the musical equipment). Our rooms, kitchen, everything in the lodge was cleaned and in order.

It was near midnight when our caravan drove out. There was very little traffic on the roads at that hour of the night. We had gotten only a few miles east, heading for the valley and we began to see red streaks coming from the center of the sky to the earth. We pulled to the side of the road and stopped. There were perhaps a dozen or more of our cars and pickups lined up, and we were the only ones there. No other car even drove by at that time. Everyone was out and praising the Lord. The sky was filled with the brightest red streaks, which solidly filled almost half of the sky. We knew it was nothing but the glory of the Lord adding His final touch to our days of praises to our God. What a night to remember!

We did have music and singing, but our praise and worship wasn't the singing alone. It was praise to God and worship, with words, with cries, with hands raised, lost in His presence as we vocally adored Jesus. It was all so genuine.

An Unbelievable Tragedy

While we were in Molalla, my first husband's mother and 17-year-old son, Dick, came on the bus from Michigan to see us and to visit Gladys and Clyde Hines, who lived in Springfield, Oregon. Dick had gone back to Springfield to go with Clyde in his logging truck. Clyde was a prince of a man and had made a permanent impression on Dick's life.

They were driving along a narrow road southeast of Springfield. There was a dangerous railroad crossing where the train tracks made a bend just before the crossing. There were no warning lights, just a small "Slow R.R. Crossing" sign off to the side of the road. If you didn't hear the train whistle, there was trouble. A witness said Clyde slowed, then drove on, but it was too late. The train came around the bend at a fast speed. Clyde and Dick were killed instantly. The locomotive pushed the truck cab about a quarter of a mile before it was able to stop. The picture in the paper showed the cab totally flattened. Louie Sinnar, road foreman of engines for Southern Pacific, was aboard the train, which was the Pacific Shasta Daylight passenger train.

Several families were left stunned and in anguish and grief that day. Dick's mother, Mattie, was still with us when the call came. It was impossible to accept it all. The rest of her family was in Battle Creek, Michigan. Some of them drove night and day to come out and be with their mother and help with all the decisions involved in shipping Dick's body back to Michigan and finding a way for Mattie to get home. Going by plane was not a common thing yet.

CHAPTER 12

This was a really hard time for me. They were all a big part of my life for a lot of years and still are.

Clyde and Gladys had a daughter, Naoma, and two sons, Clyde Jr. (we called him Junior) and Ronnie. Gladys was widowed for several years, then had a stroke and couldn't talk or move about. She had to have constant care. It was so heartbreaking to see that sweet, wonderful person in that condition.

My Physical Breakdown

I had been trying to keep doing everything, but with very little sleep. We'd house all the preachers who came to preach. I did all the cooking and entertaining, doing much more than was expected of me. I knew I was running down, but I thought since I was working for the Lord, I would be alright. I was seeing different doctors. They'd tell me, "It's just nerves; too much pressure."

One doctor told me, "If you will just throw a hammer through your plate glass window, you'll do better." He said I was "too mild, too accepting, too helpful." There was no way I would resort to that kind of action. So, weak and trembling, I kept going.

One evening, I had fried some razor clams for supper, and we had just finished eating. I went to the piano and started playing. The three kids left doing their dishes and stood behind me singing the song I was playing. Lloyd was nearby. All of a sudden, my arms went limp and my head went down as I began to collapse. They grabbed me, Lloyd carried me to the couch close by and my world was in a whirl!

I was vomiting horribly with unbelievable dizziness. Lloyd called a local doctor.

"Don't move her for anything," he warned. "I'll be right there." He came right away. He gave me a shot that was to put me into a deep sleep for several hours. It did absolutely nothing. I was so sick, and sleep would not come.

I would squint my eyes a tiny bit and could tell that someone was standing near, but I couldn't be sure if it was an adult or a child. The one phone in the house was on a stand five feet from my head, and when it rang, it seemed to go through my brain. Lloyd got word to most of the church people not to come or call. The kids were whispering, trying to be quiet, but that's difficult for three teens.

MORETA: MY STORY

I laid on the couch with the same clothes on until the third day. Our bedroom was just off the living room, and I could stay on that couch no longer.

"You have to get me into my bed and get these clothes off," I told Lloyd.

They got the bed ready for me, and I knew my husband was carrying me as carefully as he could, but it felt like he was slinging me like you'd snap a dishtowel.

The only way they could move me was to turn me with the sheet. For 10 days this went on before I should have any movement at all. The doctor had me on heavy pain and sleeping pills. It was many days before I had much movement. For about a year, I couldn't read, write or see straight.

District Superintendent N.D. Davidson came to pray for me. Also, many other preacher friends would come for a few minutes only. If anyone stayed more than about five minutes, it would begin to feel like pins and needles in my body, my hands and legs especially. My head would feel so heavy. Mentally, I was sharp, but physically, I was shot! I just couldn't cope with pressure.

Rhonda and Ormel graduated from the eighth grade a short time after this inner ear disease hit me. It would soon be summer and too difficult for all the activities of three teenagers to be slowed and quieted down.

Lloyd asked what I thought of sending the kids to relatives for the summer. I didn't want to but knew something had to be done. I don't recall if Rhonda went to her grandma's or to Aunt Jane's. Ormel went to Grandma and Grandpa Reid's in Oklahoma for those months. I believe Judy stayed with us a while. I'm not real clear about when, how or where the kids went during that time.

I had gotten hooked on the sleeping medication and pain pills during those several weeks or more but was able to be up a little at times. I had to walk slow and deliberate. I couldn't move fast and still couldn't be under pressure or around lots of noise. Once when I was alone for a couple of hours, I very cautiously got out of bed, held on to everything and walked back and forth quoting Isaiah 40:28: "They that wait upon the Lord shall renew their strength; they shall mount up with wings of eagles; they shall run, and not be weary; and they shall walk, and not faint." I would do that occasionally, but nothing was instant. It actually took a good two years to recuperate totally.

CHAPTER 12

We had gotten the new trailer house a short while before, and Lloyd took me to central Oregon, 10 miles down the Metolius River to the last campground and parked "us" (the trailer and me) a few feet from the beautiful river's edge. He brought up wood for me to have a campfire when I desired. I had plenty of food and things to keep warm. I still couldn't read or write. But I had my camera to take pictures — lots of pictures of chipmunks and robins, ducks and deer, campfires and fish baked in foil on the coals.

I was there to break my "habit" and hopefully get some sleep — without the pills. And I did! I enjoyed the peace and quiet.

I was there the last part of April, before the camps were opened for the summer. There were very few people around, but fortunately, every night, there would be at least one camper with comfortable looking people — not scary. The men were generous fishermen and would stop and talk to me and bring me fish to bake on my fire. The weather was always nice during my stay.

I would sit in the sun on my folding chair for hours taking pictures, enjoying the sights and sounds of birds and water rippling over the rocks.

My husband came to see me on Mondays and would go back home the next day or two. By the end of the next month when he came to take me home, I had a different problem to add to my first one. I was pregnant! That shouldn't happen to anybody who was my age, with my youngest child 14 years old. I began telling young married women, "If you ever get sick, don't go to bed."

It was summer when Ormel went to be with my parents who lived downtown in Lexington, Oklahoma, right across from the post office. Ormel loved to climb the many trees that were around their home, and once while playing Tarzan in one of those trees, a limb broke and he fell to the ground, breaking his arm. I hurt because I wasn't there to be with him, though I knew he was in good hands and would be alright.

He remembers one day during that summer when Grandma was gone, Grandpa was showing him his favorite 12-gauge shotgun but was disappointed that the firing pin wasn't working and hadn't worked for years. Ormel asked him how he knew the firing pin didn't work, and Grandpa said he just knew because it didn't work the last time he shot it.

Ormel kept asking questions and prying him for better answers when Grandpa got exasperated, grabbed the gun and a shell and said, "Come outside, and I'll show you." They stepped out the back door where Grandpa proceeded to put the shell in the gun, aim it at Grandma's prize petunia bed and blow it to smithereens all over the backyard.

After the shock wore off, and the enormously loud echo stopped reverberating from all over town, the two of them ran inside where Grandpa quickly hid his gun and made Ormel promise he wouldn't say anything to Grandma when she got home. I think Grandpa was not nearly as worried about what would happen if the police showed up as what he would face when Grandma got home.

That is still one of Ormel's favorite memories of Grandpa. Oh, yes, Ormel also remembers Grandma's return home and her first trip out the back door to check on her award-winning petunias.

My mother always had a pretty cat around. My dad wasn't too fond of them. This one day, he was in his rocking chair, and Mama warned, "Careful, Papa, the cat's under your chair." He gave a big *rock* and looked around just in time to hear the cat scream and shoot across the room in a horrendous panic.

"Oh, there he was," Papa said. If that cat hasn't exhausted its nine lives by now, it's probably still licking its tail.

By the time summer was over and the three kids were all back home, we told them about the new baby coming. They were so excited about it, and we let them spread the news. The arrival date wouldn't be until February. The cook and housekeeper husband felt a bit overwhelmed. He suggested we could let Judy go to our Christian high school in Canyonville if she wanted to. I said I knew that wouldn't work because she was too excited about the baby coming. We never mentioned our conversation to her or anyone else.

She went to youth camp that summer and met some interesting young people who were attending that high school in Canyonville. She came home all excited about the school and surprised us with, "Can I go to Canyonville to school?" It was amazing! God had prepared us and then put it all together for her. We couldn't afford it, but we did it! She finished the 11th and 12th grades and graduated from there.

I wasn't able to attend church very often during that year. Our churches over the state had been praying for me at the time of my inner ear problem. And now, there were more prayers.

CHAPTER 12

There were several doctors I had been seeing about all my physical sicknesses before the "breakdown" finally put me under. Then, of course, when I began turning green with my new problem — at age 37 — my doctor said that I could be starting menopause. They were running tests to see what was going on, but I was still dizzy. One doctor found a large tumor on my lower right side. With all this back and forth and still trying to fit it all together with my dizziness, it became quite interesting.

On February 1, 1959, baby Verlon arrived at the Silverton Hospital at 9 p.m. That Sunday night at 6, when we drove out of our driveway to go to the hospital, it was time for the youth C.A. service to begin. Then the night meeting was at 7. I had my little suitcase all ready to go, but instead of Lloyd bringing my things, he came out with his Bible under his arm. At my suggestion, he hurriedly retraced his steps and came out with the right baggage.

The kids got to tell everybody at church that we were on our way. Rhonda stayed in hearing distance of the phone. At 9 p.m., it was all over, and Rhonda got to tell the news to everyone who was still at the church.

With all my difficulties — not seeing straight, being slow and not able to walk without holding onto things — I had not been too interested in having another baby. And because of my hemorrhoids, I had to sit on a round plastic blow-up pillow with a hole in the middle. I just couldn't get too enthusiastic about a newborn human. But the moment he popped out and they cleaned the blood and slime off, then held him up for me to see, he was great!

The nurse dressed him in the pretty little gown I had brought and wrapped him in a blue baby blanket. As they handed him to me to hold, he was wide-awake, looking me right in the eyes, examining me like I was checking him out. I had to laugh at his big hands — just like his daddy's. I wasn't too sure he was happy with his new world, but after a few hours, he started rooting for his first breakfast and looked up at me with total admiration. Wow! He was beautiful and all mine. A real winner.

A lot of years later, after he was grown and married, I was telling of my frustrations at having another baby, and Verlon looked shocked, like I had hit him over the shoulder with a wet mop. He had been unwanted! I said, "Hey, but remember, that was before I saw you. When I held you, it was love at first sight." He will soon be 50, and I still love him more than he can ever realize.

MORETA: MY STORY

When he was a few weeks old, my brother, Admiral, and his wife, Joyce, came to see me and my new baby. I was in bed while the baby was in the process of nursing. Their 3-year-old daughter, Lori, was standing close by, wide-eyed as she watched the unbelievable scene that she had never seen before.

Her mother explained to her that the baby was getting his breakfast. Lori would look at her mother, then back at me, then to the nursing baby. She did that a time or two, then sort of breathlessly said, "Yeah, hotcakes."

District Superintendent N.D. Davidson came to see how I was doing now that the baby was here. Many times, I go against my better judgment in making statements to get a laugh out of people. This time, I really did a doozy! My ducks came home to quack with their tail feathers plucked out.

I laughed to N.D. about how the churches had been praying for me and my tumor and how I had been changing doctors to get them to say I wasn't pregnant — but I had him, anyway. Our friend N.D. knew that I was just being facetious and having fun about all the months of suffering that had turned out with the surprise of my new baby. Even though I still wasn't out of the woods with my weakness and the ability to be up and doing much, I could laugh about it.

I knew the superintendent would quote me in the same vein that I had said it to him. However, somewhere after several years of time, it got twisted and came out as though all of it had really happened that way.

My baby, Verlon, was grown and married (and listen to this). I was at Ormel's helping Sandi get ready to go with him on a trip. I was doing some ironing and listening to the radio, KCCS in Salem, Oregon. John Davis was on staff at Christian Center with Bob Cornwall. John was the speaker on the radio that morning and was saying, "This woman had been sick and thought she had a tumor, but that tumor turned out to be my brother-in-law."

I yelled, "Sandi, come here! Did you hear that? I'm that lady!" I was mortified! Shocked! Embarrassed! Angry!

"Gonna kill that guy …" Then it got funny.

Sometimes I think I don't have good sense when I forgive and laugh about things that I should hate for life. But if I hadn't had the ability to forgive and laugh at the impossible, I might have been in a padded cell by now. Or maybe just a mean old lady!

CHAPTER 12

Oh, and about the tumor? My baby doctor, Dr. Neally in Silverton, told me that many times a tumor will leave and never come again. And I have never had any symptoms of any kind. It was totally gone. Praise the Lord.

That John Davis has now been a missionary in China for several years. I love him and his lovely wife, Cindy, and I pray for them often. Since my son is married to his sister, that makes us kinfolk. I don't know if he ever learned the true story of the tumor. But, you know, it's funny how time, forgiveness and love can change things. I don't think I even had to work at forgiving. When you learn the daily forgiving of 70 times seven, it seems to become a habit. Thank You, Lord.

We had been in Molalla for four years. Things were about to change. We had loved the Molalla people and all their blessings to us. In spite of all my sickness, we had felt rewarded and loved. However, Klamath Falls was to be our next move.

CHAPTER 13

Klamath Falls or Bust

My husband had been having the same dream for three nights. Superintendent Davidson came by to see us, and Lloyd told him of the dreams he had been having of "Klamath Falls or bust."

N.D. said, "I'm going to Klamath Falls for a business meeting tonight. The pastor has resigned, and I'll put your name in."

We didn't have to send a written resume about our ministry in those days. But Lloyd told me, "We will be going to Klamath Falls to pastor." After the church voted on several pastors and couldn't settle on one, they finally called us to come for a weekend and preach. It was an interesting few days.

On Sunday night, the pastor and his wife, who had resigned earlier and were still involved, took charge of the service. They began to perform like they were the ones who were trying out for the church. They were much more flamboyant than we, more talented, more everything. Sure enough, they let the church know if they would vote them back in as pastors, they'd stay. What a switch! Lloyd was to preach, so while a song was being sung, he slipped out to the car to get different sermon notes and preached about "The Coming of the Lord."

When we were driving out of town the next morning, it looked like it was all over.

The kids asked, "Dad, I thought you said we were coming to Klamath Falls?"

"Just give it time," he answered. "We *will* be coming to this church."

It happened. In just a few days, we got a call that we had been voted in as pastors of the church. Our three jumped up and down with excitement.

We resigned the church in Molalla, and they voted in our friends David and Doris Godwin as their new pastors. I still wasn't too peppy. I wasn't totally recuperated from my sickness.

Verlon was almost a year old. Ormel and Rhonda were in the first year of high school. Judy was in the middle of her junior year

CHAPTER 13

at Canyonville Christian High School and loving it, making new friends.

We moved to Klamath Falls the first part of January 1960 and were pastors of the church for 18 years (January 1960 through November 1977). We were so grateful to have our teens in the new territory. They had done well in Molalla, but this was so different with all the ice and snow and the small lakes and rivers frozen over. The kids would go out with the young people of the church and play in the snow or skate on the ice. They'd build a big fire at night, roast wieners and such and enjoy all the outdoor activities.

The summertime had great fishing, water skiing, boating and mosquitoes. We had variety. Seldom did it rain, but it did snow or hail even in July. A big hailstorm came once in August.

We moved into the church parsonage. There wasn't an evergreen tree around in those hills. I used to say, "Not a tree to spoil the view anywhere." I missed the green and the valley with all its beauty. Our only view was the highway and a railroad track, but there were lots of pretty sunsets. However, mosquitoes were thick. Verlon was just 1 year old, and we couldn't let him go out in the yard. The mosquitoes loved that tender baby skin, and he would welt all over.

The city mayor lived next door. He said there were so many lakes around that it was a losing battle to fight the mosquitoes. However, before long, they brought in mosquito hawks from Japan. They didn't bite people but swarmed in funnel-like whirlwinds. They ate the larvae, and soon the mosquitoes were gone.

While we still lived in the parsonage and began hearing about the hot water wells, Lloyd began looking for property to build a new church. He wouldn't look at anything but in the area of the hot water so we could heat the church with this system.

The present church was beyond old. It was ancient! My husband loved the challenge of building. I think at every place we pastored through the years, we either built or remodeled the church or parsonage or both, except this parsonage that we lived in here. We rented this one out to the Air Force base and let the rent pay our mortgage payments while we built a new house for ourselves.

In the earlier years, most of the churches furnished a house for pastors to live in. The thinking had been that preachers should own nothing, drive an old car and be supported with very little. (We always drove a nice car.)

MORETA: MY STORY

That feeling was beginning to change across the country. Too many ministers were coming to the end of their lives with nothing and nowhere to put it. Our denomination had no retirement plan for our senior ministers and still doesn't. So it is only sensible to begin to acquire a home at least.

My husband had a difficult time breaking through that opinion. While he was looking for property to build a new church, I was looking for property to build us a new home. We would talk about it, then he would back out. He didn't want to hinder the ministry. He knew we should, but ...

I found a great piece of property in a new development. I put money down on it with the agreement that my husband would have to agree and sign, or they would refund my down payment. I took him to the vacant lots and gave him the papers to sign. He battled with it for a few hours — yes, no, yes, no. I assured him that I knew he would lose his doubts when we signed on the dotted line and got started. Soon he signed, and we were on our way! I began drawing plans to build.

He was forever grateful. We later sold an extra lot off our land, and that almost paid for the area where we would build our house. Plus, our land was 300 feet deep and a lovely place with a view of Mount Shasta from our south side windows.

We didn't live in the parsonage much longer than a year. We built the new home on Patterson Street for less than $18,000. We lived there seven years and sold it for $25,000.

With that $25,000, we built a new house on the hill at the end of Shasta Way. It had the most beautiful view in Klamath Falls. Mount Shasta was to the south at the end of the runway of the Air Force base airport. There were brilliant sunsets with the nightlights of the city below us.

Things Could Have Been Worse

When our young son, Verlon, was around 4 years old, we drove from Klamath Falls early one morning on our way to Portland and stopped before noon at the district office in Brooks.

In those early years, the headquarters office was in the administration building. The entrance to Bethel Park was straight in from the old highway, and there were no homes or other buildings between the road and the office.

CHAPTER 13

We had recently bought a new Buick and our district treasurer, Lester Young, wanted to go for a ride in it. My husband let him drive, and they weren't gone for more than 10 or 15 minutes. I stayed and visited with the girls in the office to catch up on the latest upstate church news.

Verlon had asked if he could go play on the swings and slide, which were about halfway from the office to the highway. There were no other children around and no reason for concern.

Before long, a police car came in, and we stood, wondering what was up. The policeman got out and, hand in hand, led Verlon up the long steps. I ran out to meet them, and when Verlon saw me, he began to cry. I held him in my arms as our car was driving up, and we all heard the story together.

Verlon had seen our car drive out and thought we had left him and began running up the highway crying. A man stopped his car and asked Verlon some questions, then drove him to Woodburn and gave him to the policeman.

He told them we had dropped him off and left him. When they asked him what his daddy did, he told them he was a carpenter. He didn't tell them that his daddy was a preacher or that he was building a church.

They asked if he was hungry, and he told them yes, that he hadn't had anything to eat. Verlon hadn't given them anything to go on, but where the man picked him up was not too far from the entrance to our campground, and the policeman tried there first.

How glad I have been that we didn't discover he was missing and have to go through what too many families have to endure in these troublesome days. That surely is one of the worst things that could happen to anybody.

Ormel and Sandi had been pastoring in Rogue River, but while we still lived on Patterson Street, they were invited to come to Klamath Falls and be with us. He was our youth pastor for that time and helped in every area needed, and *he was needed!* He also helped build our new house on the hill.

Lonnie, our first grandson, was born while they were in Klamath Falls. They were with us for two years before taking the church in Canby.

From Canby, he became District Youth Director for the state and held that position for 14 years.

MORETA: MY STORY

Looking Through My Scrapbook

During our first year while still in the parsonage, we were having lots of activities in the church. We would have two or three revival meetings each year. Also, there were lots of events with the children and young people, the women, men's times, drama and visuals with training and teaching times. Before long, I was back to my full strength. We kept every evangelist in our home and part of the singing groups.

During those 18 years, we ran a full program. We had early morning Easter sunrise services at 5:30 or 6:00 a.m. but not in Klamath Falls. We tried that just once, but the hail, snow, icicles and frost taught us to make different plans for the next year at Easter time. We had egg hunts (but no bunny).

There were graduation celebrations for our high school graduates, all kinds of showers for special occasions, many weddings, funerals and memorials. We had every kind of contest and promotional event. I was a creative thinker and dreamer, along with many of our helpers.

I was involved with the women's program, the children and the youth. Then I would fill in to most any department when there was no one else to do it. I wrote and directed Christmas plays, Easter and illustrated sermons with the young people occasionally on Sunday nights, then they would let us have the offering that night. I was the youth pastor, but being the pastor's wife, nobody paid me. Plus, I had to find ways to finance our programs.

One of the most important things we had was the women's prayer meetings on Wednesday mornings. There were wonderful answers to prayer. The women never wanted to close down for anything, even holidays, and if only a few wanted to come, I was there with them. I loved it.

One early morning, when my husband went to pray and study, there was a small black wax doll left on the door with his name scribbled on the back with an arrow through the heart. It was a threat on his life! This happened three mornings in a row, and each doll was a bit more threatening with red blood painted on the heart. We talked it over and decided we should call the police about it. They checked it out and found there was a Satanist group in town with a store that had this sort of thing. It also came to light that this group was planning a Satanist church in town.

CHAPTER 13

We showed the dolls to our prayer group. Our praying ladies went to effective, fervent prayer about this satanic thing that had come to our town. We prayed loud, and we prayed long, our voices blending together in one accord. How powerful when two or more are together with real fervent praying and fasting. We prayed that demonic thing out of town! Before long, the newspaper stated that the satanic group had left Klamath Falls because their activities couldn't operate in that area. The paper also said the group was moving their operations to Eugene. We never heard anymore about them at that time.

For three years, our youth department was number one in the state for Speed-the-Light giving. In 1974, we gave $5,383. In 1975, $5,182. In 1976, we upped it to $9,622. We made flower sprays for Memorial Day and sold them on the streets. The youth helped with it all, plus many other creative ways to reach that goal. We also made flower arrangements for Christmas that our church people could purchase.

The Speed-the-Light program for the national department raises money to buy equipment for our missionaries in foreign countries to speed their time and make them more effective in their work. Collectively, our youth bought cars, boats, airplanes, bicycles, radio equipment, printing presses and anything else to make their efforts go easier and faster.

During the age of plastic flowers, I would take some of the young people to the cemetery after Memorial Day and, with permission and even help from the cemetery manager, we loaded pickups with the arrangements that were to be discarded and took them to our garage floor. We had tubs and a place to wash and drip-dry the flowers, the Styrofoam or whatever would help us make arrangements for the next occasion.

There were lots of different ways to make money for our project. We had fun being number one in the state those three years. Then the larger churches caught on and outdid us. We still sent in lots of money for Speed-the-Light. Nationwide, we gave millions of dollars each year.

We prevailed on the powers that be to give us an area over the prayer room for our flowers. We organized them and made them workable in that special place for our business. Several girls and young married women would help me make the arrangements in that little room.

MORETA: MY STORY

One of the young women, who was helping me with the arrangements, had gone downstairs for a moment and left her little 3- or 4-year-old boy until she returned. In another part of the room, I heard water running. There was no water in that area so I checked it out. You guessed it. The child was watering my flowers the only way a little boy could. I grabbed him, showed him what he was doing and scolded, "Look what you're doing. I'll call your mother. You get out of here and down those stairs quick or I'll get you. Look what a mess!"

He grabbed his wet britches up while running down the stairs crying, "What a mess! What a mess! What a mess!" He left me laughing while I cleaned up the wet in the flower box and on the floor.

A council worked together in the youth department and in the women's functions. The W.M.C. (Women's Missionary Council) had a director, a secretary and treasurer with project committees, and the Christian Education Council had its Sunday school superintendent and separate officers. I was just the advisor and was at every planning session in all these departments for advice and to take the blunt if there were any complaints from anybody. We did lots of interesting things in every area. The planning times were fun. We had jog-a-thons, rock-a-thons, relays and serious times.

We made floats to enter in parades of the city. In Molalla, we even took first place one time. Another time in Klamath Falls, we took third place, and we used the big star and props in other decorations. J.C. Penney was discarding some of their mannequins, and I was able to get me a man. Our decorators got lots of laughs out of people as they would see the dummy at different times, in different ways and even in scary places. We used it in many ways of interest.

All this time (remember I had three high schoolers and a baby), I raised a garden out behind our fence. People said you couldn't raise a garden in Klamath Falls because the seasons were too short. I just covered things at night when it seemed frost would come. I don't know how I did it all. I also designed and made most all my clothes and the children's, and even a few for my husband.

My husband was a presbyter for 20 years. He was voted in by the churches of the section and was one of about 12 men who were leaders of the Oregon State district. We would have many preachers in our section, and their wives at times, for a special dinner in our home. Then, many from the state and wherever.

CHAPTER 13

We had lots of friends, and we loved to entertain.

We had invited all the ministers of the section to be with us this day for my specialty of enchiladas. They were all seated at the tables while I brought the hot platters of food from the oven to their individual places. Just as I was bringing the last one from the kitchen to the dining room, the platter broke and the contents spilled all across the hardwood floor and "What a mess, what a mess!"

Several of the wives rose to help, and soon, all was well. I always make extras, so the problem was solved. I don't want hardwood floors now, but as I look back on that time, how good it was!

The Original Beginning

The Assembly of God church was begun in May of 1932, when two area Pentecostal churches united to better serve their congregations. The group began the building of their first church at 746 Oak Street in 1938 with the first services held there in 1940. In June 1942, the Pentecostal organization affiliated with the Assemblies of God, thereby changing their name.

By the time we took the pastorate in January of 1960, the church was in dire need of new facilities. We began to hear of the underground hot water wells in certain areas of the city. My husband found the right place and would look at nothing else. He began to dream.

It took several months to get the package all together and money down on the property for the new church. But, before the year of 1960 ended, the 3 acres (with no buildings on them) belonged to the church.

And I began drawing plans for the new edifice. The busy program of our congregation was much alive with special happenings, new beginnings and revival meetings.

In November 1962, we began revival meetings with evangelist Fuchsia Parrish and her co-worker, Thelma Drye. Those were powerful services from the start with many miracles of healings and lives changed. We wouldn't think of closing the special move of God that was happening. Crowds were increasing each night. We took a week off for Christmas so the speakers could go home to Texas for the holidays. When they returned, the momentum continued and lasted for a total of 13 weeks.

MORETA: MY STORY

In March 1963, the last Sunday of those special revival meetings, we invited Oregon District Superintendent N.D. Davidson to be the guest speaker at the morning service and to officiate in the afternoon at the groundbreaking ceremonies on the new property just off Alameda on Henry Street.

Most always on Sundays, I would fix an oven dinner to be ready to set on the table and eat without much delay. I did so this morning especially since the afternoon service would begin at 3 for the groundbreaking, and there were so many of us — N.D. and his wife, Mamie, and the two evangelist ladies. I'm quite sure Lester Young and Mae were there with our family and a few others.

After the service that morning, when we walked in, N.D. was escorted in first. I asked, "Well, how does it smell?"

He said, "I don't smell a thing." I knew he had to be teasing. But he wasn't. The automatic oven had malfunctioned and had not stayed on. There were no KFCs or Golden Arches or Costco. I invited everyone to sit down so I could think. I had a ham (not pre-cooked) in the oven, plus potatoes and other vegetables. We took the ham out and put someone to work slicing it to fry. The rest of the things went on the stovetop at high speed, and soon, we were eating. Fortunately, the dessert and refrigerator goodies were ready to go. We had plenty to eat and were on time for the 3 p.m. service.

The construction of the $150,000 church was begun that August. The formal dedication of the new building was held on September 6, 1964, with a number of city officials and out-of-town church dignitaries conducting the services. One of the high-ranking men of the city who spoke that day told that years ago the farmers would bring their hogs to the spot where our church was now standing and scald them.

We were thrilled with the hot water area on which the new church would be built. Some churches in the city had monthly heating bills of $100-plus during the long, cold winters. The heating of our building was by hot water, pumped from a well drilled for this purpose. The water from the well was at a temperature of 212 degrees. As best that I can remember, we didn't use the water from the well but ran a (copper?) pipe in a larger pipe and let the heat come through that source. Since my husband is gone, I'm not sure who to call that would know all these answers.

For many years after we left Klamath Falls, when a new pastor or whoever would need to know about where, what or how

CHAPTER 13

concerning the mechanics of those things, they would call our home for Pastor Fosner. He seemed to be the only one who understood its operation.

The hot water pipes were run into every part of the new church and also under the wide sidewalk that ran the length of the auditorium to the front entrance. Every area of every room, including the sidewalk, was perfectly heated all the time with no forced air, no noise, no discomfort anywhere and no snow to shovel off the walkway.

However, the large parking lot had to be plowed off during the snows. Our heating bill for the whole church was only around $10 each month.

The Building of the Church

I had drawn the floor plans to scale for the new church but wasn't knowledgeable enough to do all the structure, foundation, plumbing, wiring, etc. However, the Air Force base was in Klamath Falls, and one of their architects heard of our project from an airman who came to our church.

The structure planner came to meet with us and volunteered to do the total set of blueprints free of charge. He said he wanted the experience of drawing plans for a church building. He did a great job for us.

Our friend Ray Marks, who was a church builder, came from Eugene to live in Klamath Falls while he was building with us. Also, Lyle Shrode (who was married to Naoma Hines, a relative of mine) came to oversee and slave in the cement work of the foundation. There were a lot of areas we had to hire other help, but lots of the work was done by volunteer workers.

My preacher husband would get up a lot of times at 5 in the morning to study, pray and prepare for the preaching services, then before 8, he would be on the job to put volunteers to work and keep things running smoothly. He was an efficient pusher of workers.

The building project had its interesting and challenging times. However, when things seemed not to go together as planned, we slowed or waited until the right thing came. Then we moved on with that particular part. The work never stopped. After we started, it was full steam ahead.

MORETA: MY STORY

The building was built in three stages over a period of time. The first structure was the sanctuary with a large prayer room behind the platform. An ample entrance and foyer were combined with the furnace room behind the foyer. A balcony was above these areas for future growth with Sunday school rooms and a temporary kitchen. We used the balcony for a multi-purpose room. The balcony risers were added later.

Just inside the main entrance were the church office and the ladies' room with a baby-changing area. When I drew the plans, I had weddings in mind. There was an elegant bride's primp and dressing boudoir next to the restroom. One wall was totally mirrored with a wisteria tree in purples from the floor to across the top of the mirror with a lavender carpeted floor.

The pastor's study and some Sunday school rooms were in the first structure with rooms on the second floor for classes. The second wing, which was built later, extended further on south with a youth chapel at the end, which was like a small church. I had drawn it for a wedding chapel, but it never was used for that purpose. It became the children's church, C.A chapel, and was used for other activities.

The aisle in the main auditorium was wide enough for a bride to walk with ease. We carpeted the floor with a beautiful, warm red carpet. The huge window to the south was intricately designed of colored glass. However, after about 40 years, the wood between the glass portions began to deteriorate, and the window had to be replaced. I haven't seen it since that was redone.

In a few sentences back, I mentioned that when things seemed not to go together, we stopped and waited until they did. This is one example: We had taken trucks and people to dig the stone out of a mountainside a few miles south of town. It was unloaded near the place where it was to be used. Finding the right person to do the cutting and to lay the stone in an artistic way became a difficult find. We waited.

The men of the church went to the jail each week to minister to the inmates. After one service, our men came to my husband. "We may have found our man. I think it's worth checking out." He was our answer! He would be getting out of jail in a week. The man had done the stonework on some of the large state buildings in Washington and would be glad to stay and give us a sampling of his work. We checked him out and were convinced that God had

CHAPTER 13

him there for our need. He stayed with the job until it was finished. We took care of him and paid him well. (I hope we paid him well enough since he was a *Godsend* for us.)

One of our bankers wanted to know who did the work on the front of the church. His statement: "It's the most beautiful stonework in this town." (Of course, that was almost 50 years ago.)

The third addition to the church was on the north side. It was a full-sized gymnasium with a spacious, stainless steel-equipped kitchen and eating area in the gym. A covered walkway led from the side door of the church to the kitchen and restrooms in the new building.

We acquired seven buses from schools and two new 15-passenger vans that we used to bring un-churched children to Sunday school. It was an exciting time with a hardworking team of trained drivers and helpers. All the buses were painted a different pastel color. A very capable man in the Salem area came and painted them all for us with the church name on the sides in bold letters. A beautiful array of a man's efficiency. I wish I could remember his name.

We miraculously started the Klamath Christian Academy in our facilities, kindergarten through high school. I think we started with kindergarten first, then the other grades through high school. It was a needful thing and was a great addition to reaching out.

Our first principal, Bill Park, married one of our choice girls, Renee Jones. The second principal, Ray Wunder, married Gwen Schlumbohm who was one of my most valuable workers with the youth programs. Ray was still the principal when we resigned and left Klamath Falls in 1977.

Our first graduates of the school were Tony Orton, Mary Parsons, Arlene Jannuzzi and Linden Hankins. I don't know how long the school was going after we left the church and moved to Salem. But it has been discontinued since.

Our Home and Church Life in Klamath

After we moved to Klamath Falls and were living in the parsonage, a very interesting, laughable thing (I thought) happened to the girls.

Rhonda was dating Bert Allbritton, and Judy was going with John Taylor. Judy was home for the summer from Canyonville.

MORETA: MY STORY

We seldom locked our doors in those days. We took the girls to church that night and then brought them home. They were quite disturbed, not understanding what was going on with those boys. Neither of the boys had come to take them to church, and they were not in church. When we got home and the girls walked into their bedroom, they cried out, "Oh, no! I don't believe it! I'll never speak to him again. Oh, Mom!"

By then, I was there and laughing. The girls about hated me and the boys, too. I was always on our three kids' case to "Make your bed. Clean up this room. Put this away. Pick that up."

The two boys had come in after we left for church and cleaned our girls' room!

The backside of the fireplace was made of brick, decoratively laid floor to ceiling, and it was in their bedroom. It had shelves of the brick from about waist high to the top.

I had seen their room earlier, and it was a disaster. One nylon hung from one of the shelves, the chest of drawers was partly open with unmentionables half out. It looked like a whirlwind had hit it, but now, it was spotless.

The boys had even folded their things and put them neatly inside the chest. Shoes were lined up on the floor of the closet, clothes were on hangers and all was in order.

As the girls were thinking of it all, they were groaning, "And my **** was out. And ****!" I don't think they slept all night. I really believe it helped into the rest of their lives. Thanks, boys!

I just called Judy and asked her to tell me what she remembered about this. Her answer was, "Absolutely nothing!"

I said, "Thanks, Judy, you just gave me a great double ending to my story." We had a good laugh, and she volunteered no more.

Slanguage

On this day, our three teenagers peeled apples to make about a dozen pies for the freezer. I turned the actual pie making over to the girls.

Later, when I came in, they were working on the last few pies, and Judy was marking the tops of the crusts with D instead of A for apple. I asked, "Why the D?"

She drawled, "D for darn."

We never used slang at our house, but the girls were so tired of

CHAPTER 13

making pies, it was almost earned. We laughed, but the girls didn't. They were still tired.

One Sunday, I wore a colorful new dress to church that I had recently designed and made. That morning before church began, I walked down the aisle and stopped to talk to a slightly older lady who was seated. When I stooped to say something to her, she pulled me closer and straightened whatever on my dress, and I thanked her for helping to get me dressed. She said, "Well, it's the perttiest dern dress I ever saw."

Tony Orton Called

I'm writing this on Sunday afternoon, September 30, 2007, after Tony called. He was Verlon's very special friend. Verlon, who was 14 years younger than the other three offspring, was the only one living at home by now. The others were married and had their own homes.

Verlon and Tony loved to water ski and do varied kinds of sports. He often stayed nights with us.

One summer, when his parents had a financial setback, we rearranged Verlon's bedroom, put his twin beds together to make a king-size bed for the three boys and had Tony and his brother, Toby, come spend a few months with us. They shared the work around our house. I was quite an artist at keeping jobs for the three boys. They were all in high school. Verlon had been taught that I called him only once to get out of bed in the morning.

This school morning, I called them, but they rolled over and went back to sleep. Before long, though, Verlon came rushing in with, "Mom, you'll have to take us to school, it's too late."

I said, "Oh, no, I have plenty of work to keep the three of you busy all day."

He had this happen to him once before and had learned the consequences well. He grabbed his jacket and, without breakfast, dashed out the door with a quick goodbye and ran to the end of the driveway in time to catch his ride to school.

The brothers heard the commotion and came in shortly. "Where's Verlon?" they asked. "What happened?" I calmly explained and reminded them that I had warned them last night that I only called once, and Verlon remembered. They knew they were trapped.

MORETA: MY STORY

At fun times like that, I can be so sweet. "You can make your bed, get your work clothes on and I'll have breakfast ready for you. Then you can get to your day's work." (I would go out and help them occasionally.)

We had a fireplace, and the winter's wood had been dumped in a pile behind the garage. It had to be stacked outside against the garage, some outside and some inside. Also, some kindling had to be split and stacked.

You know what? I never had a bit of trouble getting those three boys out of bed after that. They were glad to hit the floor with both feet and come out happy.

For years, I taught parents they could train their children to be obedient and they would enjoy doing it. You can read lots about things like this in my next book *You and Your Children*.

Verlon and Tony have been friends for life.

Today was a special day after Tony called me and talked for 40 minutes, thanking me for making a difference in the formidable years of his life. I hadn't heard directly from him for years, and what a treat it was to get the news of his parents, Joe and Barbara Orton, now living in Phoenix, Arizona. Toby lives in Ohio with his wife and children. Tamala, Treva and Tonya are all married and living in difference states. And each one of the family are serving the Lord. Tonya married a preacher and is involved in a special ministry. I'd love to see them all.

Tony and his wife, Debbie, and their two grown sons are totally busy in ministries in the church. They are now teaching a special series for married couples.

Two Weddings in July

Earlier in the year, we went to Bethany Bible College to meet the new members of our family (to be). Ormel had chosen Sandi Bedwell for our approval, and no way could we disapprove. We had known her parents in the ministry for many years and loved them already, but we didn't know their daughter.

Judy had found a great young man, Robert Harkins, who was already preaching and going to school. We fell in love with both the ones our son and daughter had chosen.

We had heard that it was Bethany "Bridal" College, and our kids proved it. All four had our complete approval and acceptance.

CHAPTER 13

And they have proved to be the perfect choices.

On July 2, 1966, shortly after Ormel's graduation, he and Sandi were married in our church in Klamath Falls. I was the photographer for their wedding and had mighty good subjects to work with. However, it was done in black and white. Color was just coming in, and I wasn't set up for color work yet. Ormel had become the youth pastor in the Grants Pass Assembly for Pastor Don Merrill, so after they were married, they went to Ormel's new small living quarters there.

On July 22, 1966, Judy and Bob were married in the church where Bob was assistant pastor — the Glad Tidings Church in Santa Clara, California. They hired a photographer to do their beautiful wedding in color. Bob had one more year of college. He had served in the evangelistic field for three years and had also attended Central Bible Institute in Springfield, Missouri, before coming to Bethany Bible College.

Both weddings were quite elaborate with many attendants of their dearest friends and their expertise in beauty. Wow! My weddings were sure nothing like that.

Rhonda didn't get married until a couple of years later. She had been engaged to a young man in Salem who was of Jesus Only belief. It was so extreme from our thinking, and everyone she knew advised her not to marry him. It was such a hurtful decision for her, but she finally broke it off. I'll write about her wedding later.

Alaska Moose Hunt

Shortly after our son and daughter's weddings, our church honored us with a trip to Alaska for a moose hunt and to visit the Gerald Stacks. They were a family who had been transferred from the Air Force base in Klamath Falls to the Alaska base. In fact, there were two families there at that time. Also, Walt and Jane Landes, Lloyd's sister-in-law and husband, were living there. Between all of them, they helped us get enough things together to go camping in moose hunting territory. That was a real experience! We couldn't walk in the woods because of the rough tundra. We had to find some guides to take us farther back into the area where we could find the moose. They had a large, heavy vehicle, kind of like the old Army tank that moved along on full tractor treads, but it was all open on top. It was a rough ride and a bit scary with all the uneven tundra beneath us, especially when they pointed out to us that it had "rolled yesterday, right here."

They took us back into the wild and dropped us off by a stream and left us all day. We had a blanket to sit on and a sack lunch, but there was nothing else to do but sit or stand and watch for moose of which none showed all day. There were no big trees, just a very few small scrubby-like saplings. We never saw an animal of any kind. Finally, late in the evening, the old tank came lumbering back to us. It was a welcome sight by then. They loaded us on top of the thing and ambled near the edge of the stream until they pointed out a big cow moose for us to get off the vehicle and shoot. We both got shots off at the thing until it fell. It wasn't a real thrill like Oregon hunts were. This was like shooting the side of a barn — a big object you couldn't miss, but we had our meat. They put a chain around the moose and drug it to where we had our tent. But there was no way we could cut the big critter up, so they drug it to a man not far away who could prepare it for us to travel and loaded it into our pickup. By this time, it was late at night, so we spent that night in the tent and were on our way early the next morning back to Anchorage. I think it was about 400 miles.

Walt and Jane were planning to move back to Oregon soon and asked us to drive their pickup back. Wonderful! We didn't have to ship the meat but packed it down with dry ice. We loaded our things and started the long drive home to Oregon. It took four *hours* to fly from Seattle to Anchorage and six *days* to drive back to Klamath Falls. Never again! Twelve hundred miles of gravel road is 1,200 miles in any man's land. We never saw an animal of any kind along the way, just a couple of old horses. I'm sure the roads are better by now, but it took both of us straining our eyes for deep potholes in the roads, broken up by the snows and bad weather with very little care.

When we got home and unloaded but had not put things away, our house was broken into and lots of our things were stolen. Three rifles, two shotguns, a 35mm camera and a borrowed movie camera, also our field glasses and Verlon's little record player.

The thief had broken in through the garage, and I'm sure they left hurriedly as we were coming in after church, because they went out through the double glass doors in the breakfast area. This was in September 1966. It was sad in a lot of ways. The cameras had

CHAPTER 13

our trip pictures. But almost worse than that, some of our kids' wedding pictures were still in the cameras. And, almost worse than that, deer and elk hunting seasons were just days away — and no guns!

Air Force Base and OTI

It was so great having the Air Force in our town with all its families and young men who became involved in the church. I think they were usually stationed there for four years. The Oregon Technical Institute (it was later renamed Oregon Institute of Technology) was also in Klamath Falls. We had a lot of the fellows come to church and accept the Lord as their Savior. They liked dating our church girls, and some even married them and took them with them when they were transferred or finished their term. But it was always with our blessing.

My husband talked to some of the Christian boys. "There's no need for you to come to church alone. Bring other young men with you." One of the OTI students brought Glenn Foo Sum from Hawaii. Glenn was an honor student with a scholarship to the school. He played sports, and his name was in the paper many times for his achievements. I believe the one who brought Glenn to church was Jim Moody. He was also a valued player in sports with Glenn.

When the altar call was given that morning in church, Glenn went straight to the altar and accepted Christ. After the prayer time, I was starting to explain to Glenn what he had just received, and he said, "I know. Jim has told me everything." That Sunday night, Glenn received the baptism of the Holy Spirit.

The following week, Glenn was going to California to see a relative for the Thanksgiving holiday. I wondered if we would see him again after that, but he came back just as exuberant as before. He grew in the Lord and became one of the greatest workers in the church we ever had. He later married the pastor's daughter, Billie Rentz, from Chiloquin, a town nearby. She had moved to town and was a great worker in the church, too. The pair of them was unbeatable. They excelled in every area that we entrusted them with. They are still going strong and have moved to Hawaii, where his parents lived and where he was raised. I believe they had been Buddhists in his earlier years. We can know he is still leading people to Jesus.

MORETA: MY STORY

My husband's voice had gotten bad with laryngitis, and he couldn't preach. The doctor told him he must not preach for several weeks or months. My dad was sick, and I was going to Bend on Mondays and coming home to Klamath Falls on Fridays. Lloyd had gone to a preacher's meeting in Medford for a couple of days while I was gone to Bend. I came home with the weekend ahead and much work to be done. Also, a preacher was coming on Saturday to preach the next day. (They were a family of four and would be staying with us.) I just painted this picture so you could understand the big news that I was about to receive when I arrived home on Friday.

Hawaii

With Lloyd's bad voice, he squeaked, "I'm ready to go to Hawaii."

I said, "Man, have you gone crazy?"

He replied, "Yes, do you want to go along?"

My answer was, "No."

Other than a childish dream that someday it would be nice to go to Hawaii, we hadn't thought of such things. Now he was ready to go. I asked when he would like to leave. His reply was, "Monday morning" (this was Friday afternoon). I explained that there was no way we could leave that soon. We left on Tuesday!

We had no reservations on planes, at hotels or anything else done, but somehow we were able to get it all together.

On Sunday morning, he let the congregation know we were going to Hawaii. The young Hawaiian who had recently started coming to church, Glenn Foo Sum, came to us all excited. He called his parents in Maui to have them meet us at the airport in his hometown, Kahalui. He also contacted the pastor of the Assembly of God church, and the pastor met us at the plane. The pastor took us to their home where his wife had a lovely meal all prepared for us. We had never met before and didn't know that Glenn had called them. I explained to him that perhaps he could take us to a hotel. He smiled and took us to a bedroom in his home. It was a very nice, comfortable room, and he assured us that we could stay as long as we wished. We spent some great days with them.

Of course, when the Foo Sums met us at the airport, his mother had Hawaiian leis for us. I think it was the first time they

CHAPTER 13

had met the pastor, too. Glenn's parents were so cordial and made plans to come for us the next morning to show us around the island.

The first thing next morning, they took us to their home. She couldn't believe a lady wouldn't have a muumuu. She showed me her closet full of all kinds of the beauties. When I would ooh and aah over them, she would say, "Try it on." If it fit and I acted like I liked it, she would say, "It's yours." By the second time, I learned not to say anything. But I was dressed in the right thing for the island that day.

They took us to gift shops. Their generosity continued everywhere we went, but we learned early and only received what they chose. At restaurants, Mr. Foo Sum would disappear, and when we went to pay, it was all taken care of. Seemed everyone on the island knew the Foo Sums.

Every morning when they came for us, the gas tank was filled, the car was polished and we were treated royally. They took us to a coconut grove where Mr. Foo Sum picked up a long pole that lay on the ground and knocked coconuts off the trees. They were free for the taking. We climbed through a fence to lili-koi trees and picked lili-koi (passion fruit). We went to a hillside where avocado trees were plentiful and picked huge avocados.

When we got to their house, Mrs. Foo Sum made fresh coconut pies and lili-koi pies from the fruit we had picked and processed that day. You've never tasted anything as fresh and good as those pies. There was always mango juice in the fridge for us to enjoy.

The Foo Sums came to visit us and their son, Glenn, and his family in Klamath Falls in 1974.

Lots of interesting things happened on that eventful trip to Hawaii in the wintertime of January 1969. We had no reservations — nothing except the plane tickets.

The morning we were to leave, there was a huge snowstorm that had blown in, and airplanes could not land in Klamath Falls. The radio didn't forecast the weather like they can now. We got a call from the airlines telling us that we would have to drive over the hill to Medford to catch our plane, which was due to land almost immediately. We had snow tires on the pickup, so we loaded our luggage in as quickly as we could and headed out.

Ormel was pastoring in Grants Pass. We called them to meet

MORETA: MY STORY

us at the airport and take our pickup home with them. It was a rush job for us all. When we arrived, the plane was there. We had to run for it. We pulled off our winter coats and left them with Ormel and Sandi and got on the flight to go to a warmer place.

It was a rough ride all the way with lightening flashing off the wings of the plane and black clouds as far as you could see. And going west, we got into darkness again. That storm dumped snow and ice all across Oregon, so much so that when we got home 17 days later, there was still snow blocking our driveway. We lived on a hillside and had to park down below and find our way up the side of the bank. Icicles were hanging from the rooftop to the ground after all that time.

Our friends had told us to get our tickets to the big island of Hawaii. The plane had to land in Honolulu. If our destination was Hilo on the big island, we would be able to visit all the other islands on the trip free as we made our way back to Honolulu. That was nice. However, because of the storm, a headwind had slowed our plane, and that caused us to miss our flight east on the smaller plane.

As the airplane was landing, they were calling our name to come to the front, to be the first off the plane so we could make our next connection. The man who met us had to have some information from us and detained us too long. Our next plane was gone. We had to look on the information boards to see where to go and what to do next. When we got to the baggage department, our big suitcase was gone — stolen! It had all of Lloyd's clothes and some of mine. It was quite a mix-up. We were exhausted. Now what do we do?

We were with Pan American airlines, and they treated us like royalty. While the authorities were searching for our luggage, Pan American came to the airport in a limousine and took us to a plush place with beautiful, colorful Hawaiian foliage that lined the red-carpeted walkway, which led from the limousine to the front door of our abode. Inside the room, the carpet was red, and the bedspread was a beauty. Remember, we didn't have reservations for anything, but it seemed like the red carpet was rolled out for us at every turn.

When it came time to eat, the big, long, black automobile was there with the driver in his full regalia. Wow! I could get used to that kind of treatment.

CHAPTER 13

We were there for two or three days. They hadn't found our things, but the airlines gave us money for Lloyd's underwear and things we would need while the search continued. Finally, we went on to Hilo, rented a car and circled the island of Kona to see all the beauties. While we were there, Pan Am called. They had found our suitcase and would hold it till we came back to Honolulu. We had a nice room on Hilo Bay. It was $12.48 per night in the Hukilau Hotel. We were there three or four nights, then began our short flights to Maui, Molokai and Kauai. We stayed a night or two in each place till we felt we had seen all we wanted to see, then we were on to Oahu.

At the airport, we picked up our luggage that had been stolen. The suitcase had been broken into and was held together with a belt. Several of the shirts and pants were missing, also the shorts and undershirts. The airlines had us write down everything that was broken or missing, and they reimbursed us for everything. So we got a new suitcase and some new clothes. All my clothes were still there.

There were lots of hippies and winos in the woods around Waikiki. That's where they found our things.

Other than Maui, Waikiki was our favorite place of all the islands. Everything was really inexpensive in those days, and the atmosphere was truly Hawaiian. All the women wore muumuus, and we enjoyed the Hawaiian music, the food, papaya, pineapple, sugar cane and coconut groves. Lloyd played golf several days with a foursome. We went to different churches on Sundays. We knew the pastor in Honolulu, and I got to do all the talking.

Verlon had his 10th birthday while we were gone. We had left him with a family in the church. I've kept his cards he wrote us while we were gone. He was pretty homesick for us.

When we got home from the islands, Lloyd's voice was still bad. He hooked up the trailer house and went to Sun Valley for a few weeks. I was glad to be home with Verlon.

Over the years, we took five flights to Hawaii. Lloyd took six. He went twice without me, and I went once without him. I went to American Samoa with the Oregon youth on a missionary trip when Ormel was District Youth Director for the state. Verlon was older by then and went with us; also, Bob and Judy went as speakers and workers. I was to be the chief cook, but there wasn't that much to do. The local church ladies were great to do that for us.

MORETA: MY STORY

What a beautiful place and a wonderful opportunity to see all the special Christian people. We came back to Honolulu on the way home for two days of R and R.

***

In 1974, the trip to Hawaii was a triangle flight, Hawaii to Alaska, when Jodi, Rhonda's baby girl, was born. She was an adorable baby Alaskan. Great days!

On one of the trips we took to Hawaii, Admiral and his wife, Marie, flew into Hilo, and we met them at the airport with leis. We rented a car and had the privilege of showing them the Kona Coast and other islands. It was a great time to have them with us.

More of Our Travels

About 1957, when we were pastoring in Molalla, Lloyd took a great trip to Mexico and Central America — Guatemala, El Salvador and another place or two. He went with a group of preachers from all over the nation and denominational leaders from our headquarters. Instead of flying commercial, they flew in small private planes, which made for some hair-raising experiences. Levi Larson, pastor of First Assembly in Salem, was another Oregon minister who was along on the trip. He and Lloyd went on a fishing trip together and had lots to tell about in that foreign country.

Lloyd was not interested in taking pictures, but I threatened him with extortion, excommunication or whatever it took. He had to take every 36 exposure, 35mm roll of film I was sending — seven rolls in all! He took every roll (and he had to use an exposure meter). He did really good and was able to show his slides to church groups.

***

In 1970, we went to the Holy Land for 15 days with Northwest College in Seattle. President D.V. Hurst and Amos Millard, professors in the school, led the pilgrimage. It was a great learning time. However, it changed our thinking of the whole Bible. We visualize distances of things in the Bible and where everything happened. When we were there, our thinking was all changed. Israel is a tiny

CHAPTER 13

land. Wells, hills and the burning bush — everything is close together.

We had to go back as soon as possible to get it all straight in our thinking. We got all the information, showed our pictures to different churches and gave invitations for those who would want to go with us. We led our own group in 1971. We took nine people with us, and it was greater than the first time because we knew our way around. We got into some very interesting places and experiences that we were bold enough to go into. Our group had a great time. The ones who went with us on our second trip were all from Oregon:

Reverend Lewis and Loretta Hootman from Bend
Reverend Ronald Murphy from Butte Falls
Reverend Robert Collins from Central Point
Jane Landes from Monmouth
John Studley from Klamath Falls
Jim Wagner from Klamath Falls
Juanita Tull from Bend
Grace Miller from Portland

We left from Portland and flew to Rome (Roma) Italy, the site of the Catacombs, where an estimated 350,000 Christians were buried. We saw the Colosseum, the Vatican and the Mamertine Prison, where Paul was confined until he was beheaded.

From Rome to Egypt

In Cairo, we stayed in the Shepherds Hotel on the Nile River. We went to the pyramids of Giza and to the Sphinx on camelback. The leader of the camels was heckling us all the way for money. The Cairo leader of the trip to the pyramids wouldn't let us take pictures of anything along the way as we traveled in the hotel bus. I stole a few, anyway. I set my camera in the window and looked straight ahead. As we were seeing the awesome sights along the way, I was snapping pictures.

They took us to King Tutankhamen's tomb and then for about two hours to a gift shop, where we could spend money on watches, rings, etc.

When we got back to the hotel, I said to Lloyd, "They won't let us take pictures, and I am not interested in going with them again."

MORETA: MY STORY

The next morning, we went to the steps of the hotel and slowly began to walk around the block. An Egyptian man began to follow us. He talked plain English, but we asked him to leave us alone. We just wanted to walk. "Yes, yes, of course." But he kept walking with us and talking.

There were buildings along the sidewalk but no windows in them. When we came to a door, he asked if we would like to see inside. He opened the door, and it was a lovely textile shop with beautiful materials and knickknacks of all kinds. Not junk, but unusually rich things.

As I was looking around, he and Lloyd were talking. Soon my husband came to me and announced, "I think we have found what we had hoped to find." Sure enough! He showed us his papers with his picture and told us about his job. He spoke seven languages and was hired by the hotel we were staying in. We hurried back to the hotel, took his little booklet inside and asked at the desk if this was authentic. The man at the desk rushed out to see, and it really was. His name was Moses Sam. He could stand on the big steps of the hotel, but he couldn't come inside.

What a find! I explained to him that I wanted to take pictures, but when we went on the bus, they wouldn't let us take any. He said, "I let you take pictures." He would pick us up in one hour. We had met another couple from Washington State, and when we told them what we were going to do, they wanted to go with us. Moses Sam had rented a taxi, and there was room for our friends, also, and what a morning we had. He took us to places the tour bus never took any of our people.

We saw the old city of Cairo and walked among the places where the people lived. We saw the synagogues, mosques and the oldest Coptic Church. It had been built in Mark's time. We went down in the basement to the place where Joseph, Mary and Jesus hid for three months when they fled to Egypt to escape King Herod as he was killing all the babies.

We walked the narrow street among the spices; it was the same as it was in Moses' time. And we believed it. The smells, the large sacks of spices that lined the walkway, the old scales to weigh the spices, and we had Moses Sam to explain it all.

He had instructed us not to pay when the beggars came begging for "one dollah, please." Also, when you took a picture, they wanted money.

CHAPTER 13

Moses Sam took care of all of that, and I took pictures of all I wanted. When a beggar came behind us, he chattered something to them and they scattered.

When the others of our group came in at night all tired and disgusted, we would be all washed, dressed and ready for dinner with our great tales to tell. We had our own tour guide who made Egypt alive for us. Moses Sam took us out that afternoon, the next morning, afternoon and night. By the next morning, there were 10 or 12 that wanted to go with us, and he rented a limousine, plus the taxi to take us all. We rode with him in the taxi, and he explained things to us as we went along.

He took us to the potter's house. Lloyd was really interested in that since he had preached about the potter. It was all old and typical of what you would expect in Bible times. We went to the Land of Goshen, where Joseph had become the ruler of the whole place and brought Jacob and his family when the famine was on.

While we were on this trip to Memphis, with just the four of us, Lloyd told Moses Sam that he would like to ride a water buffalo. That was the animal they farmed their little plot of ground with. Moses Sam drawled, "You want to ride a buffalo? Okay." We stopped once, and he and the owner almost got in a fight. Of course, we didn't know what they were saying, but you could tell by their actions. Moses said to us, "Come on, let's go."

After a while, we stopped at another man's place, and Lloyd got his chance but not for long. He got on the animal, and the buffalo turned and headed a few feet for his shelter. That shelter was only high enough for the buffalo. Lloyd managed to jump just in time. There didn't seem to be people around, but when that happened and we were laughing, Egyptians seemed to come out of the ground. They are interesting people and can change from fun and laughter to fighting angry in an instant.

We went for a ride on the Nile River in a rickety old boat that didn't look like it would float. It was so entertaining to see the Egyptians in their old dress-like garments doing all the work on these excursions.

Two of those ladies who had been along on the Moses Sam trips went with us the next year. We happened to go to the same Shepherds Hotel in Cairo. We went to the steps of the hotel, and Moses Sam was there. He remembered us from the year before and ran to us, kissed my hand and we were ready to go again. After

MORETA: MY STORY

lunch when we went to our room, there was a bouquet of flowers and a sack of oranges for us. Moses Sam had done things like that for us the year before, and he remembered the things I liked.

We were only in Egypt that first trip for three nights and days, but those days were filled with unforgettable memories. When it was time to leave, we were all at the airport, but two men were missing. Our college leaders had brought the men's luggage with us. We were a sad but praying group of people. The police had been notified, and the hotel was frantically searching, but we had to leave.

We were at the airport, ready to board the plane, when the two men were ushered in. Talk about a prayer meeting of praise, tears and joy to see them, and they were two thankful preachers. All was well! The hotel people had found them and got them released just in time. The men had gone for a walk that morning to take a few more pictures. Not knowing the language, the signs along the way meant nothing to them. The signs had read *No pictures in this area.*

The police saw the well-dressed men with their cameras and arrested them. They marched them about two miles down streets, into state buildings to sign papers and on to more places. All the while, as they went along, the crowd of excitable Egyptians was growing larger as they followed from building to building. Their cameras were broken into and the film removed. They were fingerprinted. They were humiliated and had something to preach about when they got home (with embarrassment). But we loved them at that moment.

From Egypt, we went to Nicosia, Cyprus. One of their national leaders, the Minister of the Interior, had been murdered that day in the hotel where we stayed. We were there only one night. It was a beautiful country with oranges hanging from streetlights and in decorative places around the city. It was during their orange festival time. From there, we flew to Tel Aviv and then took a bus to Jerusalem, Israel.

Israel

How great to be in the land where Jesus walked! To see the sights and be in the places that we had read about all our life. We went to the Garden of Gethsemane, where Jesus wept over the city,

CHAPTER 13

and stood where He was betrayed. The olive trees that are more than 2,000 years old still stand. We were inside the tomb where Jesus lay when He arose from the dead. We stood at the Wailing Wall, where many Jews stand and wail for their Messiah to come and for the loss of the commandments and the destruction of the temple. I stood and wept with them for the coming of the Messiah, too, but in a different way. They were wailing for Him to come the first time. I wailed, prayed and wept for His second coming. "Come, Lord Jesus, and come quickly." You can't believe the fervency I felt — just to think, I was there praying with the Jews about the Lord Jesus.

All the happenings in the Bible we saw, touched, felt and experienced in a heart-thrilling way. I waded in the Dead Sea. We climbed the hills by foot to see old Jericho, where the walls came tumbling down. Jericho is 350 feet below sea level.

We saw the caves where the Dead Sea scrolls were found, and we visited the new modern building where the Dead Sea scrolls are housed now. The Jerusalem University was unbelievably modern. Israel was just beginning to blossom like a rose as the Bible says it would be in the last days before the coming of the Lord.

We ate at the Sea of Galilee, then took a boat across the sea to a kibbutz, where we ate fish that had been caught in the waters there.

On a Sunday, four of us had dinner at a shop owner's home in Bethlehem. His name was George Baboul. They had two daughters and three sons, Maha, Haia, Anwar, Munir and John. That was a glorious experience. His wife was a dear woman. I have pictures of it all, and the details of each experience are so special. However, the coffee was something else! The tiny demitasse cups and black coffee lasted me a long time.

After Israel, we went to Greece. We saw guards at the royal palace, the Olympic Stadium, the Acropolis and Mars Hill, which was in the shadow of the Acropolis. It took 10,000 slaves 30 years to build the Acropolis (a pagan temple that later became a Christian church after Paul's sermon on Mars Hill). There are so many things to tell about all the things we saw!

We went to Corinth. At least 100 slaves were sold each day in Corinth, a wicked city in Paul's day.

On our second pilgrimage, we didn't go to Rome. We went to Beirut, Lebanon, which was a very modern city. The hotel we stayed in was elegant. The maidservants were hospitable, the rooms spotlessly clean and there were no beggars around. We tried to tip the maid, and she refused! That was a switch. Hearing of so much war and destruction of the beautiful buildings and country over there really grieved us.

Our last flight was Amsterdam to New York and then we landed in Portland on March 25 at 10:20 p.m. What a wonderful experience and a privilege to fulfill such a lifelong dream.

Thanks, Klamath Falls, for making it all possible on the first trip. The second time, we both traveled free for getting the tour together.

Family Deaths

My mother and daddy were living in Bend, Oregon. My mother had been anxious to go home (to heaven) for a while.

One day, when I traveled from Klamath Falls to see them, I walked into her bedroom, and on the top of her chest of drawers was something covered. As I was lifting the covering off, Mama was saying, "Do you want to see it?" By then, I was already seeing.

It was a beautiful long white satin dress. She said, "It's my trousseau. I'm getting ready to see my heavenly bridegroom." This was to be her burial dress. It had long sleeves with a ruffled, gathered wrist and lace around the edge. The high neckline had a *big bertha collar*, with matching ruffle and lace and a satin ribbon rose with long streamers from the shoulder. She had little white satin matching slippers with a smaller satin rose on them. All her underwear, including white nylons, was there. She made all these on her old Singer treadle sewing machine that she had made her wedding dress on more than 60 years before. She owned an electric machine these days, but my sentimental mama did it all with planning, love and care.

As I was looking at all this, I realized she was watching me, expecting me to scold her. I said, "Mama, this is the most beautiful thing I've ever seen. I wish everyone had a mother like you — not complaining, not whining, but looking forward to meeting her Maker."

As she was showing this to me, Papa walked in. I asked, "Can I show this to Papa?"

When he saw it, his expression was real serious as he gently spoke. "That's nice."

CHAPTER 13

Mama didn't go for four or five more years. She never took a pill in her life, not even an aspirin. She made us all promise if she ever got sick that we would not have a doctor with her. God had been her healer, and she still trusted Him.

None of us children ever took pills as long as we were at home. I had seen my mother walk the floor all night with my brother when he was sick. God always came through, and we were a healthy lot.

In his later years, Papa had ulcers and went to the hospital for a while on the advice of my brothers. He didn't like it one bit and wanted to get back to his bed at home. He was in his late 80s. One of the old men across his room at the hospital was lying there asleep with his mouth wide open. Papa said to Orion, "If you don't get me out of here, I'll soon be looking just like that old man." His mind was sharp as could be; he knew what he wanted.

My brother finally got him released and on his way home in the ambulance. When the attendants wheeled him into the house, heading for his bedroom and passing his favorite chair, he called, "Hold it right there." They got him into his chair, and he leaned back and sighed. "Now, that's what I've been looking for."

He became bedfast after a while for a short time. Pastor Hootman and Missionary Benintendi came to pray for him. They started to pray, rebuking death and praying for his healing. When he heard them praying like that, he removed their hands, rolled to the wall and said, "Don't pray for me like that; I want to go on *home*."

My brother, Orion, his wife, Elnora, and Mama and I were at his bedside as he was breathing his last. My mother walked out of the room and didn't come back right away. I went into the living room, and she was lying on the couch. I asked what was wrong. She said, "Well, my heart was pounding, and I was so weak. I thought wouldn't it be nice if I could just go on and be there to meet Papa when he comes in at heaven's gate?"

I hugged her and told her, "Mama, you can't turn the quittin' button off. You may as well get up and come back in with us." Heaven was real to my wonderful parents.

And it's just as real to me. The more family and friends we have on the other side, the greater heaven becomes and the more homesick we get to be there, too.

MORETA: MY STORY

***

My middle brother, Melbra, was coming out from his job on Christmas Eve. He got to his car and slumped down beside it and was gone. A massive heart attack. It was a real shock to all of us. He left his wife, Edna, a beautiful daughter, Deanna (who was my son, Ormel's, age), a son, Robert John, and a young son, Phillip. They lived in Pueblo, Colorado.

My daddy died February 23, 1970, at age 87.
My brother, Melbra, died in December 1971, at age 54.
My mother died June 1973, at age 82.
My dear mother-in-law, Mattie Chapin, died in September 1971.

***

I asked my son, Ormel, to write the following story. It's great!

We had just returned from a mission trip to American Samoa when we learned of my grandma Chapin being admitted to the hospital in Battle Creek, Michigan. The news was not good as she was not expected to live very long. I was also told that Grandma Chapin was asking to see me as I seemed to have taken my dad's place in the family after his death just before I was 3 years old. It was only a matter of hours after returning from Samoa that Mom and I were on our way to Battle Creek to see Grandma.

Upon entering her hospital room, I stepped beside her bed and hugged this special lady that I loved so much, but because of the distance between Oregon and Michigan, saw so few times in my life. When she saw me, she reached up with both hands and took hold of my face and drew me directly in front of her and with clear, sharp eyes began to study my face. She then smiled so sweetly, and after a moment, her first words to me were, "You look just like your daddy!"

Wow! I was shocked with the sudden wave of mixed emotions that flooded me. I entered her room with the heaviness that I may not have my grandma very much longer, but with her saying that I looked just like my dad, I was filled with such excitement and pride to know that my dad was really visible in me. There was no greater word that could have been said to me, for Dad (Harry) was and still is my hero whom I have always loved, missed, admired

CHAPTER 13

and truly wanted to be like. That was one of the most amazing days in my life. I looked like my dad.

Later that day, Mom and I were taken to Uncle Junior's (Sherman is one of my dad's younger brothers) home for a family reunion, where more Chapins came out of the woods from around Battle Creek than I could have imagined. While sitting and feasting between two of my uncles, Uncle Junior leaned over to me and said, "When you arrived, I saw you walking up to the house, and you walk just like your dad."

Amazed, I asked, "Was he bowlegged like I am?"

"No," he laughed, "but the way you walk just reminds me of your dad."

Wow! Another God kiss.

A little later, while sitting at the same table, Uncle Don (another younger brother of my dad), not knowing what Uncle Junior had said earlier, said, "I watched you while you were eating, and your hands remind me of your dad's."

Again, I marveled and said, "Did he have long, skinny fingers like I have?"

"I'm not sure," he responded, "but there's just something about the way you use your hands that makes me think of your dad."

I couldn't believe it. Three incredible statements that linked me directly to my dad truly made my day. How cool is that? I look like my dad, and he's my hero.

A few weeks after Mom and I returned from Michigan, I was in my office in Canby, Oregon, a few miles south of Portland, where I was Senior Pastor of the Neighborhood Assembly. While in prayer for my family and the Chapin clan, the Lord seemed to remind me of the three God kisses I had received regarding me being like my dad. I meditated on what Jesus said in the scriptures, "If you see Me, you see the Father," and what Paul wrote, "Follow me as I follow Christ."

It was during this time of prayer that I sensed a loving Father God gently impress upon my heart these words: "Wouldn't it be great if people who saw you walking down the street would come up to you and say, 'I recognize your Father God by the way you walk?'"

This really grabbed me and changed my life. "Oh, God, may Your life and character be in me through Jesus Christ, Your Son."

MORETA: MY STORY

I still am excited to know that in so many ways I am like my dad. But now, my greatest desire and motivation is to be like my heavenly father, and someday, I will be with them both forever.

My Old Man

On my way home from Battle Creek, the flight was delayed in Portland, causing me to miss the connecting plane to Klamath Falls. I had to be shuttled from the airport to downtown Portland and take the bus instead. I was thinking, *The Lord must have someone very special for me to talk to,* so I was content to make all the confusing adjustments.

I had to run to catch the bus. There were only two empty seats, and they were the last two seats in the back row. The bus seemed to be waiting for one more to fill the empty spot beside me.

At last, an old fellow waddled in to sit beside me — dirty, drunk and tobacco soaked. I let him get in the middle, and I sat on the seat by the aisle. I prayed, *Dear Lord, this wasn't what I had in mind.*

With his face right in mine, blowing his foul breath as he spoke, he said, "Hello, what's your name?" I tried to be respectful while ignoring his question, but he didn't give up. "I say, sweetheart, what's your name?"

The unceasing chatter continued during the long trip, and I talked to him when I had to. I asked him if he ever knew anyone who had prayed for him. "Oh, yes, a praying grandma. She never gave up." And he never let up talking and breathing. I did give a scripture or two and suggested he go to church.

Then he said, "What church do you go to, sweetheart?"

Oh my! Now what do I say? I finally told him, but I didn't tell him that I was the pastor's wife. He assured me, "I will come visit your church. I will." I'm sure he never came. At last, the old fellow laid his head on my shoulder and started snoring. Which was worse, him blowing in my face and talking or sleeping on my shoulder and quiet? The sleeper sounded better.

Three young women were across the aisle from me, having such a good time together I thought surely they had just gotten away from Papa and the kids (probably teenagers) for the day.

I called across to them, "You girls are just having altogether too much fun. I think one of you should change places with me for

CHAPTER 13

a while." That just added more life to their enjoyment.

What little *planting* or *watering* I did certainly was not done with any amount of pleasure. Nor did I feel real saintly or feel that I had accomplished anything worthwhile.

A couple of times, the old man would light up a cigarette until the driver smelled the smoke and called out, "Whoever is smoking, put it out now!"

The culprit would turn to me and say, "Pardon me, honey, is this bothering you?" And then he put it out.

At last, we reached our destination at almost 2 a.m. The bus depot was in the roughest part of town, and they locked the doors at 2. I rushed to a payphone and called home to get my husband to come get me. I let the phone ring — no answer. I would hang up and call again and again. I let it ring 50 times. I'd hang up and let it ring another 50 times.

Finally, a sleepy voice came on. (It was evangelist Claude Wood who was staying in our home while having special meetings in our church.) "Hello?"

I almost screamed, "Where in the world is everyone? I've called and called." I told him I was in town at the bus station, and please wake my husband to come get me.

He slowly drawled, "Is it comfortable down there?" Claude Woods was a preacher with a great sense of humor. We enjoyed him. (But not right then. However, it did sorta bring a smile.)

By the time my ride came, I was standing with bag and baggage on the sidewalk alone with just a few other slithery-looking characters not far away.

Recently, I had made a brand new two-piece suit that had been so wearable on the trip. It was a very pretty suit with a pleated skirt that didn't wrinkle or look slept in. When I pulled off my skirt, I discovered a cigarette burn in it!

As long as that skirt was around, I would pray for "my old man" because of the tiny hole. Even after the suit was old, gone and hardly remembered, I'd still pray, "Lord, what about my old man?"

I never saw him again, but I can't help but believe that all the times I've prayed for him and all the inconveniences he caused me were evidence that the Lord must have directed me to him so that I could water or replant what his grandma sowed. The only harvest I saw was a tiny hole in my pretty brown suit.

MORETA: MY STORY

Our 25th Wedding Anniversary

In August 1974, our children planned a beautiful celebration for us in our church in Klamath Falls. (All were there except Rhonda and her family from Alaska.) They remarried us with full dress, veil, bride's bouquet, boutonnieres, cake and all the trimmings of a wedding. We marched down the aisle, and the attendants were our offspring and our grandchildren. There were lots of laughs and happiness with plenty of pictures to capture the day. They even decorated the getaway car with tin cans and "Just Married" signs. The photographer was our young son, Verlon. The preacher who remarried us was our older son, Ormel.

Tragedies

Over the 18 years of our ministry in Klamath Falls, there were lots of unhappy and hurtful events in our church families' lives. We were a large, close family, and when hurts came to any of them, we hurt, too. There were the "in" people and the fringe ones. Tragedy came to each of them, and we were a part of helping them heal.

One man, who was a woman chaser, came home late one night after being out with some gal. (He didn't come to church, but his wife did.) His wife approached him about it. He beat her up and then left. She called us. She was alone, hurting and fearful. I dressed and went to her. She showed me where he had beaten her across her breast until it looked like hamburger.

This same man would come to church occasionally and sit on the back seat. While my husband was preaching one Sunday morning (I think he was preaching on tithing), this man stood up and loudly proclaimed, "That's a lie. That's not the truth."

My preacher man waxed loud and bold. "You sit down and not another word out of you."

If anyone had been asleep that morning, he or she came wide-awake and amened the preaching with full attention and praise.

This man's wife was leaving her wife-beating, rambling man. One of our deacons was helping her move some things. Her husband met them and beat the deacon up pretty good. That was hard on the deacon's pride, but I think he was proud of himself that he didn't fight back. I'm pretty sure it was only a short time after that

CHAPTER 13

the man was at a tavern, and another man threw him through the window. It put him in the hospital, and he died. He was a fighter and was husky enough. A couple of years ago, his lovely wife came to see us.

***

Another Air Force wife had a fire in her kitchen and grabbed the burning skillet of grease to take it outside. She tripped and spilled the blazing grease on a big part of her body, including her face and arms. They called us from the hospital. We went immediately and prayed for her. The healing and absence of scars were unbelievable, except through prayer. Her unsaved husband was a mess, too. She and her new husband came to see us recently from back East. How special to see them.

***

One of my young men had been in my Sunday school class for years. He had gone with our group of 17 to Bethany Bible College. He had gotten away from God. He was still living with his parents who had left our congregation and were going to another church, but he seldom went anymore.

This one Sunday morning, he came to church and sat through the service. At the end of the message, I went directly to him. He knew I loved him, and he loved me. I urged him to recommit his life to Jesus.

"Sister Fosner," he said, "no one can live a Christian life where I live in my hypocrite haven."

I can still see us standing in front of the big colored glass windows beside the aisle on the south side of the church with our arms around each other.

The phrase I had spoken many times to my young people, I repeated. "Nothing or nobody is worth you going to hell over." My eyes and nose drip as I write this. It still hurts! It was hard for him to walk out, but he did. Everyone knew he was far from God.

In just a few days, he was driving at a fast speed and lost control of the car, hit a tree and was killed instantly. He was drunk. It was a blow to everyone that he was really gone.

MORETA: MY STORY

***

One Air Force wife with a roving, ungodly husband was living a life of grief. She was a great worker in the church. She had three teenage daughters who came to church with her. Her man was going to leave her for another woman, but she was holding onto him, refusing to let him go. She was destroying herself with denial and pain. One night, I met her at the church for counseling. We were in a small classroom, and she knew she had to have help. I told her, "You have to come to God and tell Him that you give your husband to that other woman."

"That's not right! He's my husband. I can't give him to her," she wailed. I assured her that she had to have peace. She had lost him already, and she had to give up or go on in this distress, which was killing her. He had never been faithful to her.

"It may take you all night to say this and be able to really mean it, but by morning, you can be free from this pain and have the joy of the Lord. He is your strength, and He will see you through this painful ordeal. This is worse than death."

I left her there alone. She wept and prayed it through until daylight, until she was free. She called me the next morning with total victory. She never returned to that torture again. Soon she was able to say with assurance that she hadn't been this happy in many years. God used her in many ways in the church until she left the area after we moved away.

She later married a good Christian man and had several years of happiness before she passed away. Girls, don't ever marry an unsaved man. Fellows, you listen up, too.

***

We had one week of five different extreme happenings. One young adopted teen had given a party while her parents were gone for the night. She set the house on fire to destroy the evidence of her wrongdoings. When the parents returned, the house was gone. We were involved with all the court proceedings and getting her into a juvenile home. We grieved with families at times like that.

Another time that week, a young Indian man kidnapped his estranged wife, drove her to a country road, raped her and left her in the dark night to find her way back. We didn't know her at all,

CHAPTER 13

and he had only been in the church a few times, but we were at his trials and had an interest in his sordid life, hoping we could help him to know God's love.

The same week, one of our Sunday school teachers and her little 5-year-old boy were walking along the road near their home. A car came along at a fast speed, hit the 5 year old, threw him 90 feet through the air and killed him. When this all came about, the wife confessed to us that she was having an affair with a neighbor man. She and her husband weren't regular members, but we still cared and had to handle another sticky situation. It was traumatic and painful for the family and for us.

There were two more such happenings that week, but I think I'll just let it go. Actually, some of those people are still alive, and I'd better just leave it alone.

Oh, there were so many times in our ministry that we had to get a husband and wife together to confess wrongs. One such time, we had to chase down the other woman who had completely lost her mind over it all. We took her to the Salem institution and got her to sign herself in for a few months. We asked her husband to move her out of town. They had been there only a few months and were not longtime residents. He gladly complied. The husband and wife who had been a part of this ordeal stayed together for all these years. But, oh, what a grieving time for them and for us.

***

Once, we had a harder than usual time with such things. The man was on the board, but his business dealings were getting back to us from people in the town. My husband had to deal with him, and it became an unpleasant encounter at the board meeting. He became really angry with the pastor and was threatening to beat him up. One day, he called my husband with these threats, and my husband hung up on him, saying, "I don't have to listen to this kind of talk."

Before long, we saw his car pull into our driveway, and my husband sent me to the door. I shouldn't say he sent me, he just asked me if I wanted to answer the door. I always enjoyed a challenge and was glad to do it. I don't remember one thing about the conversation. But I think the man was glad to have it happen that way. I just remember seeing him walk back to his car and drive away. However, the church board stood with my husband on all of this man's lack of integrity. He was dismissed from the board, and he left the church. But you can't imagine the troubles we had, plus his home was on the rocks, too. Plus-Plus-Plus.

Believe me, other pastors have these kind of things happen to them, too. They just don't have a wife to publish it for everybody to read. But believe it or not, I loved pastoring and really miss it. I love people. There were so many wonderful things that happened that surpassed all these hurtful events, affairs, concerns and surprises. Only eternity will tell if we ever did anything worthwhile or changed lives for His purpose.

An Extreme Tragedy

On February 26, 1975, David Nunn was flying from Salem to Klamath Falls in a Cessna 182, when the plane disappeared from the radar screen. David had retired from the Air Force after 20 years of service. He was a teacher's aide in the industrial education department of Klamath Falls Union High School and working at Southern Oregon Aviation. He was a flight instructor and had two high school juniors with him, Mat Perkins and Jim Pryor.

It was a night flight, and the weather had turned bad. Dave was an experienced flyer. I don't know if they ever determined the reason for the downed plane. The search had gone on for months with search crews from California and many other places, but nothing of the plane or its occupants were found for seven years.

Dave left behind his wife, Jean, and four lovely daughters, Leilani Jean Johnson of Hawaii, Lena Joyce Hoskins of Salem, Liann Janelle and Linda Jeanette who were both still at home and in school.

As soon as Jean got the word near midnight that the plane was down, she called. We prayed, and I went down and stayed the rest of the night with her. She had had a premonition of his going. When he kissed her goodbye as he was leaving, her thought was, *The kiss of death.* She had gone to sleep that night and had awakened with what she thought was Dave with his hand on her leg. She raised up, expecting to find him coming to bed. She drifted back to sleep until the phone call, and she knew *that was it!* It's so great of the Lord to prepare us ahead of time about extreme things to come.

CHAPTER 13

We had no choir leader at that time, and when a ministry was needed, I would step up and do whatever was necessary. I had developed an extremely beautiful what I called the Sunset Package. I had a 34-member choir. We had practiced this and were ready to go with it.

When I was with Jean the night of Dave's disappearance, I told her about this choir that was ready for presentation. She was so convinced that Dave would not come back, she said, "I want that for Dave's memorial." I just knew that God had prepared it all for this time. We had the memorial on a Saturday afternoon, April 5, 1975.

A great technician, an artist and a lot of help put it all together. (I never liked a baptistery with a hole up high in the wall above the platform, so when I designed the building, I planned the baptistery on the level of the platform with a wall that made it unnoticeable until it was being used to baptize converts.) It was quite an ordeal to get everything together for the choir production.

The workers made a large golden sun on a device above the baptistery that set so slowly, you couldn't see it was moving. Just at the end of the program, it set and left us in semidarkness. A spotlight came on above where two large fluffy clouds had been seen and now were parting, and an 8-foot Jesus appeared with hands outstretched. A trio was singing, "What a day that will be, when my Jesus I will see; what a day, what a day that will be."

Other songs sung were songs with emotion and feeling like "If you go first and I remain to walk this road alone." Tony Orton, with his rich bass voice, did a solo on this with the choir background.

We also sang "When Jesus breaks the morning, the hosts of heaven sing. Hosanna in the highest, Christ is our conquering King."

While all this was going on and at the right time (I had made pictures of sunsets that I had taken on trips and wherever through the years), these sunsets were being shown on the large wall on the right side of the platform. Oh, what drama and beauty it all was for almost an hour.

Jean had prepared a long table down in front of the platform with Dave's picture and the plane and with his medals and honors from the service. There were lots of them.

MORETA: MY STORY

She and the four girls stood by the display as people came around and showed their concern and love to them.

We had moved away at the end of seven years when Dave's body was found, but we went back and officiated at the graveside and witnessed his burial.

Helpmate

I was a widow.
I married a preacher.
There were three kids, then one more.
He did the preaching.
I trained the kids.
We did it!

We fished in the ocean.
He piloted the boat.
I pulled in the fish.
We went hunting.
I shot a deer.
He got a bigger one!

He preached.
I played.
A necessary twosome.
He taught from the pulpit.
I taught in the class.
They got the message.

He was the Reverend.
I, the photographer.
That came in handy.
He gave the Word.
I made the picture.
We worked together.

He brought it in.
I paid it out.
We made it work.

CHAPTER 13

At times, things were good.
At times, they were bad.
I worked it out in the darkroom!

He dedicated their babies.
I loved on them all.
We were a team.
He baptized the converts.
I encouraged them on.
I was his helper.

He specialized in teaching the Bible.
I specialized in weddings and babies.
They got the picture.
He married them.
I shot them.
He buried them!

Moreta Fosner

CHAPTER 14

The Hunting Trips

In all of our 57 years of married life, I don't believe there was ever a year that we didn't go deer hunting. After our first year, Lloyd bought me a gun of my own. I had to stay at home that time because the kids were in school. Lloyd went hunting with the men. When the children were in school, I went out to Warren Cornelious' ranch (they were preacher friends) east of Springfield and went hunting by myself.

When I hadn't gone far, I saw a small yearling with barely legal horns. I shot him. Now what do I do? With no man around, I had to gut it out myself. I took my hunting knife out and started whittling. I slit its throat to let it bleed.

Then to the gory part. I slit it from the neck to the bottom, rolled my sleeves up and started pulling stuff out. I was hunkered down, next to the brush, and I'm sure my nose was all crinkled up. I heard laughter. It was the preacher, Warren! He heard me shoot and knew I would need help.

As I was telling a lady friend about it, she said, "Why didn't you try using two sticks to get the gunk out?"

I said, "I did!"

That was the picture Warren saw when he came up. There I was with two sticks in my bloody hands and a smirk on my embarrassed face. I gladly turned the job over to him.

After a nice lunch that Muriel fixed, I was on my way home with my bounty. When the kids came home from school, my little horned deer was in its deer bag, hanging in the garage. The men came home that day, skunked — no deer. Our three never let their daddy live it down.

***

When I was about six months along, before Verlon was born, it was doe season, and I had a doe tag. We were camped by the Metolious River and were road hunting. Lloyd was driving when

CHAPTER 14

we spotted a nice deer. I carefully slipped out of the car and shot it. I didn't have to clean this one. Thank the Lord for a man.

***

Another time, we were camping in the northeastern part of the state with our daughter-in-law, Sandi's, parents, Ernie and Neva Bedwell. The deer were bigger in that area than usual. Neva didn't hunt, but she went out with me that morning. She sat by a log, reading. I had gone a few steps farther where I had a view of a large open area below me. A beautiful three-point buck (our friends in Michigan would call it a six-point) came around a bend, and I laid it down with one shot. Neva came running, squealing with excitement. I began blowing my whistle for the men to come help. I slit its throat and waited. I have a cute picture of Neva holding up one leg of the deer while the men did the dirty work.

***

Seldom did I hunt with the men. I would get on a trail alone, with my gun over my shoulder, a camera, binoculars, my water canteen, my sharp knife, a pocket full of peanuts and a candy bar. Sometimes I would come out of the woods with a part of a bare limb, evergreen boughs, pinecones or anything I could use for decoration or for a skit with my young people to use back at the church. I liked to hunt at my own speed and not feel like I was in the men's way. I had a whistle that I blew when I needed help. We always had other hunters with us, and I accused my husband of going the other way when he heard my whistle so somebody else would have to clean my deer.

During our times of hunting, I shot several deer. The last few years, we had wonderful family camps with my parents, brothers and their families. The kids would make all kinds of playhouses, churches and preaching times. They have big stories of what went on, who preached and what they said. The preachers were usually my boys when they were little. They got good training out in the woods, close to the camps and were all eyes every time a deer would be brought in.

There was always much fun and laughter with all the ones who stayed in camp. Plus, you can't imagine the good food we enjoyed

MORETA: MY STORY

out in the open woods, around the campfires and visiting from one RV to the other. We had a city out in the wild made up of our trailer houses, motor homes, tents, hunting equipment and toys. It's been rough to get too old and have to give up the hunt.

Our young ones and their kids are now married and mostly moved away to other states. They miss the camping and hunting times we enjoyed for those many years. Oh, how rich I am because of my heritage, my great upbringing and my dear family and friends along the way.

More Hunting Stories

We were camping with another couple, Johnie and Ruthie Hoskins. She wasn't a hunter. It was during doe season, and I had a doe tag. We had all fanned out not too far apart and were making a drive through the area. (For you non-hunters, that's several hunters walking through the woods stirring up deer.)

I shot a nice big doe and blew my whistle. No husband — but Johnie came. When Johnie knelt down to start to work on the deer, he said, "If you'll go bring the car closer, I'll clean out your deer." As I walked past him, he squirted milk across my path and suggested, "Bring a milk bucket back when you come."

Our hunting times with different people and in different parts of the state were exciting, fun times with lots of laughs around the campfire.

***

Oh, yes! There was the time, shortly after we moved to Klamath Falls, that we went deer hunting with two or three couples from the church. Around the campfires at night, we usually heard the hunters' stories of the day. Some of those local couples had a ritual — if anyone told of shooting and missing his buck, he got his shirttail cut off. Katherine Palone was always handy with the scissors and did the cutting from the hunters' garments. So again, there was plenty of fun and laughter and wonderful food together. At the end of camp, we had four small squares from shirttails.

Ormel was in high school and was hunting with me. We heard a shot just over a little rise. I said to Ormel, "Now, watch right over

CHAPTER 14

that clearing. If they missed the deer and it comes our way, it will come right through there."

No sooner had I made that statement than the deer came over the spot. I was ready with the shot, and the deer went down. Ormel said, "Where'd it go?"

"Let's just stand still a few minutes and give it time to die, so it doesn't jump up and run away." (I've seen that happen.)

When we got to the deer, it was a nice four-point! I said, "Well, Ormel, get your knife out."

He answered, "If I had shot it, I would clean it." I began to blow my whistle. Nothing. No one came. We finally began to do the dirty work.

Someone once said, "When you pull the trigger, the fun is over." And that's the truth!

We had it almost done and another hunter came along. He had a hatchet that was needed to cut the bottom bone to finish the job, and he offered to do it. We lucked out on that. He came along just in time. We got the deer into camp. The men skinned it and hung it on the camp pole in its deer bag with the horns showing. *Nice!*

The next morning at daylight, I was out there again. Grandma Mocabee, who had kept our kids at times when we needed to be away, was on the camping trip with us. She was not a hunter but loved the meat and had a deer tag. She went out with me so she could tag a deer when I shot it for her. Sure enough, we hadn't been out long when a nice forked horn came along. I did it again, and we had her meat. So I had two deer hanging on the meat pole.

The next morning, I walked out not too far from camp to find a stand just in case a deer came through. As I was walking along, I found a set of horns — a three-point. That was a rare occasion. You just never saw horns out in the woods. I brought the horns to camp. The ladies in camp were ecstatic with it all and helped me gather small limbs and branches to fake a deer body. We put it in a heavy non-see-through bag, let the horns show above it all and hung it beside my other two deer.

Fortunately, a game warden never came along. It's unlawful to have untagged horns.

That night, when the men came in from their hunt and found that I had my third deer, it got quiet until one of them discovered the truth! What a fun camp.

MORETA: MY STORY

My Most Embarrassing Time

When I think of this, I begin to get a headache, blurred vision, backache and start hurting all over. So I quit!

I'm back, two days later.

I'll copy this just like I wrote it a few days after it happened and not try to put it in my words after 35 years. Maybe it's gotten worse by now. I doubt it.

I'm sure I will have times of grief, sorrow and disappointments during the rest of my lifetime but surely never a more embarrassing day than this particular Sunday.

We pulled our camp trailer about 20 miles from home on Friday so we would be at our hunting location for the opening day of deer season. Since my husband is pastor of a church, we would have to be home for Sunday. We camped in the yard of one of our parishioners who had a 150-acre farm and hunting land with a large mountain behind his place. We had a lovely chicken dinner and visit with them that night and retired early so we could get up at 5 Saturday morning to begin the hunt at the break of day.

The family had talked about a deer that someone had shot in the leg before season last year, and they had nourished it back to health, then turned it loose. Occasionally, it would come back and play around the farm. They sure hoped no one would shoot it this year, and yet, they knew he couldn't escape. He had one long horn and one short one. It never entered my mind that I might see the deer, or what I would do if I did.

That evening as we were hunting back toward home, I had just come out of the timber, and I saw the head of a deer about 75 yards away. I stood completely still until he looked away, then put my binoculars on him and saw horns. He jumped over a fence nearby and watched me again. I could see the one long horn and the one short horn. For at least three minutes I watched, standing perfectly still when he looked my direction. I sighted him in with the gun when he turned. *Should I, or shouldn't I?*

Eleven hunters had come in view the last hour of the hunt. Some of them were strangers, and some were college boys I had met during the day. I began to reason, *Any minute, one of the strangers will step out of the timber and see the deer, and that will be the end of him. I may as well pull the trigger and finish him off myself.*

CHAPTER 14

With my sights on a perfect shot and my trigger finger trembling (boy, I sure hate to say this), I did just that! I stood there a while before going to him, thinking, *Oh, I wish I hadn't done that.*

Then one of the college boys stepped out of the edge of the forest, and a couple minutes later, before I went to the deer, the owner stepped out. Believe me, I was sick! I said, "I'm afraid I got your pet deer."

He helped me find it, stopped and, almost in reverence, said, "Yes, that's Bambi." I wanted to faint, run, die, anything. That's the first time I'd heard his name. Then he took out his knife and slit his throat — the deer's throat, I mean. I began to shake and feel like a criminal. I was so relieved when my husband and young son, Verlon, drove up in the pickup and took over. Nobody was saying much.

The farmer decided he would walk on home and feed the cows. I asked him not to say anything to his wife and children for a few days. He said he wouldn't. But their teenage daughter (who was in my Sunday school class) heard the shooting, jumped in the car and came just as we were loading him. She wanted to see what I had. I didn't want her to see, but my husband insisted I may as well tell her. When I did, she said, "Oh, no! Bambi?" When she saw I was so distressed, she got hold of herself and said, "Oh, don't worry. It's just a deer, and someone would have gotten him, anyway." That was sweet of her, but it didn't help much.

The two college boys needed a ride into town, so we brought them in. I knew it was too late for them to get anything to eat at the dorm, so we brought them home with us and fixed supper before taking them on to the college.

The boys helped my husband hang the deer and skin him while our son helped me fix something to eat. We talked of my terrible feelings about the deer. I finally said, "You know, if I hadn't shot that deer, the college boy, Gary, would have because he stepped out of the woods five minutes after I shot."

Verlon said, "No, I don't think he would have because Mr. Splodger (not his name) saw the three of us today and told us of the one long horn and one short horn and asked us not to shoot it."

I groaned, "Oh, no."

As we were eating supper, I mentioned this at the table, and Gary said, "If I had seen him, I would have thought, *Oh, boy,*

MORETA: MY STORY

horns. I would have shot and thought later." Everybody was trying to be kind to me.

My husband quipped, "I made up my mind when they talked about it last night that if I saw him, I wouldn't shoot."

"Why didn't we talk this over before we went out?" I asked.

Sick inside? You bet! I didn't sleep well at all. I kept wondering how I was going to face the family at church on Sunday and wished I didn't have to go. But teaching the high school and college class of almost 40, including Julie (not her name), I had no choice but to face it with a smile, or so I thought.

After visiting with several people in the foyer of the church, I went to my classroom about 10 minutes early where several of the students were already assembled, chatting cheerfully.

When I walked in, one of the career girls, who loves to hunt herself, said, "Congratulations, I hear you got your deer."

I didn't look too exuberant as I spoke. "Yeah, I got a small one."

She declared, "Well, that's more than the others got."

And now the bomb explosion! One girl, who had just come in, said, "Did you really shoot Splodger's pet deer?"

"Do what? Who said such a thing as that?" I asked.

She replied, "Your husband did as we came in the door."

My son looked as shocked as I felt. I absolutely couldn't believe it.

"See you later," I said and walked out as they began to laugh.

As I walked down the hall, all I saw were people who looked like they knew how cruel I was. So I headed for the prayer room. I was sure there would be no one in there. But to my surprise, the choir director's husband was there. I was ready to burst into tears. He stood there, not knowing whether to leave or ask what the problem was. I felt like I had to run or tell him, so I blurted it out. It must have been funny because he began to laugh.

When I walked back through the auditorium, there sat the grandma of the deer family. I was glad (really) and sat down by her, hoping no one had already told her that I had shot Bambi. I would tell her myself. When I told her, she said, "Oh, I'm sorry." But when she saw my distress, she put her arm around me and consoled me by saying, "Someone would have shot him. It's alright."

When it was time to start the class, I was back with my young

CHAPTER 14

people, ready or not. I knew I would have to tell the whole story. So I told it the first thing. It seemed to strike most of them funny again, until my tears started rolling. I was able to give them a very beautiful lesson that I had learned through it all. (I hadn't realized I had learned anything until I heard it come out of my mouth at that moment!) The lesson was: Think things through clearly and definitely before you become emotionally involved.

In dating, decide the kind of person you want before the commitment and why you would date this one now.

In marriage, decide before you become emotionally involved. Marry a mate of like faith, good character, one who is efficient, ambitious and one you can endure and enjoy for the rest of your life.

In schooling, your profession, your own attitude for life, etc.

A burning desire of mine was for my class to know that one wrong decision, one thoughtless act or one night of sin can bring distress for the rest of their lives. However, though their earlier hurts, troubled lives or loss of reputation can still bring extreme guilt and grief, those pains can be the very thing that will be used to minister to others who are going through heartbreaks that have led to inner anguish. God can take what Satan meant for evil and turn it around for your good and for God's glory. Don't dwell on your problem. Turn it over to God and come out with peace.

With complete amazement, I discovered that my horrible experience gave impact to the lesson I had planned for, studied for that week and gave to them with total concern and sincere tears. I wanted them to prepare in every way for those waiting years ahead. This was one of the subjects some of the class members had asked to be discussed in class.

My dear grandchildren, are you sure you want to be a teacher, preacher, leader or in any service to help others? That, for sure, is what I want for you if that's what God has planned. But I'm convinced that no one is worth shucks until they have gone through the rough places in life and can feel what they are teaching or preaching. But His grace is sufficient! The night can be dark now, but joy comes in the morning.

This was the first time I had realized that this terrible, embarrassing Sunday morning experience could be a part of the lesson and perhaps was taught with power. Is it possible that the young people of that class could have been changed for life? Yeah, it's possible, but I fear the main thing they remember is their crazy teacher out hunting.

However, think of what grandson, Phil, had gone through in his early life. Every part of it is being used to help others around this nation and several countries around the world.

Think of Phil's father-in-law, Dave Reiver, who was wounded so horribly in the Vietnam War. Think of the price he paid for his ministry today and his worldwide travels in ministering to the many wounded servicemen in Iraq and throughout these many years since he was wounded. Everybody loves Dave Reiver, and it's not because he's so handsome. Nor is it because he's so scarred. But he gave his scars to God, and God has used them to help other's scars to heal.

When class was over that morning, I had to walk the hall and foyer and meet people. I imagined that everyone I met was thinking how awful I was. I greeted a few new people as I made my way into the auditorium, then I went to my usual place in the front. I cringed inside. I was hurting!

Really, I don't know how I heard the sermon that morning with my new wig over my ears, but much to my dismay, my husband brought a very good message, and being the sweet soul that I am, I even told him so. I don't think it helped me much to tell him, but he probably enjoyed hearing it.

In the afternoon, a missionary couple was to come to speak for us in the night service. They were missionaries from Africa! Big game country. As I looked at my poor little 150-pound strung up, skinned "Bambi," I just couldn't face it. To explain or to hear it explained? Something had to be done!

What you are about to read is something that no one on this earth has heard. Not my husband, not any of my children; absolutely no one but me knows what happened next. If I've ever had an enemy, they would love to gloat over this whole story. Especially when they know …

The Rest of the Story

Being the criminal that I was, I needed to get rid of the body. While my husband was taking his Sunday afternoon nap, I knew it was now or never. I backed the car close to Bambi and pulled and tugged, but I couldn't budge him. Finally, backing completely

CHAPTER 14

against the thing, I was able to swing him into the trunk, and with much effort, I managed to get the "stiff" inside and close the back. I wiped up the bloodstains and rushed him away.

When Lloyd came out later, I heard him looking in the garage, the washroom and even the refrigerator. Before long, he came in and asked where the deer was. I told him I had eaten all the deer I wanted, and if he wouldn't ask any questions, I wouldn't tell him any lies. He grinned and walked away. My man never heard the rest of the story. You are the first to know. I really hate to tell this, but I took that little thing to the mission downtown.

My thoughts were, *I would never be able to smile again.* Though, in the next day or so, as I wrote this all down and then heard myself read it aloud, I was laughing at my stupidity. But I wasn't laughing very deep. For all these years, this has been total pain for me. If I ever thought more highly of myself than I should, all I needed to do was think of this.

As I put my gun away that day, I thought that would definitely be my last hunting trip. But, you know, that's a good-feeling gun, and it has always felt great to pull the trigger. I decided to just keep it around. Maybe if I go hunting next year, there won't be a deer with one long horn and one short horn. And you know what? I never missed a year of hunting trips, and I shot several deer after that.

When I Killed the Chicken

When I was a child, I had seen my mother wring the chickens' necks and was sure I could do it, too. Someone in our church had brought us a live chicken to kill and eat. No problem. When the day came and no one was around, I took the hen out in the backyard, took it by its neck and gave it a twist like I had seen in my earlier years.

However, it wasn't as easy as it looked. I felt all the gristly things in its neck scrunch, the bird yelped a hideous scream and flopped out of my grasp! It went flopping all over the yard, howling and shrieking as I was trying to catch her. It was quite a chase. Eventually, I was able to corner the old girl.

She was still squirming and squawking. Now what do I do? I can't leave her like this. Oh, well, where's the axe? I had to stretch that long neck out again, put it on a block of wood and *not miss!*

MORETA: MY STORY

At last, the bloody kill was over.

Now to get the water hot enough to scald her so I could get the feathers all pulled off. What a mess; what a mess. I then had to get all the guts out of her without breaking the bile jigger and ruining the meat. When at last I got all the blood, guts and feathers cleaned up in the house and in the yard, I could cut the animal up and enjoy fried chicken. It had been a murderous day's work. People, don't ever take your preacher a live chicken.

And Then, There Was This Cat

We most always had cats around when I was a child. I liked cats. My husband had to kill one or two that had caused ringworms on young Verlon. He did not like that job and informed me that if I brought another cat in that had to be killed, I would be the one to take care of that little chore. Well, another stray came along and adopted us. He was small, skinny and simply loony, and it didn't improve with age. The longer we had it, the crazier it got. It would follow me everywhere I went, trying to hang onto me, crying. It would literally try to climb my legs. I had about all I could stand.

My husband was gone elk hunting. Verlon was in bed, and I was in the garage with this cat trying to hang onto me as I walked. I thought, *This is the time to take care of this skinny little dying creature.* So I picked up a two by four and hit him as hard as I could. He came alive! Screaming, clawing, climbing and driving me to murderous thoughts.

Now blood was smearing up the floor of the garage, and I hit him again, and again, and again. Believe me, cats do have nine lives. I'd grit my teeth while going in circles to escape that crying animal. I did everything to kill him but stomp on him. He would not die. I knew I had to bring this to an end before Verlon heard the noise and woke up. I'm not sure if I ever killed him, or if he even died, but I did manage to catch the thing and get him into a sack.

There was blood splattered everywhere, on the walls even. Now to dispose of the body and all the evidence. I camouflaged and wrapped him in several newspapers and sacks so he couldn't get out if he came alive. Hopefully, the garbage man wouldn't get too suspicious when he saw that bundle.

CHAPTER 14

You know? I think I can relate to how a murderer might feel trying to hide the evidence. When I shot the pet deer, I didn't feel like a murderer until I had to dispose of the body, clean up the blood and destroy the mess. When I killed the old flopping chicken, I kind of took on murderous feelings as I had to chase her around the yard. But when I killed that cat, it was pure murder from start to finish.

Fishing

About the last year in Klamath Falls, we bought a new 17-foot outboard boat with a partial top. We took our RV and the boat to the Klamath Lake and kept them in a little marina there. After church, on a Sunday or Wednesday night, we would go to the lake, stay in the trailer house and go fishing at daylight the next morning. By noon, we were back home and ready to keep our busy schedule. The fishing was a great getaway time for us, and it was close to home. We caught large 5- to 8-pound rainbow trout — real fighters! The fish were fighters, not us.

CHAPTER 15

Our Six-plex in Bend

My brother, Orion Reid, in Bend, Oregon, decided to sell the six-plex he had built a short while before. All six units were filled with renters and in a great location. My husband declared, "My, I wish we had the money for a down payment! I'd sure like to own that property for retirement days."

I surprised him by telling him, "We have $10,000 in the bank." I did all of the bookwork, paying bills, banking and all that was needed in that area. I had also received a small inheritance from my parents a short while earlier that he hadn't thought about. Plus, I had been taking out a small amount each month to put into savings. So a few months before we resigned the church, we were able to buy the very nice property in Bend.

The six-plex rentals paid the monthly payments and about $100 a month extra. It's hard to believe, but a few months after we bought the plex, our interest on the loan went to 22 percent for a while. We scraped, scrounged, borrowed and stole (not really) everything we could find to get that loan down where we could live with it. We were able to borrow money from Lloyd's brother and his sister in Portland. We always paid them back with whatever interest they asked, so it was a source of great help for us.

Our last two years in Klamath Falls, the Sunday school attendance average was 432 and 436. The bus ministry was still going good, and many people were great workers. Lloyd was having lots of physical problems, and we felt we should resign and move to Bend.

Some had said to us regarding our lovely home on the hill: "It will be hard to give this place up if you ever decide to move." But I had resolved years earlier that no place would hold onto me when time comes to go.

We had a huge garage sale and sold lots of sets of dishes (such as a set for 12 of Desert Rose Franciscan Ware with lots of extras at the price of $150 — don't cry, girls). You can't imagine all the pretties I sold.

CHAPTER 15

We were moving into a mobile home, 70 by 14 with 3 bedrooms, two baths and not much room for all my treasures, which my husband called my idols.

Lloyd moved into the mobile home in Bend and went to work for my brother, Orion, on his construction projects. I had to stay in Klamath Falls for a few months before our house sold. I kept a bed in our bedroom, a table and two chairs and a recliner in the kitchen area where I sat and read most of the time. It was winter, and I kept the hall and other rooms curtained off. With the baseboard heaters, I was warm enough. I drove to Bend on weekends and went to church with Lloyd.

Young son, Verlon, was in Northwest Bible College in Seattle.

Daughter, Judy, and Bob were pastoring not far away in Lyons.

Daughter, Rhonda, and Paul lived in McMinnville, Oregon, at that time.

Son, Ormel, and Sandi were still living in Salem. He was Youth Director for the State of Oregon with the Assemblies. Sandi was State Missionette Director, then later became Women's Ministries Director for several years.

Our New Life in Bend

We moved our mobile home into a really nice mobile home park beside the canal. We had a great view of the five Sisters Mountains with the desert sunsets. Then in springtime, the water was turned on in the canal where the ducks and waterfowl lived and played. The mother duck would bring her babies in front of our place and show them off.

Along the banks of the canal, I planted hundreds of tulips and daffodil bulbs, then in summer, I had lots of petunias, so the place sparkled with beauty. I would go out and call the mama duck, and she would answer me with a "Quack, quack, quack, quack, quack" and come quacking around the bend of the canal with her little family. How sweet it was! I put lawn furniture on top of the canal bank where we could entertain our friends. It was an enjoyable, relaxing place to be in that Central Oregon atmosphere. We were only a few blocks from my brother's home, and many other friends visited us, too.

My husband added a nice large deck onto the mobile home and built a storage shed on the other side in back. We were quite

MORETA: MY STORY

comfortable. Friends would come to go fishing with us in lakes and rivers around Bend.

However, Lloyd was still having physical problems and had to have two or three operations while we were there, so it wasn't all sugar and vanilla. Lloyd would work for my brother between hospital times. It was convenient to be near our six-plex. When a renter moved out, we were there to prepare for the next occupant.

There was a need to build a home for the camp director at our Oregon youth camp located between Blue Lake and Suttle Lake in Central Oregon. Sandi's dad, Ernie Bedwell, and my husband were asked to do the building. After a short while, Lloyd decided he needed a more comfortable place to live while working there. He had seen a beautiful motor home on a lot near Bend and checked it out. When a man starts looking at vehicles, you may as well say, "Uh-huh!"

He bought it! I guess he was sicker than I thought. We did get it paid for eventually, and it was nice. I don't remember the name of it, but it was 32 feet long with lots of luxuries and was said to be the Cadillac of motor homes.

During camp meeting at Brooks, Oregon (nine miles north of Salem), that summer as he was still working on the building, he thought I should take the motor home over the pass from Bend to camp meeting. I could park it in the campground, then he would come on the weekend and be with me for the services.

The big vehicle was fun to drive, and I blew my bubble gum as I drove along. However, a loaded log truck was coming through the back window (it seemed), and the built-in bed that was over the driver's seat came loose above me. I had to hold it up with one hand and keep driving. There were no turnouts on the road in those days, but I made it fine.

Our dear friend, Earl Book, was District Superintendent of Oregon by then. After a few months, Lloyd let him know that we would be available to fill in for churches that needed help for a short while. Soon, we were asked to go to Newport as interim pastors.

We accepted the invitation and moved to Newport in our motor home. We parked it in the trailer park area of the Embarcadero and would walk to the boat docks to watch the fishing boats come in with their catch. Newport was a fairyland to us, and we loved it. I didn't enjoy backing the motor home up, though, with the boat

Chapter 15

attached to launch it into the water. It was too far from the driver's seat to the boat. I couldn't see the boat and had to stick my head out of the window and listen for the yells. It was scary.

We had been going south in the wintertime for several years, but we were here now with no desire to leave. There were many days of sun and beauty. It wasn't all fog and rain as we had heard. We would go out in the ocean and fish for bottom fish before salmon season opened and, of course, there was crabbing in the wintertime.

Now that we were pastoring again and could see that we would be in Newport for a while, we didn't need the motor home. I put a For Sale sign in the front window, and the first person who came by to see it said, "I want it, but let me bring my friend to look it over. I'll be right back." She had walked through it one time. She was a worldly-wise woman and knew what she wanted. I put a price of $20,500 on it. That was $500 more than we had paid. She gave us cash, and we moved into a townhouse apartment not far from the church.

Newport, Oregon

When I came to Oregon in 1939, we came to Toledo, just seven miles east of Newport. I loved Oregon then, and now to be back in the area was just too good. Newport, being right on the ocean, was better yet. I still love the ocean, the beaches and all the coastal beauties — birds, fish, shells, skies, sunsets, whales, rainbows — God's gifts!

The dear church people in Newport needed lots of attention. We were not a part of the problem, so we could enjoy the task of helping to pull it all together. We came to Newport in 1979, in May, I believe.

My heart had always been with young people. I started a Saturday night prayer meeting for the youth (high school and college age). Someone said, "You can't get enough of that age together to begin." I declared that if I had just six for the first prayer time, it would be a good start.

That first Saturday night, there were six young people present, even though some of them didn't seem to know what prayer was really all about.

Three of the ones at that first prayer time were from the

MORETA: MY STORY

Becker family, Robin, Mark and Dave. I'm not sure about the others, though I'm positive one was a visitor.

While we were there, my husband handled the services and business with wisdom, and we felt loved and welcomed. We were there for one year and nine months. The youth group grew and became a happy lot. We had great services, great play times and unusual get-togethers with plenty to eat. We often had times of fasting and prayer.

Our first Christmas there, we rented a large house on the beach for three days and the whole family came. We decorated, baked, ate, played table games, ate, walked, played on the beach and ate some more. It was a different kind of Christmas for our family, but it was still traditional — turkey, dressing, laughter, loving, talking, planning, praying and gifts as we celebrated Christ's birthday.

The second summer in Newport (1980), we had an all-night prayer meeting with the youth group. Cliff and Ortha Passmore (an older couple) had a few acres south of town. They let us come out, pitch tents and set up for the young people to begin the night of fasting and prayer in the wooded area behind their garden. After school Friday afternoon, we gathered at the church and went to the camping spot. We built a fire in the open with logs around to sit on. The evenings are usually cool on the Coast. The fire was mostly for atmosphere, and it was cozy.

Before dark, after a time of prayer and instructions, we had each of them take their Bible and find a place to be alone — just them, God and the Bible — to spend an hour in prayer and seeking God. The boys were on one side of camp and the girls on the other. They were to write down what they felt the Lord had ministered to them, then share it with us later around the fire, if they would like.

It was a night to be remembered. Every hour had been planned, but room was made for any change that God might have in His order of things. The night was filled with the presence of the Lord — exciting times. They were totally involved until around 5 a.m. when we sent them to their tents. I'm not sure many of them slept, but it was a time of rest until they were called at nearly 9 a.m. All were up, dressed and ready for a prayer time of thanksgiving and praise. Then everybody helped prepare a hearty breakfast and a time of playful activities. That was the only food that had been served out there. Later in the day, we left for home.

CHAPTER 15

Our young son, Verlon, who was in Northwest Bible College and preparing for the ministry, had brought a young girl that he was interested in to meet us. They were with us for the all-night prayer meeting and were a big help. They were also totally involved in the services. He was an intern with us in the church that summer. That was a requirement for his schooling, and we were so glad to have him with us to help and to have a small part in his training.

Verlon was working in Salem with builder Loyal Peterson and was staying with our older son, Ormel. The girlfriend was the daughter of our friends Al and Marylou Davis who lived in Salem. We hadn't known they had a "Melodee" before, but we were impressed.

Verlon found a time for us to be alone so he could talk to me about what I thought of her. I was convinced that he was making a wise choice. Verlon was 6 feet 3 inches, and Melodee was a charming 5 feet. He said, "But, Mom, you've always told me not to marry a girl that was short — to save them for short men."

I'm sure I made him happy when I declared, "Yes, but that was before you found this one. If you feel this is the right one, the one that can help in your ministry and that you can love and make happy, you get her quick."

We loved her parents, also, and felt honored to become family with them. Verlon and Melodee were married that winter on December 13, 1980. He had one more year of college.

They married in the church her parents were pastoring in Dallas, Oregon. It was a most beautiful, elaborate wedding with many friends as attendants. Both preacher dads did the honors of tying the two together, and it holds beautifully to this day. Three wonderful additions have come along and are beginning to find their way in the ministry and finding their mates. I love that pack of kids!

Ray and Annabelle Hall were in the Newport church. Ray is the one that my husband fished for many years before after graduating from Bible college. The Halls still had their fleet of boats and were always faithful in church.

We had our little 17-foot boat and took it out on the ocean to fish for salmon and all sorts of bottom fish. We enjoyed that boat, but we didn't go out much while we were pastoring. However, Melvin Beachy took Lloyd up the Yaquina Bay in his boat to fish.

MORETA: MY STORY

They brought in two huge 36-pound, 45-inch Chinook salmon and two 18-pound ones. Lloyd was sure his call to the ministry was valid, and he was where he belonged, right there in Newport. We moved back to Newport two or three times after moving away. Of all the places we lived, we chose Newport as our choice place on earth.

Time With Grandkids

Each summer, we had our four grandkids stay with us for a week, then only one at a time after they reached the second grade. Judy's two were Loreesa and Shereena, and Ormel's two were Lonnie and Chad. At Christmas time, I had given them each a scrapbook. They could choose what they would like for their scrapbook — birds, flowers, animals or pretty girls. Chad chose birds, Lonnie took animals, Loreesa the flowers and Shereena chose pretty girls. I would save pictures from magazines or wherever, and they were to do the same and bring them with them when they came the next summer.

At times, we would take them in our motor home to a lake or some picturesque place so I could teach them how to take good pictures with their camera. We took them in our boat out fishing in the ocean, but the girls didn't go for that too well. The boys, especially Chad, lived for that time.

We would sit and cut out pictures and arrange them in their scrapbooks. Some nights, we played table games with Grandpa. We had super special times with each one.

When the church was finally ready for a pastor, we resigned. Ken and Debbie Franks became the new ministers. It was his first church.

Waldport

We rented a new house right on the beach in Waldport. Our yard was all beach sand. Chad loved that when he came to see us that summer.

Lloyd's two brothers, Harold and Shirley, and their wives lived nearby in Seal Rock. They were both failing in health, and we thought we could be of help. We had never lived near them until now.

CHAPTER 15

We were there in February 1981, for my "whatever" birthday. The ladies from the Newport church came and surprised me with birthday gifts, cake and all the goodies. Every gift they brought was red or wrapped in red. They knew my favorite color — how special! It was a red-letter day for me.

When we resigned in Newport, we bought a trailer house, and while we were in the area, we took it to Siletz for a month or two to fill in for that church. Lloyd had pastored there with his first wife. Both their girls, Judy and Rhonda, got their start in life there.

Tillamook needed a fill-in, so we took our RV and were there for seven weeks.

In the spring of 1981, we took our little home on wheels and our boat to a marina on the south bay in Newport. We had a lot of visitors while we were there. Grace and Thaine and Jackie and J.R. from Michigan came. It was so special to take them out in the ocean, show them the area around our favorite spot on earth and watch them try to pick up the crabs. They enjoyed all the good ocean seafood. We loved those people!

Of course, our families would come at times to fish or just to be at the beach, to enjoy the food and hear our latest stories.

The last part of September 1981, we stopped fishing to get ready for hunting with our extended family. We had moved back to Bend to our apartment (number 30). Usually, by the last week of September, the way was cleared for us to head for the woods.

Back to Bend

As usual, the big deer hunt was a wonderful time. There were 27 of us camped in the woods. My two brothers and their families, plus my married kids including Verlon and Melodee that year. Then there were in-laws and out-laws (not really), plus a few extra friends.

We girls would go on our hunts alone (not with the men). I got a pretty forked horn that year as Sandi and I were standing and talking (quiet, of course). The other girls were all around us. I have a cute picture of Melodee standing by a stump with a gun. Probably the first and last of her hunting experiences. Verlon got a nice deer that year, though.

To smell the aroma of foil dinners at night as they cooked in the huge campfire was always something to behold. Then to come

MORETA: MY STORY

in from the early morning hunt and smell hot biscuits, gravy, hash browns, eggs and corn relish that Carol would have "just about ready" was great. And she always had enough for everybody! That's Carol!

All our times around the campfire were indescribable. We would tell tales with much laughter and listen to the coyotes howl. The kids would howl with them until the animals would come closer and closer to camp. Then the kids would begin to snuggle up to a parent until all was quiet.

Sandi's dad could call the elk up at night. However, we didn't do that close to camp. We'd load up and go farther away to hear those sounds until the hair would stand up on our necks as we heard the elk coming up the canyons, closer and closer to Ernie's calls. We could hear grandpa elk, mama and young elk bugle as they were thundering through the woods toward us. Then we would begin to nestle closer to someone, get in the car and head back to camp.

When deer hunting season was over, Lloyd went elk hunting with five other men — my two brothers, Lawrence Crook and, I think, Ormel, along with others. They each limited out (one each), and Lloyd got a prize set of huge horns! He boasted forever, and I didn't blame him.

That 1981, Christmas was in the apartment in Bend. A big, big snow had come, and it looked a lot like Christmas. The grandkids, Loreesa, Lonnie, Shereena and Chad, built a fort and a snowman in our front yard. It was another great time together!

In January 1982, the snows kept coming. We left it behind and went south. We visited John and Lori in Sacramento. We drove to San Diego for a night and went sightseeing with Larry Morse and his family. We went to Yuma, then to Covina with Lorene and Albert and visited with Imogene. Then we camped in Palm Springs and Desert Hot Springs.

Verlon graduated from Bible college in 1981, and now was a youth pastor in a church (I don't remember where at this time). He had made this remark: "I can't wait to retire. My folks have so much fun all over the country."

The last part of May 1982, while still living in our apartment in Bend, we went back to the Newport Marina where we had camped before. Our friends Lorene and Albert from Covina brought their RV and camped there with us for a couple of weeks. They loved all

CHAPTER 15

the fishing and crabbing, too. When we came in from the early morning ocean fishing with our limit of salmon and bottom fish, we would trudge up the hill to our abodes with our catch and fix dinner at noon. After we ate, the real work began. The fish had to be cleaned, wrapped and put in our little freezer that we had brought along. Then the boys would go down to the docks, pull the crab pots and bring up the crabs, which had to be boiled and picked out of their shell. We would eat all we could and put the remainder in the freezer or give to friends. Finally, exhausted and near bedtime, we would play a few hands of rook and laugh ourselves silly. But we were ready to go to bed and do the same thing early the next morning. We thought we had fun! Now it makes me tired to think of it. Other friends and family came to visit us there, too. It was great!

Lorene and Albert went with us back to our apartment in Bend, then to Klamath Falls to conduct the memorial for the pilot David Nunn whose plane had gone down seven years before and had just now been found. His wife, Jean, and all four daughters and their husbands were there, plus lots of the Klamath Falls people from our church. It was a special time. Then we went back to the marina for a while longer.

There was a prize offered by the marina for the largest fish caught each week. Once while there, I won the prize. I caught a 13-pound lingcod and won $50 and a free meal. The next week, I did it again. But another man caught a 13-pounder, too, and I had to split the $50. The $75 cash wasn't bad, though, and the two meals in their restaurant weren't bad, either.

An Interesting Change Coming Up

One day, when we stopped at the post office in Newport, Pastor Franks saw my husband and asked if he might know of a good youth pastor or if he thought I might be interested. Lloyd said, "Well, I don't know. She's out in the car; you can ask her." They came out, and we talked.

Pastor said, "We're having a board meeting tonight, and I'll put your name in." He did, and they voted me in 100 percent. So, in my 60s, I became a real live youth pastor with an office of my own, my name above the door and a salary for the first time in my life.

MORETA: MY STORY

I had done it all, seen it all, said it all and thought it all, but no one had ever paid me. So, I was back in the saddle again with pay! My son, Ormel, was now the oldest state youth director in the nation, and his mother was perhaps the oldest *official* youth pastor, and I loved every minute of it.

We moved from our apartment in Bend back to Newport and into a nice large rented house a half block from the ocean in 1982. We could see the whales spouting, the boats and all the happenings on the water from our windows. That's nice in Newport! And I loved the same group of young people that I had when we were pastors shortly before.

While I was youth pastor, my husband would go to other places and preach for churches when needed. He filled in a few weeks for the church in Yoncalla, where we had pastored when we were first married. He really didn't like to go alone to these places, though I loved it. So my career with pay didn't last as long as I had hoped it would. Not much more than a year later, I felt I had to be free to go with my husband. But I left a great group of young people. I still hear from some of them occasionally.

We kept the rented house in Newport for a while and filled in for the church in Seaside, where we had pastored years before. We lived in a mobile home the few months we were there. That was a special time. They treated us royally with gifts and lots of love. In January, we went south again for the winter to Palm Springs.

Another Move

From the Newport house, we went to Garibaldi for five months. That was in 1984. We moved bag and baggage into the small parsonage, but I liked the old house. We could see the Tillamook Bay from our window, and there were sweet people in the church. Rod Sanborn was soon ready to come be the new pastor, so we moved again.

On August 1, 1984, we moved to a brand new house in Bay City, which is a small town five miles from Garibaldi. Our family came for a great Thanksgiving.

It was a young couple's dream house, but for some reason, they couldn't keep it. We were only there nine months. That's where we lived when I caught my 48-pound Chinook salmon in Tillamook Bay.

CHAPTER 15

It took one hour to land the big bruiser. I didn't always carry a lot of pictures of my grandkids, but I carried the picture of me with my big fish for quite a while.

Back to Bend

On a Friday night at 5:00, Duane Brown, Jim and Dianne Coon, Willie, Ken and Kevin helped load the truck and U-haul for us to move back to Bend. I had put an apple pie in the oven and served a piece to them after loading. We were tired and ready for bed by 10 p.m.

Saturday morning at 3:30 a.m., Lloyd woke up and said, "Get up, let's go!" We had rented a house on Seward Street in the north side of town in Bend.

We moved back and forth from Newport to Bend to wherever we were filling in for several months. At times, we lived in our 27-foot Traveleze, an apartment or in a mobile home that the church might provide. We were constantly on the move. Our things were stored in all kinds of places and with different people. I began to really want to settle down, but it would be a few years yet.

My brother, Orion Reid, and his family had built the Orion Greens Golf Course with a clubhouse and restaurant in Bend, where my husband could golf free anytime. That was nice. We loved being near my brother and his wonderful family. This is where my parents had lived and were buried. Our young son, Verlon, and Melodee were youth pastors in the church in Bend at that time. We had lived there before and had our six-plex close by, so there was a real draw to come back to Bend between times. Verlon's second daughter, Courtnay, was born while we were in Bend. Also, their older daughter, Lindsay, had been born earlier in Bend.

Where Do I Live?

Returning from Battle Creek, Michigan, where I had been for two weeks at a family reunion, I met with some difficulties. I flew back to Portland on Tuesday evening,

August 27, 1985. Lloyd hadn't gone with me because of our rental property business. His sister, Ruby, met me at the airport, and I spent the night with her. I had left my car at her place and told her I might awaken early and slip out. At 5 a.m., I was on my

MORETA: MY STORY

way home. I stopped for gas, breakfast and chips to keep me awake while driving. I arrived in our driveway at 521 NE Seward in Bend at 9 a.m.

There was a small trailer house sitting there. As I walked past the garage, I glanced in the window, and nothing was ours. Everything looked so different. I tried the front door, but my key didn't fit. I walked around in back and looked in the glass doors, and the place was empty! A shocking thud hit my chest and went to the pit of my stomach. It's obvious I didn't live here, but where do I live?

Sitting in my car for a few seconds, I decided I'd go to my brother's. Maybe he could tell me where I live. On the way to his place, I had to pass our six-plex. Oh, yes! It began to come back to me. Maybe the next place to look was at 30 SE Craven. When I got there, there was no pickup and no one home! Now where do I look? Then I remembered that we had the master key to the apartments in the ashtray of the car and sure enough, I could get inside.

When I unlocked the door, it was just like heaven inside. You know, the Bible says, "You can't imagine or think what it will be like." Well, I had tried to suppose what I might encounter and had determined that I would take it all as a dutiful wife — a perfect Christian, a trusting soul, the sweet, kind, loving, good kid that I am — but I hadn't imagined or thought of this.

Lloyd had called me in Michigan to tell me the owners who we rented from had sold the house and wanted us to move as soon as possible. I told him, "No way! We have a month to get out, and I will be home shortly." He said that our apartment in Bend was empty, and we could move into it. But I thought we had settled it. I couldn't believe he had done such a thing!

All along, I told him I did not want to move back into the apartment, but he had been determined, so what could I say? For sure, I couldn't say much now, but I did! Maybe it was good that he wasn't home when I got there.

Now, where do I begin? I walked into my jumbled bedroom and saw stacks of big boxes and sacks and things everywhere. I unloaded the bed, found some sheets and made it up. Then I unpacked my suitcase. I had taken a little pair of scissors with me, and I opened the sewing machine drawer to put them away and found the drawer was empty. Oh, no! I checked the other three drawers — empty! Then a horrible thought — No, it couldn't be! I opened one drawer of my dresser, and *it was empty!*

Chapter 15

I began to bawl. I couldn't believe it.

My dresser and nightstands have 19 drawers. There were big boxes in the room that were scrawled with "Moreta Dresser." I refused to look inside any of the other drawers or the boxes.

If I needed anything, I'd just go buy it. I would NOT sort all that stuff out and try to put it in order again. I would be the messiest housekeeper he ever saw. I bawled. I squalled. I would just give all that stuff to charity. I didn't want any of it! *There was nowhere to start doing anything.* I went to bed.

When he came in an hour and a half later, I was in bed. He rushed in cheerfully, saying, "What brings you home so early? I thought you weren't coming for a couple of days yet?"

I drawled, "This was the day I was to come, and I supposed this was the place."

"How was your trip?"

My scornful reply was, "It was fine until I got here."

"What's wrong?" I guess he thought I must be sick since I was in bed.

"Why in the world did you have to move before I got home?" I asked.

He explained, "They were rushing me. They sold their house and were giving possession by the first, and they wanted to paint and re-carpet before they moved in."

"But we had 30 days. You didn't have to move."

"Now, I did the best I could, and there's no need for you to get all out of joint about it," he blasted and walked out.

He had been to the storage shed to do some rearranging to get more stuff in. I don't know why God protected him from my first unholy thoughts. Or maybe He just let me enjoy my first hour and a half of torture in peace, quiet and tears alone.

There was no need to lay in my anguish any longer. I got up, washed my face and came on out.

He was looking for the phone book and asked me to help. Then he needed a paper that was in my secretary desk. I opened the drawer — yes, empty! There was a large box sitting beside the desk. He suggested it was probably in that. Another shocker, but the first thought wasn't as bad as the real thing.

The secretary has three long drawers, plus the pull down door with the small separated compartments in the back with things all organized, or it was at one time. I was not going to try to separate and reorganize that. I'll go buy what we need, but he has to have that business sheet, and oh, yes, it's time to pay bills, and they will all be in there.

As I started digging through boxes with stationary, all occasion cards, sympathy cards, birthday cards, Christmas cards and addresses, I realized the card boxes had come open, and everything was all mixed together. I sniffled and found no bills. Finally, as I knelt on the floor beside the big box, I just began to throw things out on the floor as I bawled.

Then I whimpered, "Why did you have to empty all the drawers? I can never get all these things together again."

He said, "It's too hard to move things with full drawers."

"We've never emptied drawers before," I whined as I threw out a mixture of the cards. The bottom drawer had been full of cloth napkins, probably 150 of them. They were all tossed with the contents of the secretary. And would you believe it, the bills were in the very bottom of the box! The record books, check statements, stubs, bankbooks, all of it in the very bottom.

There was nothing to do now but sort it all and put it back in the secretary. 'Twasn't fair. I was just gonna leave it and not go through it!

Then there was the desk! It had three long, narrow drawers across the top, with two file-size drawers and a smaller one on the side. He had been real wise with the three smaller ones and emptied them separately into large grocery sacks. I peeked into one and remembered how I had had each item organized into small compartments. Now, here were the upset boxes with thumbtacks, paper clips, stamps, pencils, pens, rulers, different size papers and this year's snapshots in order (now out of order). Several years' worth of separated negatives, different kinds of typewriter paper, lined paper, graph paper and everything you can think of were in there. That box is still sitting. I may never need anything out of it. If I do, that will be soon enough to work on it. (I took this from the copy I wrote a few days after this experience.)

The tall four-drawer file cabinet had been emptied into open boxes. I'd have to get them in place as soon as possible. They really weren't mixed too badly, and I think I got them reloaded pretty much in order. Praise the Lord for that.

The next day, I would just sit in the mess and read a book. Ho-ho-ho. Of course, I couldn't help but put some things away (all the

CHAPTER 15

groceries) and repack all the good crystal, sets of dishes, glass serving dishes and all the special things. I kept only the one set of everyday Corelle and just enough things to sort of camp with. We were ready to move most anytime, but prepared to stay for life.

Thursday and Friday, I puttered around doing very little and resting whenever I needed to. I made trips to the shed with him, feeling old, mean and ugly. But no more tears since the first day. By Thursday evening, I was sitting at the piano, playing and singing. I'd thought I would never smile again. Now I was singing — ridiculous!

No way would I go through the boxes from my 19 large dresser drawers, though; I'd just give it all away!

However, Saturday morning, I had to wash and put my hair up. No curlers! I dug through a box, still no curlers! Another box — none. The only thing to do was put things away since I had to get into it, anyway. There were about three or four drawers of things emptied together in each large covered box. Can you possibly imagine fur collars, a wig, silk flowers, wires and supplies to make small arrangements for the house, a camera, flashgun and other camera supplies, plus a small bag of spilled mothballs and three corsages all mingled together? All the artificial flowers were crushed under the weight of yards and yards of new material.

Then there were hankies, slips, nylons and panties all mingled with a lot of jewelry, cards of bias tape, patterns and other sewing supplies. And this is the truth! Those curlers were in the very bottom of the last big mixed-up box!

Then there was the sewing machine. I wouldn't need to ever sew again. But by Saturday morning, the sacks were in my way, and I gradually began on them. I probably have 75 spools of thread, and they were mingled into a variety of interesting places. I did put them into place.

Two weeks after I wrote this, I reread it, and it all sounds so mild — it wasn't!

I've trimmed it down in the writing until it almost sounded like fun — it wasn't!

I've almost made myself sound sweet and good — I wasn't!

(I'm still copying from what I wrote.)

And yet, when I think all that terror was just a few days before, I must be an angel or an idiot to have forgotten, forgiven and feigned it all so sweetly so that by now, already, I don't even care.

MORETA: MY STORY

And I knew if I didn't write it all down, I wouldn't remember to hold it against him, or maybe thank him for doing it all himself. Never, ever!

After the first day, I didn't cry anymore, but four or five days later, when I'd start to think about it or tell someone about it, my nose would start dripping and my eyes start watering.

On the first Sunday morning, I sat in bed early, reading and praying. I began trying to think like he might be thinking (I'd never know for sure). He knew I hated to move again. (This would be the fourth time in about 14 months.) He could have been thinking, *I'll just surprise her and have it all done.* But I could also hear him griping with every breath because I have so much stuff.

He had floored the whole attic to put boxes of things in. He had worked himself to a frazzle to get it done. He had taken the food I had canned out of their boxes and put them on shelves in the storage shed. I'm sure he felt he had done a super job. Then he comes in and finds me slinging tears and unhappy with all his accomplishments. That perhaps was a shocker to him. Maybe.

Aren't I the sweet one to even think such thoughts? And now, I realize I must tell you how I came through this with any amount of sanity.

With my longing to have happy, loving closure, but with his actions and reactions, it left me muttering to myself and gnawing on it for hours every night, even all night long. I didn't want to forget any of it. I knew if I kept this up, I would be totally destroyed. I had to refuse to dwell on these thoughts, and it was not easy! I had to fight with all my might, really! Satan would like to heckle me and take my mind.

Finally, I began to sing a song every time the tormenting thoughts came (in my mind, of course, quiet and in the middle of the night). *Praise the name of Jesus. Praise the name of Jesus. You're my rock, You're my fortress, You're my Deliverer. In You will I trust. Praise Your name, Lord Jesus.* I knew I had to have deliverance, and the fight was difficult. I learned that when I couldn't do anything to make it better, I had to forgive and make it a happy ending, anyway. Sweep it under and go on. In some cases, you have to *live and let live.* That's not the best way, but if it's the only way, then make it happen. To bring it up again would be tragic. So, case closed!

Now, I can laugh about it after all these years.

CHAPTER 15

***

There's always somebody, though, who can outdo you. I was telling a friend in another state about my dilemma. She could sympathize with me alright and could top mine with an unbelievable story.

They had to move to another place. She was sick and unable to help with the packing, so her good husband had to do it all. However, when they were all moved in, she had to get well fast. Her *helper* had taken a bed sheet and emptied everything from the cabinet shelves — salt and pepper, toothpicks, butter on a saucer, oils, cans of spices, vinegars, silverware, about everything you can think of — and tied the corners of the sheet together. That's what she found when she went in. I think it was worse than anything I had seen. We both survived and kept our husbands.

***

Case closed? No, the case was not closed. I had to deal with my attitude. Face it head-on. Talk it out. Pray it out. Forgive and do good in return until I came out with peace and even joy, plus hilarious laughter. But sometimes, that last part takes time.

Speakers at camp meeting, District Council, retreats or on the TV would put me under the bench with their stories that always ended amazingly well. They would tell us "how to do it and make it work." I had tried that way, and it hadn't worked. So, what's wrong with me? The Lord or "the Lloyd" (one or the other or both) would let me know how wrong I was.

Sister Carnahan in our Molalla church told of a mother with two little girls who had clashed over something. She told them to go apologize to each other and ask forgiveness. She heard the sweet one say it all, and the feisty one answered, "Well, I'll forgive you, but shame on you." Case closed, or was it?

There are problems in some marriages, some families, some working conditions or between some siblings that can't always be fixed with an easy one, two, three, press the delete button. But there's hope and help for everyone.

If your life's arrangement is one of peace and beauty, thank the Lord, and treat it with all the love and care in the world. But, know this, not every home is so blessed. There is an answer. There is a way through every problem, but at times, there has to be a crucifixion before there can be a resurrection. Don't run from it. Stay put!

When there's friction, both suffer, but you can come forth with joy, with peace, with blessing, with honor and the glory of the Lord upon your countenance.

With joy: "The joy of the Lord is your strength." (Nehemiah 8:10)

With peace: "And the peace of God which passes all understanding, shall keep your hearts and minds through Christ Jesus." (Philippians 4:7)

Keep happy: "Rejoice in the Lord always, and again I say Rejoice." (Philippians 4:4)

Guard your thinking: "Finally, dear ones, whatsoever things are true, whatsoever things are honest, whatsoever things are just, whatsoever things are pure, whatsoever things are lovely, whatsoever things are of good report; if there be any virtue, and if there be any praise, think on these things." (Philippians 4:8)

Let Him renew your youth like the eagles and give you strength: "They that wait upon the Lord shall renew their strength; they shall mount up with wings as eagles; they shall run, and not be weary; and they shall walk, and not faint." (Isaiah 40:31)

CHAPTER 16

Tillamook, Oregon

January of 1986, we went to Eagle River, Alaska, to visit our daughter, Rhonda, and family. We had a great time playing winter sports like ice fishing. We cut holes in the deep ice on the frozen lake, though we didn't catch many fish. We went for rides on their snow vehicles. I don't remember what they called them. All the ice and snow sure made the fireplace feel good when we were inside.

The last part of January, we went back to Tillamook to fill in as temporary pastors for the church and were there a year and eight months. We couldn't find a house to rent, so we lived for a while in our 27-foot Traveleze trailer house that we parked behind the church. After a few months, we found a nice house to buy with a big yard and room for plenty of flowers. I filled the yard with dahlias, rhododendrons, azaleas, tulips, daffodils, gladiolas and lots more.

The church had a Christian school, K through 12. I enjoyed having access to so many young people and children to work with. I wrote songs and trained a trio of 6-year-old girls to sing one of my songs. Angela Larson, Nicole Rogenes and Sarah Kujak were incredible little girls. We were invited to sing for a statewide women's conference in Portland. My small girls stole the show. Their mothers had made really nice matching dresses for them to wear, and they sang with feeling and with ease.

We had Easter plays, special Christmas services, skits and dramas for all occasions. There were great families in the church. I had the women's prayer meeting each week with many healings and lives changed. We had prayer every night for one week and urged parents to bring their whole family. Many of the families came, and they knew how to pray in unison and in one accord. We felt we needed a Pentecostal move of God. The atmosphere was a definite change after that. God still answers prayer when we pray. Not if we pray, but *when* we pray.

After a few months, I started the young people's service on Saturday nights and have seen several of them married and living

MORETA: MY STORY

in a close relationship with God. Some of them went on to a Bible college and are in the ministry today.

My husband found time to fish. Don Widener took him sturgeon fishing, and he caught several big ones. One was 36 pounds and 49 inches long. That's a big fish! Every bay, every lake and every river has a different way of fishing. We had to learn how to catch salmon in the Tillamook Bay (which is in Garibaldi). It's tricky, but we learned.

***

Judges 1:7 states: "As I have done, so God has requited me."
(I'll write what I wrote then.)

We were loading the boat from the Garibaldi Bay yesterday. I was up on the tongue of the boat trailer cranking the winch. The water was beneath me. My wet shoes slipped, and I fell into the water on my back. My head was downhill, but it was out of the water. All of me was wet except the right side of my tummy to my knee. Two men were right there. "Are you hurt?" they asked as they helped me up.

"Nah, just mad as an old wet hen," was my reply. They didn't laugh. They treated it as serious.

Earlier in the week, Lisa Brown had gone fishing with her boyfriend, Jeff Coon, in his small riverboat. They rounded a curve in the river, and the boat tipped, dumping them both into the Wilson River. We were at the Browns' home for dinner that night, and I laughed at them and told her, "Usually, they wait till they get you to dump you." That was just Monday. This was Thursday, and I was in the watery bay. He didn't dump me. I give myself the full credit!

Years ago, when a person would receive what they gave out, my friend Siama Southwell, with a swirl of her tongue in Norwegian, would say, "Drouka." That meant "It will all come back to you."

Jeff and Lisa were married not long after that time. After all these years and five or six kids later, he still hasn't dumped her. They have been pastoring in Garibaldi for a few years. They are a dedicated pair to God, man and each other. I love them and bless them.

Chapter 16

***

I still have some dear friends in Tillamook, Duane and Betty Brown and their family. We see them at district meetings and visit with them occasionally. We had successful fishing times with them in the rivers around that area. We saw their children grow up, marry and go into ministry, where I have had the privilege of visiting their church.

We were treated so royally in the Tillamook church. I'm still using my first microwave oven that the church gave us. I had wanted one since I first heard of them, but had not been so blessed as to own one. There were many great friends that we loved and who blessed our lives in so many ways.

After we resigned, once again, I was obliged to stay in Tillamook to sell our house while my husband went to Newport to build our next house. My birthday came during that time, and the ladies of the church started coming to my house that morning to visit. Each one would bring me one or two carnations. At the end of the day, I had had wonderful visits and a big bouquet of different colored carnations.

You've noticed, no doubt, that I have all the answers. I know how. By this time in life, I should have a few know hows, right? (I'm writing what I had written before.) But I just came out of a trial that was unbelievable!

It started very simply, no problem at all. I just quit sleeping — one, two or no more than three hours a night and some nights none. After about a week of that, I was exhausted and trembling inside and out. Then a minor problem hit, and it was like a mountain. It began to grow.

When we get down physically, many times, Satan moves into the emotional and spiritual areas of our life. I gnawed night and day on the problem. Still no sleep. I was a mess. I must be dying. Maybe it was my heart. My three brothers and one sister have had heart problems — one died and one had two bypass operations. It must be my turn. There were pains around my heart, pains under my arm and a red spot on my lymph nodes. I was losing weight. (I discovered the scales were out of whack. I changed scales and no problem.)

I really began to think of death, then I fell into self-pity. I'm here all alone, too weak to keep going (though I still liked to eat).

MORETA: MY STORY

But who cares? Sure, the grandkids would care, but they've got their families, they'd get over it. They'd miss my prayers, but they probably don't know that yet.

Oh, the thoughts and the tortures I had those days. I even thought of suicide. I'd never commit suicide. I don't like blood and guts and pain. And I know where you go when you murder. Thank the Lord for the fear of God that I was taught while a child at home. Teach your children the fear of the Lord. There may come a time in their life when it will spare them from Satan's final clutches.

Finally, I called the doctor for a complete physical. I was bawling so much, I could hardly make them understand me, and I'm not a crier. I might if it would do any good, but it never helped. When you cry, you cry alone, but when you laugh, the world laughs with you. But now, there was nothing to laugh at and no one near to care.

On Friday morning, our friend Pastor Emerson's funeral was in Portland, and I wanted to go, but how could I? I had had no sleep, I'd had a night of depression and I was feeling like I couldn't go on. I was too weak and shaky to drive. But why sit here till I die?

When I rolled out of bed that Friday morning, I was free! It was like I had come out of a tunnel. The depression was gone! Somebody, somewhere, had prayed for me. Still weak and trembling but feeling strengthened as the day went along, I went to the funeral. The day before, I couldn't face anything. Today, I could face it all and was free from the depression.

I had felt there was no one to talk to. Don't face your trial alone. Tell somebody. Get help. Not one time during those three weeks did I think of all the answers I've given people through the years. I can't believe it. Talk to somebody.

Before the report from the doctor came, I was alright.

During the time I was alone, the new pastor had taken over in Tillamook. On Sundays, I drove to Newport to go to church there. Finally, the house sold, and I was able to go be with my husband in the trailer house. It wasn't long after that the new house in Newport was finished, and I was ready to move in.

Retiring In Newport

We built what I thought was our retirement home, and we

CHAPTER 16

would never have to move again. We had found a beautiful view lot at the top of the hill on NE 47th Street overlooking the ocean, the bay and the bay bridge. All the homes on the dead end street were new and very nice.

The house was designed around the view. Our breakfast nook, dining room, living room and master bedroom were all on the front side with big windows everywhere. There was 21 feet of windows in the living area, with large ones in every room. The tall trees of the evergreen forest were about 20 feet from our back door.

Our driveway came up the steep hill to the back of the house, then leveled out into the garage and on behind the house and to the small backyard.

Verlon and Melodee (our young son and his wife) were pastoring the church when we moved there. It was great to be near the grandchildren and have them with us during those times. They were three super great kids, and they were ours. I had fun filming them and surprising the parents with their picture stories at special occasions.

We had put in a large bathtub with jets in it. All three of the children loved to get in the tub together with bubbles to their necks and make funny bubble hairdos, mustaches and eyebrows while I took pictures of them.

The youngest of the three was Brenton. He was born while they were pastors there. He was the only hope of carrying on the Fosner name. And, now, it's up to him to carry on the Fosner name further.

We weren't a part of the church staff at that time, so we did a lot of fishing in our 14-foot boat. We caught many salmon and even started going out 14 miles in the ocean to the halibut reefs. The first time we went out, we caught nine big halibut, but only two were keepers. They had to be a certain length — one or two of them were only a half inch too short. I tried to step on them to make them longer, but they would not stretch.

Halibut are heavy fish to pull from the bottom of the ocean. We would get one up to the top and it would go *zing*, back to the bottom, then we had to do it all over again and again. Finally, when we wore the fish out (and me, too), we could get it up to the boat. Then we had to kill it so we wouldn't be a victim of a broken arm or leg as the big flopping catch had done to others.

MORETA: MY STORY

With the experience of pulling the big fish in and the fast bumping ride across the swells of the ocean coming and going to the halibut grounds, my back gave me some extreme problems, and I had to stop fishing for a while. My two brothers, Orion and Admiral, came from Eugene and Bend for a few days at a time to fish with my husband. They had great times.

One day, when Admiral and my husband were fishing, Lloyd caught two big halibut. One weighed 93 pounds and the other weighed 85 pounds. That's a lot of fish.

My back had been bad all winter but was getting better by spring. I was watching the weeds take over my flowers, and I just couldn't handle that. I went to the yard, sat on an upturned 5-gallon bucket and began pulling the weeds.

I prayed, "Lord, You know how much I enjoy this dirt. I'll be real cautious and begin with one and a half hours a day until my back is stronger. Just help me, Lord."

With the rake, I'd pull the weeds to me and then put them into another container.

My Blue Jay

That first day, as I was enjoying my work, a blue jay came, sat in the tree at the corner of the house and scolded harshly. I looked at my watch. It had been exactly one and a half hours. I said, "Okay, the time is up. I'll quit. Thank you."

Next morning, the same thing happened. Then the bird would fly away, and I wouldn't see or hear it again.

Wednesday, I didn't go out, but Thursday, I was weeding on the bank in front. When the hour and a half was up, same bird, same tree, same scolding. I just stood there and laughed, thanked him and quit.

On Friday, I was at my work again. Lloyd came out and was spading up the front yard. He knew nothing of my hour and a half commitment, or about my bird, but when time was up, he said, "You'd better not overdo it. You'd better quit." The bird never came.

Saturday morning, I worked on the north side of the driveway. Lloyd came out, and I asked him to dig up some sallal bushes that were too hard for me to dig. In about an hour and a half, he told me I should quit. I agreed, and the bird didn't show.

CHAPTER 16

In the evening on Monday, I worked on the north side again, and at my allotted time, two blue jays sat in my neighbor's tree that was close by and scolded until I picked up my tools and walked away.

We had lived in that place for two years at the time of this happening, and we lived there four years longer. We had never seen a blue jay there before, nor do I ever remember seeing one after, though I landscaped and worked outside for many hours and many days at a time.

There's More to the Story

Shortly after limiting my time, I was doing much better and didn't have to watch my time so closely. I was weeding on the bank, up in back by the big fallen log. It was such a beautiful morning. The birds were singing in the forest beside me, and the ocean was bright blue.

A small bird was in the tree just above me. He was trilling clear and cheerful. I'd weed a while, stand up and thank the Lord for all the beauties and thank Him that I was able to work. I'd talk to the Lord, and I'd talk to the bird.

"Hello, little birdie. Thank you for singing so beautifully for me today."

"Thank You, Lord, for sending the birds to sing to me. Thanks for my health." (I spoke many other words of thanksgiving to my Lord). How great it was to work and enjoy all this. I'd weed between times. I was stooped over, pulling weeds, and I saw a flash come past me. The little bird flew from the opposite direction and landed on my shoulder! I felt his little claws, but when I turned my head to look at him, he flew away.

I stood up and said, "Lord, this is just too much. I can't believe all Your goodness to me."

My one and a half hours a day was all I needed to grow lots of flowers with a garden mixed into my flowerbeds. From the backyard up to the level of the forest, I had built a circular terrace of rock, three rows high with flowers that bloomed all summer.

We had gone south of town and dug the pretty rock out of a pit and hauled it to our backyard. When my back would hurt too much to work, I would lay rock for only 10 minutes at a time. It was amazing how many rocks I could lay in that short time.

MORETA: MY STORY

From the front yard down to the street, the steep bank was filled with bright beauties year after year. There were rhodies, azaleas, Pfitzer junipers and bright blue low flowers by the driveway wall. It was all lots of work, but what beauty!

We had only been there a couple of years when our son, Verlon, resigned the church in Newport to become the pastor in Ashland. So we lost our fun time with the grandkids. We knew better than to try to keep up with our preacher sons. However, this had been our first choice of a place to retire, so we didn't fall apart.

Our new pastors were Todd and Chris Wagner, a dear couple with two children. We became involved with them in the church. I also became like the chaplain of the 90-bed rest home when the former long-time chaplain died. I could go into the facility at anytime, day or night. The home would call me at times when I could be of help or comfort to a grieving patient.

I had a Bible study on Tuesday mornings with the patients and saw several of them turn to Christ. What a thrill to see them accept Jesus into their lives and to know that when they died, they would go into the presence of the Lord and be free from their suffering. I have a lot of interesting stories of their lives after they became Christians. God is so good!

The ladies' Wednesday morning prayer time at the church became my responsibility, too. We saw many lives shaped and answers to prayer during those days.

It was during that time that an unexplainable sickness hit me. The doctors couldn't find an answer. My grandchildren began to cry. It seemed my time had come.

My Miraculous Healing

In May 1991, I began having serious problems — fevers, sweats, hard coughing, spitting. I was too weak to do much in the house. I spent the days reading biographies of great Christian lives. I lived in the Word and in much prayer.

After about two weeks, my husband asked if the Lord was telling me anything about this sickness. The Lord had begun ministering to me, but I wasn't telling it yet.

"For thus saith the Lord God, the Holy One of Israel; In returning and rest shall ye be saved; in quietness and in confidence shall be your strength: and ye would not. And therefore will the

CHAPTER 16

Lord wait, that He may be gracious unto you, and therefore will He be exalted ... blessed are all they that wait for Him." (Isaiah 30:15, 18)

"... thou shalt weep no more; He will be very gracious unto thee at the voice of thy cry ..." (Isaiah 30:19)

"And though the Lord give you the bread of adversity, and the water of affliction ... but thine eyes shall see thy teachers." (Isaiah 30:20)

"And thine ears shall hear a word behind thee, saying, This is the way, walk ye in it ..." (Isaiah 30:21)

"Ye shall have a song as in the night ... and gladness of heart ..." (Isaiah 30:29)

"Hast thou not known? Hast thou not heard, that the everlasting God, the Lord, the Creator of the ends of the earth, fainteth not, neither is weary? There is no searching of His understanding." (Isaiah 40:28)

"He giveth power to the faint; and to them that have no might He increases strength." (Isaiah 40:29)

"Even the youths shall faint and be weary, and the young men shall utterly fall." (Isaiah 40:30)

"But they that wait upon the Lord shall renew their strength; they shall mount up with wings as eagles; they shall run, and not be weary; and they shall walk, and not faint." (Isaiah 40:31)

"... and thou shalt know that I am the Lord: for they shall not be ashamed that wait for Me." (Isaiah 49:23)

All of this didn't come to me in one sitting. It was just in my daily Bible reading. I have read the Bible through each year for lots of years, and many times, He gives me guidance and help day by day as I read His Word.

Just minutes after one of these precious times with the Lord, I walked past the telephone when it rang. I turned around and answered it.

A niece, Marlene Reid, from Bend, who had been so concerned and had been calling every day and knew I had been seeing only the local doctors, said, "Aunt Moreta, you must see a specialist. I have made an appointment for you with Dr. Hall in Corvallis." (This was 50 miles from our home in Newport, Oregon.)

Instantly, I remembered what the Lord had *just* given me. "... a word behind thee, saying, This is the way, walk ye in it ..." (Isaiah 30:21)

MORETA: MY STORY

My husband drove me to Corvallis many times for tests and experiments. Antibiotics, Penicillin, x-rays and blood tests did nothing. Then they found a nodule on one lung. Soon, there were multiple densities and many spots on both lungs. I was still coughing, spitting up and experiencing fevers, sweats and extreme weakness even worse than at first.

The prognosis grew more threatening each time I went. But I still had peace. I had had a Word from the Lord, and I had a God-given peace! I would even feel guilty for being so peaceful when many people were so concerned for me. Whether this sickness would be long lasting or if it would end in death, I crossed it all. I got so excited about going to heaven, I was afraid it wasn't going to happen.

When the symptoms continued and the report worsened, I called my two preacher sons about the seriousness of it. They prayed for me over the phone. Their churches were praying as were many others across the nation. This one day, after so many had come, called and prayed, the coughing stopped at night but was still with me during the day.

Another day, when my prayer meeting ladies came and prayed, my appetite returned. (I remember hearing one of them pray, "Lord, give her back her appetite.")

I weighed the same 126 pounds every time I went to the doctor. My days were still miserable. There were cat scans, bronchoscopies and biopsies. There were tests for tuberculosis, various fevers and much more. They determined, "There's something very serious going on down there. We just have to find it."

There had been many trips to Corvallis to see the doctor. On July 12th, after more tests, he said he would call me the first part of the week with the latest report of his findings. He didn't call until Thursday afternoon, the 18th.

Everything I read in the Bible during that time was about strength, confidence, healing, rejoicing, praise and singing, plus many other verses I have underlined in my Bible. How precious His Word was to me in those days.

On Tuesday, July 16th, Hosea 6:1, 2 became mine. "… for He hath torn and He will heal us … After two days will He revive us: in the third day He will raise us up, and we shall live in His sight."

That evening, our daughter-in-law, Melodee, called from Livermore, California, where they were pastoring. That morning in

Chapter 16

her ladies' prayer meeting, they had prayed for me with such fervency. She had wept and prayed, "Lord, You just can't take Mom; I need her." After she called, I realized it was during her prayer meeting time that I had received from His Word the exciting scripture that was mine.

When the doctor finally called on Thursday afternoon, the 18th, his findings were different than he had expected. The report was: No tuberculosis, no cancer, no tumors, no asthma, no pneumonia and on and on.

He explained, "We have decided it's a specific kind of bacteria of the lung. But that shouldn't have anything to do with the anemia and sedimentation. We don't know what it is. But I want to try one more special kind of antibiotic." He informed us he had called the prescription in to our local drugstore.

My husband went down immediately and picked it up. It was $85 for a one-week supply! Special? When he got home with the prescription, I said, "Oh, I wish I had been with you, we wouldn't have bought it."

He asked, "Why not?" Then I told him what I felt I had received from the Lord on Tuesday, and I expected to be healed before the day was over. He didn't say anything. I was sure he didn't believe me. After a little while, he suggested, "Well, they're paid for, and we can't take them back. You may as well take them."

I replied, "You can set them right over there. If I ever need them, I'll have them." All that same day (July 18), I still had the weak voice, coughing and every symptom of my sickness. I never tried to make my healing happen.

My two brothers were visiting us and had been out fishing all day. They came in and helped prepare the evening meal like they had been doing each evening. As we finished eating, I noticed they needed more iced tea, so I got up and refilled their glasses. It was as if someone turned on a light in a dark room. Instantly, my voice was normal! I was flitting around, bubbly and my old self. I stopped and exclaimed, "What in the world!"

My brothers were all eyes and questions. I sat down and told them the story.

There was no more coughing, no more spitting up the horrible stuff, no night sweats, the fever and weakness were gone and my voice was strong again. I was healed instantly and completely! And, of course, I never needed the $85 pills.

MORETA: MY STORY

My next appointment with the doctor was Wednesday. My husband thought I should keep the appointment and tell them what happened. This time, I drove to Corvallis myself. I walked in straight and perky with a strong voice. The doctor met me and shook my hand (for the first time) and wanted to know what had happened to me. I told him I was fine. I was well.

He said, "We finally found something that worked." (He was talking about the $85 pills.)

I explained, "Well, no, that isn't exactly what happened. I didn't take the pills."

He came closer and said, "Tell me about it." I did. I told him the whole story with scriptures and all. He was elated and commented, "It's obvious that the Lord must be doing something special in your family, and I want you to know I'm thrilled about this." He was in no rush. He had all the time needed to hear my story and ask questions. It seemed he had never heard of such happenings as these.

Then he said, "But, before you go, let me check your lungs again." I sat on his table, and he checked the back and then the front. When he was convinced, he got right in my face and declared, "Your lungs are clear."

Then he was thoughtful as he told me, "But, before you go, I want you to go down the hall to the lab and get another set of x-rays and blood tests. I do want to warn you, though, don't be too disappointed if something shows up in this."

I said, "You know, it won't disturb me one bit if something shows up. I know I'm healed."

This was my fifth set of x-rays and blood tests — five big tubes of blood each time. It was no wonder I became anemic and had low blood pressure.

Doctor Hall was so cordial. He shook my hand and explained that he would call with the results of these tests. After a few days, his nurse called and said, "The doctor wanted me to let you know that your tests were almost perfect." I was sorry he hadn't called, instead of the nurse. But I knew I was totally healed, and I was certain they knew it, too.

Actually, after the first couple of weeks of my sickness when the Lord gave me the scriptures to wait and He would wait, I did not pray for myself or for my healing. I was completely willing for whatever would happen to happen. I was in His hands.

CHAPTER 16

What a happy, peaceful place to be, even in those 10 weeks of suffering.

Our pastor, Todd Wagner, had asked me to give my testimony in church on Sunday morning after I received my healing on Thursday. When he called me to come to the platform, I walked as snappy as usual and spoke with my normal voice. Everyone was so amazed. They couldn't believe I would be so completely healed and back to normal.

The ladies' prayer meeting each Wednesday morning and the weekly Bible study were yet in my care, and I assumed the duties at the Lincoln County rest home again. I had neighbors that I loved and had led to Christ. I was sure Newport would fold if I wasn't there to keep it straight!

However, after about three years, my husband came in and said, "I'm moving to Salem. You can go, or you can stay." I didn't know he was even thinking such thoughts.

I said, "You can go. I'll stay." Of course, it wasn't that easy. There was only one thing to do and that was to change my thinking. He was a man of few words, but after trying to discuss it a short while, I knew he was serious. After a few hours, I told him, "Okay, but I don't want to have to spend days looking for a place to move. I need to know if this is really the right thing to do."

The next morning, we drove to Salem to see what we could find. Everything we looked at that was already built had tiny bedrooms and many things we felt we couldn't live with. We looked in West Salem at other new housing developments, but there was nothing. We decided we would have to build.

We found a phone and called a realtor. It was getting near noon. She would meet us at 1 p.m. in the area we are living in now. Before 2 p.m., we had purchased a corner lot in a new development in Northeast Salem, and we had the builder who would start construction shortly. We had to use one of their builders for the construction, but my husband could help with a lot of it and do the painting. Plus, we could use our own plans and choose what we wanted. So, we were in business — draw plans and move to Salem!

Salem, Oregon — Our Last Move

Our daughter, Judy, and her husband, Bob, were building a new home in Salem. Lloyd had brought our trailer home from

MORETA: MY STORY

Newport to stay in while he helped them in the building and painting. I would come over on the weekends and go to church with him, but I had no idea he was thinking of moving there.

He was a man of so few words that I'd just have to figure out what he was thinking after a while — mostly after a long while. Some of his thoughts were:

His 98-year-old sister, Ruby, still lived alone in Portland, and we were her only relatives. We had to be with her and help a lot. Salem would be easier and closer to her.

In Salem, he would have more doctors to choose from and better emergency help when he needed it.

Salem is more centrally located, and our kids could see us more often and, of course, Judy lived there.

It would be easier for our daughter, Rhonda, who lived in Alaska, to get to us.

Our son, Ormel, and Sandi, who were living in Bend, would be coming often.

Our son, Verlon, could see us more as his wife, Melodee's, parents, Al and Marylou Davis, lived in West Salem.

Our district church headquarters was located there. And there were several larger churches in Salem to go to. However, Lloyd had already chosen People's Church, and we have continued to attend there.

Many of our preacher friends had retired and moved there.

The ocean sports fishing had been cut off. The guys at the top had given preference to the sea lions, and the salmon fishing was nixed out. No need to stay around for that. We practically had to give our nice boat away.

Actually, all these issues made me very happy that his demand was "Salem!" How special of the Lord to direct my husband to move here. It's fearful to think of living anywhere else during the extremely trying times we've had these last few years. We had access to our family, friends and especially my wonderful neighbors. I could not have made it without them!

Our Neighbors

The building of our house started in February, but the builder was building a "spec" house at the same time, so our home wasn't finished until August 27, 1994. There were very few houses in this

CHAPTER 16

new development at that time, but eventually, every lot has been built on, and it surely is the most desirable place to live. It is close to everything and quiet. Another plus about this place: Every home on the circle had all retired couples, except two women who were younger and still working. There were no restrictions.

A couple of months after we moved in, we acquired new neighbors in the house beside us, Paul and Dora Davis. When they saw the place and was told that an Assembly of God preacher was next door, their search ended. Both of them felt God had surely led them here, and they bought the home on the spot. They were the greatest friends and neighbors, and our church was their church.

While our house was under construction, I began praying for all the neighbors. I'd pray for the house on the end, the yellow house, the white one, the one across the street, the one next to my garage, the one on the corner, etc. I prayed for them every day and at night. I would take flowers and garden stuff to them, and I had fun with neighborhood gatherings on our patio. I love having friends and close neighbors. And you know what? Not one of them has ever made a nuisance of themselves. They're not nosey, not demanding, but just the greatest friends. They all know I pray for them always.

This is February 2008 as I am writing this. Paul and Dora have moved back to be near their kids in California, and I miss them so much. They were like family and helped my husband with so many things, it was embarrassing. He called on Paul for everything, and Paul kept encouraging it. They loved Oregon, they loved Salem and this neighborhood; they loved it all, but health wise, it was time to go be near their children.

This writing is frustrating. I want to spend several pages on help from my neighbors during these Salem years. Kids, I hope this isn't boring to you; just take notice and do to your neighbors what my neighbors did to me. I just have to write some about such dear, helpful people. I don't think I could have lived without them.

I want my children and grandchildren to be doers and not hearers only of what I am now writing. When Jesus used anyone or any of their things, He always repaid them bountifully; they and their friends were blessed. Read in your Bible in Luke 5:1-7.

Also, Proverbs 19:17 (this is powerful!): "He that hath pity upon the poor lendeth unto the Lord; and that which he hath given will He pay him again." And I happen to know that "He" pays big

MORETA: MY STORY

interest on it all! There is a lot in the Bible about giving to the poor and helping the widows and orphans. He will repay! Many times, when those who have helped me are sick or in distress, as I am praying for them, I ask God to love them especially for me. Kids, your pay may not always be in cash but in healing, health, peace and so many other ways. He enjoys paying you His special interest.

I must write more.

There was John and Dixie who lived down at the end of the block — what special people! She was a seamstress supreme and blessed all of us with her pretties. One Christmas, I was making a booklet of my poems for all my kids and grandkids. I didn't have a computer, printer and such, so John said, "Let me do it for you." I took it to him, and he put it all together with pictures and the works. That was a big job! Thanks again, John. I miss you both since you moved away, and I pray for you often.

Cletus and Betty have since moved but only a short distance away. They were neighborhood helpers, too. One neighbor, Tom, had terminal cancer and became bedfast. Cletus would mow their lawn and help in so many ways. One day, I teased Cletus, "How come you mow her lawn and you don't mow mine?" (I didn't have a lawn; my yard was all bark.)

He mumbled, "I don't do it for her, I do it for Tom." Tom didn't live long, and Mariette moved away. I looked out my bathroom window one evening and Cletus was on his ladder trimming and tying up the limbs that had drooped down on my tall Mountain Ash tree. Betty came over, and we sat visiting on my back driveway. They both were and are great friends.

Lawrence and Kay live directly across the street to the north of me. Kay's first husband, Bill, died, and she was a widow for about five years. Lawrence's wife, Marie, died, and he and Kay married not long ago. They didn't move away and have been the most helpful two people anywhere. I accuse them of stealing all my weeds. They trim, cut, dig, spread, fix, put up, take down and do so many things for me. I'll always be indebted to them for all the times they have done the impossible for me. They share their garden, fish and lots of goodies with me. They are real friends!

In the short space of a few months, we lost five husbands and three wives from this circle and several more, including mine, in the following years. That's what happens when all are retired and most are in their 70s. It doesn't take long to grow old.

CHAPTER 16

Then, in the last couple of years, several of our group sold their house and moved to be near their children, mostly because of old age, too.

However, the new ones who bought their places are just as wonderful and are seemingly God chosen and are great neighbors and friends. I wish everyone had neighbors like mine.

Larry and Joyce live right beside me. How special they are! Always helpful, giving, caring and sharing whatever they have. They make me feel like I could call on them anytime if an emergency should arise or if I just want to sit down and talk. They also have helped correct some of the chapters in my book. It's really great to have two retired schoolteachers and a master gardener near me. He cut down a tree and dug the big roots out of the ground.

Oh, my! This is terrible. I keep thinking of more things.

If you could meet Ron and Sandi, who live on the corner across from me, you would see what a dear couple they are. I just recently purchased and am learning the computer. Sandi bails me out anytime I call, and that has been embarrassingly often. She has never complained. Ron has come to help me hang a picture, fix a leak in a faucet, put up lights, move a table and stabilize it, make the printer work right and do so many things I don't know how to. And he thanks me for calling on him.

And then there was Clyde and Esther. Before Clyde died, he was a fix-it man and had repaired a broken dining chair for me. He and Esther were great friends, and we shared some special spiritual times together. I fully expect to see Clyde in heaven. Esther still lives in her lovely home a few doors down the street from me.

Other neighbors across the street, Vern and Mae, had hospital rental equipment. When I was down, they brought the bedside commode and other things for me to use. When I was well, I visited them before and after he passed away. Now she is alone. A very lovely lady.

Harvey and Lana (like Vanna) are new neighbors across the street to the south, a great retired couple and enjoyable to be with. We help each other with our mail. They have gone south for the winter, and I have enough mail to keep them busy for a week when they get back. They call often while they are gone.

More new ones directly across from me are a couple from the Ukraine. They are younger with a 1-year-old baby. At Christmas time, I went with them to their large Russian church. What a beautiful group of people. It was a great service, and I enjoyed it.

Ken and Carol are a dear Christian couple — real friends. We have shared times together through these years. They live in the second house east of me. We girls have gone shopping to thrift stores, then to Lum Yuen's for Chinese food afterward. We need to do it again with some of these new ladies who have moved in. Ken goes golfing with the neighborhood men a day or two each week.

My prayers are still for some others who have moved away and have not accepted the Lord. I pray they will live next door to Christians who won't let them rest until they call for help. I told some of them that I was going to make it hard for them to go to hell because of my prayers.

There are more new ones that I haven't gotten acquainted with yet.

***

Shortly after we moved here, I became involved in the church. I had a ladies' Bible study in one of the homes in Keizer every Tuesday for a few years. Then I ran the women's prayer meetings at the church each Wednesday. I also taught a Sunday school class, but when my husband began to get too difficult, I quit it all. However, I still play the piano for different things and different churches when needed.

From here, life gets really interesting, unusually so. My husband's 98-year-old sister, who lived in Portland, had to make a change, but no way would she agree to anything. Lloyd would go to be with her for a few days at a time, then I would go. She was a bit more yielding to me, but not much.

It was difficult. I was elected to go do the dirty work. I had to find a way to make it happen.

99-Year-Old Ruby Staten

Ruby was raised in the same godly home as her brother, Lloyd. She was the oldest child of five, he the youngest. Lloyd was an Assembly of God minister. Since her late 20s, she had been totally absorbed with the many facets of the occult world — Unity, metaphysics, meditation, reincarnation, calling up the dead, spirit

CHAPTER 16

guides, lords and gods, feminine gods, gods within, yoga and mystic things. New Age all the way.

Through the years, she would fly from Oregon to Florida, California to Maine and many places to hear some great "teacher." She constantly preached her doctrine and prophecies that "came through to us" to anyone who was around. Not one of the prophecies that she told us ever happened. But she didn't seem to notice.

When her godly mother was in her 70s, she fasted and prayed for 21 days for the salvation of her five children and their spouses.

Ruby would have given all she owned to be able to get into that physics realm. She did all the practices, followed her mentors, read every book, paper and listened to every tape. She was never able to become so used. She just had to take others' (mostly ladies) word for it all. I was always convinced that her mother's prayers kept her from that experience.

My husband, Lloyd, was her only living relative, except nieces and nephews. Her husband, Elliott, died about 12 years before. She had lived alone in Portland, Oregon, until just three months before her death. Her wonderful neighbor, Mrs. Wardwell, checked on Ruby every day and took care of her or called us when an emergency came up. Ruby should have been in a care home several years earlier, but she refused. We wouldn't force her until there was no other way. That day finally came.

Something had to be done. I was with her for several days, but when I found a good home for her, she would not go. Finally, I said, "Ruby, I have to go home today, and I can't leave you here alone. Either you go home with me, or I'll have to call the authorities, and they will see that you get into a home. That will cost you thousands of dollars each month."

It was yes, no, okay and no again. But, at last, she disgustingly said, "Alright, let's go."

Hurriedly, I threw things together and got her into the car. It was difficult. By the next morning, she was so much worse off that I couldn't have gotten her to the car.

We had her in our home until she got so impossible that we had to put her in a retirement place with five people. She was nasty to them, too, but she was only there for a couple of months. She became weak, not wanting to eat or drink. We knew she would not be here long. When an occult life comes to the end, to leave this world, it's bad!

MORETA: MY STORY

Because of our many years of praying and her mother's prayers, I had to know that Ruby was ready to meet God. I fervently began to ask God to help me know how to reach her. She was so hard of hearing that we had to write everything on paper. Her eyesight was good until the last few days, even without glasses. Her mind was sharp.

This one very early morning, as I was praying and fasting, my prayer was, "Lord, I can't do anything if You don't show me how. Lord, keep her alive until ... Prepare her heart and thoughts."

In my nighttime, wide-awake praying, I interceded further. I reminded Satan of Mother's prayers and commanded him to stop his tormenting spirit, to leave her alone. She belonged to God, and we were going to have her.

Then calling on God, I requested, "Oh, Lord, please open her ears so she can hear me. Remove any thoughts of the occult that has bound her these many years. Make her voice strong enough that I can hear *her*."

What a miracle morning! All that I had asked for happened. I went into her room. I talked slow in a mild tone of voice, and she could hear every word I said.

"Ruby, I've come to talk to you this morning about Jesus. I want to talk to the real Ruby — the Ruby who desires to know the one true God who sent His only Son, Jesus, into this world."

When I named the name of Jesus, Ruby began to speak. She was so weak, I had to listen closely. There was quietness between words. It was a real effort for her to speak. This is what she said: "Just--this morning--something--beautiful--happened to me--. Jesus--came into my room--and said--" Then her voice trailed off into a mumble so low, I couldn't understand what she was saying. It really didn't matter. I knew Jesus had come and prepared the way. I told her that was wonderful.

I began giving her scriptures about Jesus. I didn't give her chapter and verse but spoke in my own words. And she could hear me. I kept close to her ear and talked slowly and medium loud.

Wherefore God also hath highly exalted Him, and given Him a name which is above every name. That at the name of Jesus every knee should bow, of things in heaven, and things in earth, and things under the earth; And that every tongue should confess that Jesus Christ is Lord, to the glory of God the Father.

Chapter 16

Neither is there salvation in any other; for there is none other name under heaven given among men, whereby we must be saved.

Calling her name, I said, "Ruby, you're leaving this world." She nodded. "And I'm here to help see you out of this life and to make sure you're ready to meet God His way. You're going to love me through all eternity for this day."

Jesus saith unto him, 'I am the way, the Truth, and the Life; no man cometh unto the Father, but by me.'

There is a way which seemeth right unto a man, but the end thereof are the ways of death (torment, damnation, hell).

Ruby was so near death, there was no time to soften anything. I may not know much about Hades or Sheol, but I know what hell is, and that's the word I used.

"And, Ruby, I can't let you go to hell. You are going to face God in a few minutes, and I have to know that you are prepared for that moment." She was listening.

All have sinned and come short of the glory of God.

The wages of sin is death, but the gift of God is eternal life through Jesus Christ our Lord.

God commends (stands by, offers, guarantees) His love to us, in that while we were yet sinners, Christ died for us.

For God so loved the world that He gave His only begotten Son, that whosoever believes in Him should not perish but have everlasting life.

Then I asked, "Ruby, can I pray for you?" She nodded her head yes. I prayed the scripture. I prayed to the one true God, to Jesus who died on the cross and rose again. We are saved by the blood of Jesus, and I prayed for Him to prepare Ruby to meet Him. She was nodding her head at the right times as I watched and prayed.

"Ruby," I said, "it isn't enough for me to pray. I must hear you pray with your mouth, with your voice. The Bible says, *If you will confess with your mouth the Lord Jesus, and believe in your heart that God raised Jesus from the dead, you shall be saved. For with the heart man believes unto righteousness and with the mouth confession is made unto salvation.*"

She began to point her finger toward the dresser, saying, "Book."

I ignored her for a while, but she kept pointing with persistence. My purse was there, and I thought of my little red Bible that I carry. I got it out and held it up. She reached out her hands and

MORETA: MY STORY

took the Bible in her left hand and began leafing through its pages, as though she was looking for a special place. I knew she was not even seeing it, nor could she read its fine print. Her eyes were almost closed. She was so near death and yet so alert.

She stopped turning the pages, put her long, boney finger in one place and held it there. When I kept talking and wasn't looking at it, she pecked her finger hard two or three times at the same verse. I decided to look now!

Our seniors' Sunday school teacher, Tex Rutledge, had been teaching for two or three months on "God is able." There were times I would try to apply that to Ruby's salvation, but how could it ever be? This is the very verse that she had her finger on!

That scripture was: *And being fully persuaded that, what He had promised, He was able also to perform.* Powerful! *With God all things are possible.*

She prayed with me. The occult won't pray the word "Jesus." But Ruby prayed to Jesus. With that simple prayer and refuting all her false gods, she was *born again.* She became a new person, her countenance changed, her room had a different atmosphere.

I began to sing: "Jesus, Jesus, Jesus, there's just something about that name. Master, Savior, Jesus, like the fragrance after the rain. Jesus, Jesus, Jesus, let all heaven and earth proclaim. Kings and kingdoms shall all pass away, but there's something about that name."

Ruby very reverently said, "His name is Jesus."

I sang "Oh, How I Love Jesus" and "Jesus Is the Sweetest Name I Know." She would move her head closer to me and say, "That's beautiful. Sing it again."

I called all our children and told them the story. They couldn't believe it. "Mom, Aunt Ruby?" My husband, Lloyd, wept. The next day at noon, our daughter came from work to see for herself. We stood by her bedside and sang a duet of those beautiful songs.

And, again, Ruby would say how beautiful they were and ask us to sing some more. Judy was able to let her aunt Ruby know how thrilled she was that she had accepted Jesus and to tell her goodbye. And, of course, her brother, Lloyd, was there to see her at times.

The next day at 11 a.m., I was there. While I was with her, the death rattle came. Exactly 48 hours after she accepted Christ, she took her last breath and went into the presence of the Lord.

CHAPTER 16

That was the biggest miracle of my life. For a 99-year-old person to turn to God is a marvel of God's mercy. What a privilege that I could be a part of that miracle!

CHAPTER 17

Life in Salem and Family

Granddaughter, Shereena, had her beautiful wedding April 12, 1996. She is an excellent florist, and it showed in every detail of her wedding. Josh Gering, her groom, was young and just out of Bible college, preparing for the ministry. They are having a very successful ministry, especially with the youth.

The Reid and Fosner families took their RVs to Cultus Lake each summer for a week or two of play with catamarans and water toys of all kinds. There was hiking, fishing, campfires and food, food, food!

Each fall at hunting time, our families camped out in the woods together in tents, motor homes and trailer houses. Retirement days took us to the lakes, woods, ocean and mountains. Then, for several years, we went south for the winter. Life was good.

But with the good, it seems the crushing has to come along too often. Rhonda, our daughter in Alaska, got the dreaded report: cancer. We were devastated. She took chemo and radiation and lost her hair. Then she was in remission for a few years. They'd come for Christmas, weddings and family celebrations. She stayed on her job at the school, and her workers adored her. After a few years, the cancer returned with a vengeance. Her suffering and pain during those times were unbearable!

Toward the last, she wanted to come home to be with us. She had to change planes in Seattle. We had no idea that she was that bad or we would have met her there. When she got to Portland, she was suffering and almost too weak to make it on to our house in the car. This was on Saturday, January 24, 1998. By Monday, we had her in the hospital here. The doctor said, "If her husband wants to be with her, he'd better come." He came as soon as he could.

All three of their children, Ryan, Troy and Jodi, were living at home yet and were working or in college. When Rhonda's condition worsened, they all left their duties and came. For two months,

CHAPTER 17

she was in and out of the hospital. There was nothing to ease her pain. It was breast cancer, and it spread to her lungs, kidney and brain. On March 25th, in the middle of the night, in the bedroom of our home on a hospital bed, Rhonda suffered her last and went into the presence of the Lord and the heavenly hosts and all the beauties of heaven. There was no more suffering for her.

It was horribly sad for all of us, but glorious for that sweet girl. What a day that will be when we see her again. And, according to scripture, that day is coming very soon. It was so difficult for her husband and children to have to go back to Alaska *alone.*

Life Had to Go On

We kept busy with our involvements in three churches, with our many friends and all our "busies," but the most cherished of all was to be with our family. We were learning how fragile and short this life can be.

The following year, we celebrated our 50th wedding anniversary in Brooks, at the same church where Rhonda's funeral had been. Rhonda's husband and family from Alaska came. Lots of relatives and many friends from our former pastorates were there. My two brothers, Orion and Admiral, with Don and Lawrence Crook, sang their quartet like they had sung it for years. Our children had many surprises and beauties for us that day. But there was a big gap in everything that no one could fill — Rhonda.

***

In July of that same year, I went to Battle Creek, Michigan, for a family reunion. While there, my in-laws, Junior and Jackie and Grace and Thaine, took me for a three-day trip to Mackinac Island. No motorized vehicles were on the island, just horses, carriages and bicycles.

We went across the Mackinac Straits to the tiny island by ferry to see all the beautiful mansions, government buildings, shops, eating places and flowers. Few live on the island during the winter because of ice and snow. When Lake Michigan freezes over, the only way in is by plane.

We saw the five-mile long bridge with Lake Michigan on one side and Lake Huron on the other. We went to the Soo Locks and

MORETA: MY STORY

watched a 1,000-foot long barge come through the locks. How special to be blessed with such a trip.

When I was in Battle Creek, I sent postcards to my neighbors. In the one I sent to Esther, I wrote, "My relatives here are treating me like royalty, and I expect the same treatment when I get home."

After I was home and out in the yard, Esther came by and warned me, "You know, your husband won't treat you like that, and the rest of us won't, either." I loved it. That's how great my neighbors are.

***

In the wintertime, we flew to Palm Springs and to Sky Valley for a month to be with my brother, Admiral, and Marie in their lovely park model home. They took me with them to Flagstaff, Arizona, to visit our nephews, Lanny and Paul Calahan, and their families. Lloyd chose not to go with us. He felt it would be too long and too busy. While we were in Flagstaff, we went to the Grand Canyon. No picture has ever shown it as vast as it is. I was thrilled beyond words to be privileged to see that unbelievable place and to take all the pictures.

Nephew, Glenn, and Shirley came from Grants, New Mexico, to see us while we were in Flagstaff. That was great, too, especially since we lost Glenn to cancer not long afterward.

We rode home from Sky Valley to Salem with my brother in his motor home in March. When we left Oregon in February, nothing but heather was blooming in the yard. When we drove into our driveway, there was color everywhere, daffodils, tulips, azaleas, magnolia, flowering plum trees and rhododendrons. What beauty, and what a marvelous trip!

***

In April, I went to the Southern Gospel Quartet Convention in Sacramento. I went with Evelyn Roller and her two daughters, Marjorie and Marie, and little 70-year-old Amy in their small car. We met their brother, Mitchell, and their sister, Melba, and their spouses along the way.

Attending that three-day quartet convention was one of the greatest things I ever did. We went to the convention center about

CHAPTER 17

4 each evening, and the last quartet would sing until midnight, and then we would find a place to eat. Now, that's the kind of nightlife I enjoy. I pray often for that wonderful family who took me with them.

The next year, 2001, three other women went with me to the quartet convention on the tour bus with the Knox Brothers Quartet — Betty Nicholson, Eleanor Gallihugh and Maxine Unger. It was another special time with reserved seats at the convention and everything taken care of. While there, I met Patti Palone and Richard and Carol Roberts from our church in Klamath Falls and a few others I knew from other places.

***

Our minister of People's Church, Pastor Markese, died of cancer during the year 2000 at the age of 52. It was such a shock and hurtful time for the church. The church invited our son, Ormel Chapin, to come and fill in. They pastored the church for nearly a year, and he was asked to consider becoming the permanent pastor, but Ormel just couldn't get a leading from the Lord to do so. They were so loved while they were here, and I would love to have kept them here as pastors.

We took our Terry trailer house and vehicles to Paulina Lake to fish for kokanee in May for several months. In September, when salmon fishing was on, we moved to Alsea Bay, on the Coast, to fish for the big salmon. We sure hated to be gone all summer since Ormel was filling in at our church, and we came home often during that time, but Lloyd had planned this a long time ago and wouldn't be deterred.

Granddaughter, Lindsay, on her 18th birthday, graduated from Northwest University in Seattle as Student Body President. We were there to enjoy the celebration with them.

***

My husband realized he was not able to keep up with all the strenuous boating that we had enjoyed all these years, so we sold the boat to our son, Verlon, in Seattle. Their three teens and friends enjoy the water skiing and boating.

MORETA: MY STORY

***

We love our new pastors, Scott and Bonnie Erickson, who came to us from Maryland. However, because of my husband's health, I had given up most of my involvements in our church. He wasn't going to many things anymore, but he didn't mind my going. I think he liked being alone and quiet.

***

While camping again with the Reid families at Cultus Lake, my brother, Admiral, Tracy, Dick and I took a three-mile hike to an old cabin and lake back in the woods. Then three miles back to camp, but the weather was perfect, and it was delightful. My dear niece, Tracy, a senior in high school, was chosen Homecoming Queen that fall. She's one great, beautiful young lady.

***

In December, Alvina Sparks asked if I would like to go with her to Los Angeles to the Trinity Broadcasting Network in Santa Ana. We flew there and were picked up at the airport and taken to our hotel room. We were at their services and saw all the extravagant decorations and met some wonderful people. We were there two nights and enjoyed every minute of it. That was another great experience of a lifetime. Thanks again, Alvina. It was so special of you to take me with you.

***

By 2003, we had our last summer camping trip at Cultus Lake. Then the last family hunt in October. We couldn't have done everything to get ready for camping but for our neighbor, Paul Davis. Lloyd was unable to do the necessary things to prepare all the equipment for camp, so Paul helped with all the trailer preparations, loading heavy batteries, etc. And when we got home, Paul was available to empty the holding tanks, unload the heavy things and do anything that needed to be done. Paul, I'm sure God has loved you many times for us — I've asked Him to.

CHAPTER 17

Bloody

Around 5 a.m. one morning, Lloyd came pounding on my bedroom door. "Come help me, I'm bleeding." When I stepped out of my room, I realized I was stepping in warm blood. There was blood all the way to his bathroom. We stood in a large puddle of blood where he was bending over his sink. Blood was pouring out of the top of his head from five different holes, like a saltshaker.

"How did it happen?" I asked.

"I must have fallen out of bed."

His face and head were covered in blood. I washed it off as best I could, held a towel over the fountains of blood and led him to the kitchen sink. Remembering some former experiences of my family, I filled the holes with cayenne pepper, and the bleeding stopped immediately!

Some years earlier, our son-in-law, Bob, had been in the woods, cutting shingles for their new home. The power saw slipped and cut his knee to the bone. He jumped in the pickup and drove himself the few miles to his home with the blood pouring. His daughter, Loreesa, happened to be there and knew about the cayenne pepper. She filled the wound with cayenne, and the flow stopped instantly. She was able to drive him into Salem to the ER.

With the blood out of my husband's ears, eyes and hair and a clean shirt on, he was able to go to the clinic to get cleaned up and patched up.

He was sure that I didn't need to go along, so I gladly let him drive himself. I was busy most of that time cleaning blood out of carpets, off cabinets, sinks and even walls where it had splattered.

As I cleaned his bedroom, I saw what had happened. Because of the sun on his balding head, he had to have moles, brown splotches and growths taken off his head about every three months. These five holes had turned to scabs.

He had the exercise bike in his bedroom and must have fallen against the peddle of that. That's the place the blood had started, and I even found some of the scabs there.

Then he had taken a few steps to look in his mirror, then out and down the hall to my room. Because of the flow of blood, it was easy to track him.

When he got back from the clinic three or four hours later, I should have taken his picture. They had bandaged his head from

MORETA: MY STORY

his ears, neck and over the top of his head with strips of cloth, gauze and tape. He looked like a Sikh.

Be sure and keep a supply of cayenne pepper in your house. I add cayenne pepper and garlic to most things I cook. It has so many healing qualities.

And, no doubt, if Loreesa and I and the cayenne pepper hadn't been there, what do you suppose would have happened? The cayenne pepper does not burn in an open wound. Just don't get it in your eyes.

***

January of 2004 brought a beautiful, big snow here in Salem. I love snow and made a tall snowman in our front yard. There were icicles two and three feet long on the back of the house and RV. That spring, we sold the trailer house and traded his *pride and joy* pickup in on a newer car, a 2003 Buick Park Avenue.

***

My brother, Orion Reid, had his 90th birthday in March. It was a fabulous celebration at their home in Bend. We both were there.

***

Ormel's son, Lonnie, and Tiffany, daughter of pastors Greg and Roxanne Hickman, were married June 12th. And you know what? After more than three years, they are still in love. Adorable! I love them to pieces.

He gave up his Nashville career for a while and became music and youth pastor in Fullerton, California, in his father-in-law's church.

Five of my first husband's family in Michigan came for the wedding. Junior and Jackie Chapin and Thaine Crandall drove out. Darlene and her daughter, Renee, flew to Portland from Battle Creek.

The five came to my house the day after the wedding for dinner, then we went to my first husband, Harry Chapin's, grave in Eugene. It was so nice to be with them at that time.

CHAPTER 17

***

Grandson, Phil, and Kim were youth pastors in Aloha, Oregon, and would come help me many times with things around our place. He sprayed for the moss on my roof, power washed the patio, driveways and sidewalk and dug big roots from trees that were causing problems. One time, he even brought his college-age young men to help with the outside work, and Kim brought her young women to work in the house. They did the vinyl blinds, washed windows, deep cleaned showers and the tub, vacuumed, cleaned carpets, scrubbed the vinyl kitchen floor on hands and knees and polished furniture and cabinets. Oh, they slaved all day, and all I did was feed them three kinds of good soup with plenty of iced tea and cold water.

***

In August of 2004, Lloyd had a knee replacement. When he came out of the anesthesia, he was never the same. By October, he was getting more difficult to care for, and as caregiver, I was becoming more and more exhausted. I knew something would have to be done soon. I began to search every avenue to find what was best. I needed help! Verlon came from Seattle and Ormel from Bend to help me determine the right steps to take.

It Was Alzheimer's

I called Verlon, Ormel and Judy and asked them if they would bring their spouses and come for a night and day of fasting and prayer for God's direction in this troublesome time. All three of them had been involved enough to know that there had to be a change.

I had to get Lloyd on Medicaid, and that was a lot of red tape. Both Ormel and Verlon had been with me at different times on that project. Sandi had been with me to check out different homes that might be the one for him. Judy and each of the others had spent some nights here to help with Lloyd during the night. They fully understood.

After the night of seeking God about this, all of us fully agreed and decided the action to take. The next day, the boys sat at the table and explained to Lloyd what was happening and that I couldn't take care of him any longer. *He would have to go to a home soon.*

For two months after he had been diagnosed, I kept him here. Caring for him all night and day was just too much for me to do alone. Also, he was getting worse by the night.

He couldn't find his bathroom, which was only 10 feet from his bed. He began cutting things up, mostly his clothes, and when I hid the scissors, he used the big butcher knife. He told me one day that, "Nothing looks right anymore. I know I live here, but nothing is familiar."

Having read and heard that this disease can be coming on for 20 years, I surely believe it. In the very recent years, he had become extremely health concerned and was spending money and doing many unreasonable things, costing an average of more than $1,000 a month.

For several years, his actions toward me were things the family never saw. He could be nice to everybody, and they didn't notice that he was ignoring me when they were around. One time, though, when I had to inform the children in his presence of what he had done, he said, "She drove me to it."

He had been ornery to me for so long that it's hard to remember when he was ever nice. But as you have seen in the former stories, we had many wonderful years together. Alzheimer's is such a cruel plague.

When he had the knee replacement in the local hospital, seemingly, he was quite normal when he went in. He was in there for a week and came out totally *off. H*e would yell at the nurses. He'd get out of bed and fall and wasn't himself at all. He really gave them fits, and he never recovered from that time.

The doctor said, "If this disease was on its way, a trauma like the knee operation could bring it on." Both of his doctors urged me to get him into a home and not try to keep him. One of them told me of his own mother who had Alzheimer's, and his dad had kept her until it brought him to his death ahead of her's. Then, they had to put her in a home.

He said, "Don't do it." However, I kept him until I positively could not have kept him a day longer.

The nurses said he was a "sundowner — awake all night." He was that, alright.

CHAPTER 17

The last day he was home, I had to leave him here alone while I made a trip to the CEP office on the south side of town to have them sign some papers for me. Then I would have to take the papers to the north side in Keizer to the Medicaid office.

The CEP offices had recently moved to a new location, and I had a hard time finding it. When I got there and rushed to the door, the sign read "Closed." I went back to the car, sat there and cried. Soon a man came out and locked the door behind him. I rushed to him and asked if he could let me in for a very short time. I'm well acquainted with most of them. He probably recognized me and let me in.

I took the elevator to the front desk. Anita was still there and asked what I needed. I couldn't say a word. I didn't cry (that's too dainty); I bawled. Another longtime friend stepped up about that time, and they both took me in their arms and cried with me. I had come to the end of my endurance and couldn't hold up much longer. They hadn't known what was going on in my life. And, of course, I didn't make it to the Medicaid office that night.

A few days before, I had signed all the papers and made all the arrangements at the Alzheimer's home, but had decided I could keep him and had canceled. But his last night at home was disastrous. He ordered me out of his room. "You get out of here, and let me do what I want, and you do what you want." Plus, there were lots of other antics all night. So, in the morning, I called the home and asked if they still had his room.

They said, "It's all ready for him."

I called Medicaid and said, "This is it." I called his daughter, Judy, and before noon, we had him in his new home.

It may sound heartless. It was one of the hardest times of my life, but when there's nothing else to do, you do what has to be done. Though the many days to come became harder and harder.

October 8, 2006 was an impossible day for him to have to bear. Having to be locked up with no car, no money and no say about anything and with all the others around him who were the same but different. And strangers had to take care of his every need. For a while, he could dress and do things for himself, and I went every day to help him, sometimes two or three times a day. We had chosen a home that was only five minutes from me. At times, he would get upset with me. Someone suggested that I might be going too often.

MORETA: MY STORY

So, after that, when he would get cranky, I'd leave and wait a day or two before going back. From then on, he seldom showed his anger to me.

The date of October 8th was exactly 10 years from the day that he had been so aggressive, and he had to live with the consequences of those actions for several months. I'm sure this disease was coming on for some years before that.

We made his room very nice. Ormel and Judy brought pieces of furniture, pictures for the walls, etc., and we took special things of his from his room at home — his television, chairs, Bible, books, family pictures and things to make him feel it was as much like home as possible. It was attractive and comfortable.

He would tell us all kinds of tales, hallucinations, fears and even things we could laugh at. But overall, it was a horrible time for him, and for us, to see him have to live like that. He always knew everybody, though, and could be mentally alert at times. There were days, I thought, *He shouldn't be in here; surely I could take care of him.* But when I'd go the next time, I knew that was the only place he could be.

When we first put him in the home, he was in the building with others who were not so bad, but after a month or two, they moved him into the place next door with a courtyard dividing the houses. The ones there were more progressed in the disease. We hated to see that for him, but it was necessary. When he had been in the home for eight months, I had an excruciating change in my life and wasn't able to see him for many weeks.

The Living Room Tumble

The morning of May 19, 2005, I had tidied the house, done the wash and put all the clothes away. I made some casseroles for the freezer, emptied the dishwasher and finished lunch. I had just listened to one of my favorite TV preachers, John Hagee. I thought, *I'm so weary. I'll just sit down and relax a while before going for my nap.* It was 1:30 p.m. As I kicked off my sandals, I got off balance and grabbed one arm of the *swivel* rocker. I fell in slow motion. I felt like it had thrown me to the ceiling, and all the way down, I was crying loud, "No! No! No!"

Finally, after lying there for a long time, I began to move. As I put weight on my right arm, my shoulder came out of its socket. I

CHAPTER 17

screamed in pain as I whirled my arm around, and it went back in place. It took me half an hour to pull myself across the room to the telephone.

The dining chair had never been kept by the phone, but for whatever reason, it was in the right place. I got myself to the chair and pulled myself up, but when I reached for the phone with my right arm, the shoulder went out of its socket again. More screams. I finally was able to dial 911. Fortunately, just a night or two before, I had decided that I should start leaving the door into the garage unlocked at night, in case of an emergency.

The only thing the person on the phone with 911 needed to know was the combination for the garage door opener. They were able to get right in and get me on the gurney and to the hospital. Every bump of the road was nearly unbearable.

When I called my close neighbors, they weren't home. But before the emergency vehicle drove away, the neighbor returned and came running to see what had happened. I told him that I had fallen but was alright and would call them as soon as I could. They remembered our daughter's name, Judy Harkins, and called her. She came as soon as she could get there and was with me the whole time. She called my son in Bend. He called his son, Phil, on the cell phone. Phil was attending special meetings on the East Coast. Phil called his wife, Kim, in Aloha, Oregon, not far from me, and told her to get to me as soon as she could.

In the hospital, they took x-rays and all kinds of tests. When they were x-raying my arm, the shoulder went out again twice. I think you could have heard my screams for blocks. I was in terrible pain in the back and pelvis area. They tried to get me up to go to the bathroom, but, of course, I couldn't. They brought in a bedside commode. Neither Judy nor I could make them understand that I couldn't move. I was in there for more than six hours. They said there were no broken bones — just walk and give it time.

The hospital attendants wheeled me to Judy's car and carefully got me inside. When we drove in the front driveway, my neighbors, Paul and Dora Davis, and their son-in-law and Kim were waiting on the front porch. They had the lights on in the house and welcomed me with loving care and tenderness.

It took half an hour to get me to my bedroom with them helping me as I tried to walk. I almost blacked out by the time I got to my bedroom door, and they had to wheel a chair under me until I could move again. They finally lifted me onto the bed as carefully as possible. I always thought I could handle pain, but this was very different.

Because of the wrong evaluation in the emergency room, my days and nights were painful. I couldn't do anything for myself. Living alone, I had to have someone with me night and day for several weeks. Kim stayed the first night and day, and another granddaughter, Shereena, came from Portland for the next night and day. After that, different ones came to stay with me as they were needed. Jan Voris was with me for three days and nights. I had to be bathed, cleaned and was totally dependent for every little thing. My two granddaughters got a helpful education at the bedside of their grandma.

When I was finally able to slide off the bed to the commode and do a little for myself, I could be alone during the daytime. When the night person left, she would leave the front door unlocked so someone could come in and help at mealtimes. When I had Meals On Wheels, the volunteers could get in to bring my lunch. I'd have them bring the food into my bedroom and set it on a dining chair beside my bed, then I'd try to eat with my left hand.

After two weeks, I was still suffering so much and felt if I moved, I would break something. I called 911 again and went back to the ER. I told them my concern was in the lower back and pelvis area. They did more x-rays and told me, "No broken bones. There is nothing we can do." They advised me to see a specialist and gave me his number. I kept trying to call and was given the runaround. Finally, I got a voice and an appointment. I found out later their office had been closed for the month because the doctor had been on vacation. It was actually five or six weeks from the time I fell before it was possible to see the specialist and get the true evaluation. (My doctor, of course, wouldn't come to me but just prescribed more pain pills.)

The diagnosis was a broken pelvis in two places, three broken ribs and the right shoulder cracked from front to back. Even I could see it on the x-rays. I was able to get a little more action after that. The therapy people began coming, sometimes three at a time. I'd have to call them and say, "Please, no more than one at a time."

Each therapist had their own specialty. One evaluated me and set up the program. One was there to help me shower. Another one was to work on my arm. Still another was there to work on my

CHAPTER 17

legs and hip. There were a few others along the way. They were all super great, but it was really exhausting.

After a while, I could get around a bit with a walker. Jan, the one who stayed with me those days, had recently lost her 103-year-old mother and brought her walker for me to use. For a while before that, I could be put in a wheelchair and wheeled to the table to eat — with my left hand!

My friends (and seniors' pastor) Jim and Patsy Macauley brought a wheelchair from the church for me to use until I graduated to the walker. The walker was great progress and gave me hope for better times.

Later, I was able to get around some on the walker. My husband was thinking I was dead, and I just couldn't take it any longer. Very carefully, I slowly made my way to the car in the garage, got myself inside, turned the key on with my left hand through the steering wheel and backed the car out. I drove to the home where Lloyd was, got the walker out of the car and made it to the front door. One of the workers saw me coming and came to help.

When Lloyd saw me, he seemed to try to get it all together. Finally, he said, "Well, it's sure good to see someone from heaven."

"I'm not from heaven. I'm your wife, and I'm very much alive," I told him. He still studied about it. I questioned how much he really understood, but I'm sure it helped.

I didn't stay long that day. I was too weak and shaky. I made it home without incident, all left-handed and slow and easy. Then it was another month or two till I was able to go see him again. Altogether, I couldn't go visit him for about four months.

Seeing and hearing of so many who used drugs, alcohol and tobacco, I had criticized them because they wouldn't put themselves in a padded cell and get off the stuff. Now, because of my suffering and those several months taking Vicodin and Ibuprofen pain pills every four hours and less, then more and more of them, I realized what was happening and said, "That's enough." I began to cut back, then decided it was going too slow and it wasn't helping, so I quit! Actually, it was when the doctor prescribed more drugs for me to take that I stopped.

Before I had ever thought seriously of writing my book, I had made the statement, "I'm going to write a chapter in my book called When Grandma Went Cold Turkey." So, here it is.

MORETA: MY STORY

When Grandma Went Cold Turkey

After the days of therapy and trying to recover, I felt the time had come to stop the drugs. Those times were worse, I think, than all the pain I had suffered during the healing time of the fall.

Having to be alone most of that time made the nights unbearable. I still could hardly turn in bed, and my arm was in a sling (nearly all the time). I would freeze and burn up at the same time. I would slide to the edge of the bed and hang my feet over the side in cold water, trying to cool them.

With the electric blanket turned on high and held tightly around my shoulders and middle, I would chill and shake and burn. My body would itch and burn and even flake from the heat. There was twisting, moaning and literally crying for daylight to come. Maybe that would help. Nothing helped. And this didn't stop after a night or two. It lasted for a week or more. But, believe me, I'm glad I did it!

The recovery time took a full year for everything to heal completely. My shoulder was the slowest to mend, but I am as good as new. I can sling my arm around and lift it or do anything without pain. Oh, maybe I experience some 85-year-old pain, but not because of the fall.

Lloyd's Final Months

The earlier period of time, during which I hadn't been able to see my husband, he thought I was dead or had remarried. It must have been terrible times for him. After I could start seeing him again, he asked who I had married. "Then, who are you dating?"

I tried to explain. "Lloyd, ever since we have been married, I have not seen a man that I wanted. I wanted no one else — I just wanted to win you." Then emphatically, I declared, "I don't want nobody, and nobody wants me! Not even you."

He got real quiet. There was silence for a moment, then I started talking about something else. I realized I had lost his attention, but I kept telling him things about our kids or people he knew. After a long while, he slowly said, "Well, I want you." Man, I loved him at that moment more than I had for a long time! My sympathy almost got the better of me. He hadn't been saying things that sweet.

CHAPTER 17

Sometimes, he could be really alert. Ormel and Sandi came to see him as often as they could. Sandi would sit in a chair right against him with her arm around him, and Ormel knelt at his knees, holding his hands. Before leaving, they would always ask him to pray for them. He would pray his intelligent, vibrant blessings over them as clearly as at any time before. He could still pray.

However, there were times he could be funny. Once, when we were there, he was telling us that the place was making some changes. They would be having Sunday school, and he was the preacher.

"What will your first sermon be?" Sandi asked.

"Well, I'm going to preach on tithing," was his response.

Then he told of a fictitious time before when he had preached about tithing.

Then Sandi asked, "Dad, what happened after that? Did you see a difference?"

"Yep, I was no longer the pastor," he answered.

We usually tried not to laugh at him, but this was too good. We burst out laughing. He watched us for a second, then his big jelly belly began to bounce with us.

In the last few weeks, there wasn't much to smile about. He was falling so much, he couldn't walk and he became depressed.

He could always feed himself and liked his food. The cooks there were excellent, and Lloyd never lost his appetite until the last few days when he was shutting down. He could still stand enough to help get himself from the chair to the bed.

During this one day, I had been to see him, but after church on that Wednesday night, I stopped in to see him again. He was in his wheelchair in the living area. All was quiet, and not many were in the room. I talked to him and petted him. I tried to get him to kiss me, but there was no response. I'm sure he knew it was me, but he was hardly there.

The girls were ready to prepare him for bed, though they were in no hurry. I rubbed his back, arms and neck and kept talking to him. Finally, I told him that it was his bedtime, and I would go home and take a nap, too. I kissed him on the forehead and said, "Goodnight." I left about 9:30 p.m., and the girls started wheeling him to his room.

About a half hour after I got home, the phone rang. This is the story the girls told me the next day.

MORETA: MY STORY

Earlier that morning, he had pointed up and said, "I'm going home today, where I won't fall anymore."

When they started to take him from the wheelchair to put him into his bed, they lifted him up, but he went limp. They knew they had to move fast. They gave him a quick turn and pushed him onto his bed. They got him straightened out, covered him and made him comfortable.

They noticed how peaceful he looked. In that moment, he took one deep breath and relaxed. They knew he was gone. It was August 2, 2006.

However, the nurse was right there and called 911. The paramedics had come and were rushing him to Emergency when they called me and told me they would be gone by the time I could get there. So I went straight to Emergency.

I asked if I could see him. I spent some time with him — just him and me. But he wasn't there; he was already gone. It was another *alone time*.

After a while, the hospital chaplain came in. He was so wise and let me talk it out.

I told him that August was my month.

My parents had married August 22nd.

My brother's birthday was the 27th.

We had moved to Salem in August.

My first husband, Harry, and I were married August 31st.

Harry was buried the day before our seventh wedding anniversary — the 30th.

Lloyd's birthday would have been in a few days, August 18th.

We had married August 21st.

And now, Lloyd has died on August 2nd.

Talking more to the chaplain, I said, "Just a week ago, Lloyd had fallen and was in Emergency. It had seemed he might die at that time, but he had survived, and now it has happened."

The chaplain said, "He had to wait till August, didn't he?" He prayed with me, and you can't believe the peace that God gave.

They asked if I felt I could drive home alone, and I could. It was midnight.

My Praying

I'll copy this pretty much as I had written it.

CHAPTER 17

Lloyd was in the home with Alzheimer's. Such a hideous, torturous thing for any man to have to endure. It began when he went to the hospital for a knee replacement in 2004, almost two years ago.

On July 3, 2006, in the nighttime, I was praying and was so concerned about Lloyd's condition and whether this was going to continue on and on, maybe for years.

As I was seeking the Lord, I thought of the scripture: "The effectual, fervent prayer of a righteous person availeth much." (James 5:16)

In meditation, knowing that Satan doesn't care that we pray half-hearted prayers, think a prayer, call off names in prayer, go down my list day after day with repetitive words, walk around saying, "Yes, Lord, amen," moan, "uumm," drawl, "Thank You, Jesus." God hears our groaning. There are times we have to get fervent, loud, determined, bold and come against the powers of Satan and storm the gates of hell.

"Submit yourself therefore to God. Resist the devil and he will flee from you." (James 4:7)

This was the time to rise up with authority against Satan. I became vocal, loud and clear. He had harassed Lloyd and tortured his mind with fear, hallucinations, lies, evil thoughts, inner turmoil, torments, anger and more. Lloyd had been a proud man. Now he lived with embarrassment and degrading hurts.

Also, Satan put me on my bed for months. All of these two-plus years' worth of the torments and evils he had done to me were over!

Yes, I talked loud to the devil, letting him know this had to stop. This wasn't a conversation with the devil. I gave no place for him to talk back. I had the floor, and I kept it. I was demanding, determined and I took my authority in spiritual warfare until I felt all hell had heard me and all heaven had been listening. I prayed through!

Then praying at length in the Spirit, with peace and anointing, I prayed with joy, with laughter and in my heavenly language.

Afterward, I sat in my chair just loving and talking to the Father, the Son and the Holy Ghost. I prayed myself to a calm, trusting inner spirit. I was on believing ground.

Anything could happen. But I knew God was in control, and I knew it was alright.

MORETA: MY STORY

Remember, my main concern was, "Will Lloyd's condition continue on and on, maybe for years?" I had to have help.

As I sat in my chair just loving the Lord, I reached for my Bible, not to find an answer, but to read in my daily reading place. To my total surprise, in Genesis 41, the very first few words of the first verse were: "And it came to pass *at the end of two full years* ..." Those seven words stood out bold and clear. I knew it was for me. I began to weep and praise the Lord.

As I began to think about it, I didn't know if the two years would be at the time of him going into the hospital for the knee operation, the prognosis or the time we placed him in the home. But I didn't try to pin down any of those dates. It didn't even concern me. I knew the Lord had spoken, and He would do it all just right.

Feeling like I wanted the heavens to know that I could keep a secret, I told no one about what the Lord had given me. But I was comforted, and the time went fast.

A short time later, I began to find other scriptures that added to the first one. I picked up one of Pastor's sermon notes, and on the edge of the paper, I had written "Habakkuk 2:3," and beside it, I had scribbled, "Look it up. Meditate on it." I looked it up now.

"The vision is yet for an appointed time, but at the end it shall speak, and not lie: though it tarry, wait for it; because it will surely come, it will not tarry." How powerful is that!

Later, after all was over, at 4 a.m. as I was reading all the good things that the Lord had given me, I read Habakkuk 2:2. Listen to this!

"And the Lord answered me, and said, 'Write the vision, and make it plain.'"

As I was reading this at 4 a.m., I wrote, "So, here it is. Now, I'm going back to bed!"

A couple of weeks after his death, when I went back to Genesis 41:1, I hadn't remembered or even noticed the first few words: "And it came to pass."

God and His Word are so marvelous!

***

Lloyd's burial was Friday evening at 5.

It was a beautiful time of sharing things about him around the

CHAPTER 17

open casket at the cemetery. Most all the family was there, including Rhonda's husband, Paul, from Alaska and nieces and nephews and family from near and far.

There were laughter, tears, prayers and loving on each other as we honored Lloyd and our God for all His goodness to each one of us through the years. The service was an hour long. When it was done, our son, Verlon, said to the undertaker, "I'd like to close the casket." He carefully folded the satin cloths over his daddy's body, closed the lid and locked it. It was a touching moment.

Afterward, we all went to a restaurant to spend time together.

Ormel and Sandi spent the night with me. Early the next morning, I thought the phone rang. I quickly jumped up in my usual hurry, wondering, *Now what has happened? Emergency? He's fallen again?* Heavy, so heavy. Then I lay back down, realizing I was reliving the anxiety I had felt for so long. (The phone hadn't rung. I was dreaming.) After perhaps a few seconds, which seemed like minutes, I realized, "We buried him last night!" All of that extreme heaviness left me and never returned. I just lay there praising the Lord and thanking Him for Lloyd's beautiful homecoming. He hadn't suffered at the last. He just lay back, took one big breath and was gone.

The Memorial

His final service was 10 a.m. Tuesday morning in Salem at the People's Church, where we had attended since moving here in 1994.

Verlon, Melodee and their three, Lindsay, Courtnay and Brenton, came on Monday and stayed the night with me. It was so great to have them with me and to enjoy their youth and vibrancy.

Each son and daughter and their spouse and the grandsons and granddaughters shared memories and things about their daddy and grandpa. There were times of laughter and tears with pictures and stories of the past.

Pastor Erickson praised Lloyd and prayed. Then our children conducted the complete service, which lasted for an hour and a half.

Just now, I sat down and listened to the whole tape. I wish you could hear it. Several people told me it was the greatest funeral service they had ever been to.

MORETA: MY STORY

It was a beautiful celebration time about his life and his departure from this life.

Daughter, Judy, and her husband, Bob, did his total obituary as they told his story. They had visited with him on Sunday before he died on Wednesday. He was crying while they were there, and Judy asked, "Dad, are you sad?"

His answer was, "No, I'm just so happy." He asked them to pray that the Lord would take him home, "Where I can walk and not stumble."

Judy said, "We prayed and released him to go be with the Lord."

Bob ended their sharing time with, "His vital signs were strong, and there were no big physical problems, but God took him without pain, without struggle. He was crashing through the gates of heaven."

Ormel had prayed and released him, too, at his request. He had also asked me to pray that the Lord would take him. Verlon hadn't been privileged to be with him those last few days, but we were all in one mind about his going home.

Ormel also told of a time he came to see Dad after they had been to Indonesia and hadn't seen him for about six weeks. Dad looked up as he walked in and said, "Son, I guess you've heard that your mom is ruling the world now."

"Yes, Dad," Ormel said, "I've known that for a long time."

Another story Ormel told about his dad was when he went elk hunting with my brother, Admiral, and several other men. My husband wouldn't hunt on Sundays, and if at all possible, he went from the woods into town to church.

This particular time, Lloyd brought a shirt, suit and tie and drove into Elgin to attend church. When he got back to camp, the men were in from their early morning hunt. Some of them chided him for being so dressed up and going to church instead of the hunt.

Next morning, on his way out to the hunting area, Dad was having a little talk with the Lord and said, "Lord, this would sure be a good time for You to show these boys how You can honor them if they will put You first." That morning, Dad got his prize antlers. (Ormel brought out the big rack of horns that he had hidden behind the rail.) It was huge, and the people oohed and aahed, laughed and clapped long.

CHAPTER 17

Each of the grandchildren told of or showed their intentions in preparing for the ministry.

Verlon told of his dad's big hands and how he had used them to build in most of his pastorates. And how his own big hands were being used in the same way. In fact, when Verlon was born and I looked at his hands, I remarked, "Look at those big hands."

Young grandson, Brenton, when he and the girls were talking at the service, showed his hands and said, "Just like my grandpa's." He and his daddy are hard, fast workers, just like Dad was.

Verlon also told of his dad being a man of few words with several stories of how those few words had taught him in his growing-up years. "Three words at a time." But when he was preaching, he preached with power and anointing and knew where he was going. He was a student of the Word.

(Lloyd had told me that in Bible school they had taught him to "Get up. Speak up. And shut up!" That was his practice. When he preached, you didn't have to guess what he was saying. He thought it through, he made it clear, and you could feel it. But when he was through, he quit. He didn't ramble on.)

When the memorial was over, we greeted people in the lobby, and then the church had a scrumptious meal for our extended family in the dining area. Pastor Erickson came in with us for that time. That meant so much to us. Everyone was unbelievably wonderful during that healing time.

Thanks, People's Church, for all of it.

If all the poor of America would get into a church, be at every service, be sincere, be baptized, find their place of ministry and pay their tithe, there would be very few hungry people in this country. During times of sickness and grief, there's nothing better than a church group of caring people. These people have become *my family.* Our churches care. Our churches take care of their own. The Bible is the answer. Believe it and do something about it now! And, when we obey the Bible, God restores. He gives back. He heals, and He prospers His people when we learn to give and help others.

I Traveled

A couple of months before Lloyd died, I flew to Battle Creek, Michigan, for a family reunion with the Chapin family. Sandi had gotten a great price for our plane fare on the Internet. I questioned if I should go with Lloyd's condition and my brother in Bend not doing good. But I went for five nights. I stopped to see Lloyd on my way out and again on the way home. I drove to Portland and left my car in the parking lot at Motel 8, near the airport. They shuttled me to the airport at the right time, and when I got back late at night, they picked me up, and I stayed at the motel and drove home the next morning.

Ormel and Sandi had left earlier to go to Chad's in Nashville, then Chad came with them to Battle Creek. I changed planes in Chicago. They did, too, and we met there about the same time and went on together with the same arrangement coming back.

All four of us stayed together at Junior and Jackie's. Early on Sunday morning, June 10, I got a call. My dear brother, Orion, had died. We had been calling each day and knew the end was near. It still hit hard! It was so nice to have my son and his family with me to hold and comfort me. Ormel was preaching that morning and night in the church there in Battle Creek, and the day was busy with church and the large family gathering with those who had come from Arizona and other states. Some I had not seen for years, and some of the new ones, I had never seen. The next day, we were on our way home.

***

My brother, Orion Reid's, funeral was a beautiful time together. He had been a businessman in the Bend area for years and was well known. Flowers lined the large platform, three deep, wall to wall. He looked wonderful in the open casket. Our Christian funerals are not morbid, they're celebrations. However, his four lovely daughters, his grandchildren, his brother and I (his sister) and all who knew him miss him terribly. We hadn't been ready for him to go. His mind was still sharp as always, and he was lots of fun to be with. He was genuine! Then, of course, my Lloyd left us six weeks later.

***

Two weeks after Lloyd's passing, his dear friend, Vernon Klemin, died. I think he was in his late 90s. They had hunted

CHAPTER 17

together, camped together and preached together, and we had visited in each other's homes, eating, laughing, playing and enjoying a close friendship for many years. Now, it's just Anita and me. We get together often.

Hot Air Ballooning

My neighbors, Larry and Joyce, took me at 5 a.m. one morning in August to the fairgrounds in Albany to watch our other neighbors, Ron and Sandi, inflate their huge hot air balloon, alongside about 40 others. How exciting! Ron had taken up other paying passengers, and when he landed, we were right there to see it all. They had thought I would be too afraid to go, but Ron gingerly asked, "Would you like to go up?" I started climbing in. I couldn't believe I would ever get to do such a great thing. It was wonderful. We were in the air for 45 minutes, just above the houses and fields. Such a perfect morning and an unforgettable experience.

Ten Days in Bend

My grandson, Chad, brought his girlfriend, Teryn, from Nashville to meet the family and see beautiful Oregon where he had lived. I had driven to Bend the day before and was with the family to meet them when they flew into Redmond the last of August. I went with them to Mount Bachelor and a lot of places to show her the sights. Then we had a big outdoor celebration to announce the engagement with lots of friends and relatives. Verlon came from Seattle, too. After he put Teryn on the plane for Nashville, Chad had to fly to New Mexico to play for a concert. Then he flew back to Bend, and the four of us went to Paulina Lake, fishing for kokanee. That's a landlocked small salmon. That was the first time I had been fishing for too many years. That night, we cooked a glorious barbecue fish dinner at Ormel's. I was with them in Bend for 10 days.

August had been so busy after my husband's death, there wasn't much time to grieve. However, the family had been grieving for months before. It really had been *the long goodbye.* Between times of traveling, I worked on legal stuff and tying up the loose ends. I needed to get the yard in shape, clean house, take all Lloyd's clothes to the mission, handle the correspondence, choose and order the gravestone and many other things. Life had been difficult for a long time.

To Nashville

On October 14th, my grandson, Chad, and Teryn were married in Nashville, and I was there! It was so nice to meet her three pretty sisters, her mother and her dad, who had been a professional wrestler, Nikita Koloff, "The Russian Nightmare." Now, he is a preacher! They are fun loving people.

All the Chapin family was there. The ones who didn't stay with Chad in the home of Michael Tait (where Chad and another "DC Talk" band member lived) stayed together in an inn that had been reserved for us. Talk about an exciting, marvelous time! It was unbelievable. Michael calls me Grandma, and he's my "'nother grandson." He's a fun loving guy and treated us all royally.

Chad's brother, Lonnie, and Tiffany and her family were there from California.

His brother, Phil, and Kim and their girls, Kali and Kennedi, from Colorado were there and, of course, they were all in the wedding. His dad, Ormel, and her dad, Nikita, performed the wedding vows with lots of laughter.

Our granddaughter, Loreesa, and her husband, Bryan, from Arkansas came and were in the same inn where I stayed. It was so great to be in the same place with my kids and friends for those five days.

To California

My brother, Admiral, called me from Eugene, Oregon, and said, "We're leaving for Indio in a couple of days, and we think you need to go with us." (They go each winter for about five months.)

"You know, I've only been home for about 10 days," I said.

"Yeah, I know that," he replied, "but you need to go again." He explained that they were taking two cars, and I could ride with Marie, and she wouldn't have to go alone.

When I was a kid, my dad used to tell me, "Sis, all I hear is 'go, go, go.' When anyone comes to the door and says, 'Let's go,' you say, 'Wait till I get my coat' and you're gone." I guess I'm still about the same way.

CHAPTER 17

The next morning, I called my brother back and said, "I'll be there."

The early morning of November 1, 2006, I left my car in their driveway, and we left for Indio. We had a great day, but there was stormy weather all the way until we stopped beyond Sacramento for the night. The next morning, the sun came up, and it was clear the rest of the way.

What a wonderful time in that beautiful, warm place. Their condo was on a little lake that had a swimming area with ducks and geese all around. I was meeting their friends and seeing ones I knew, also.

The swimming, exercising, attending church, eating at different places, shopping and keeping busy was what I needed. Plus, lots of naps! I was there for three weeks and loved it all. It was so nice for them to put up with me for so long.

My grandson, Lonnie, and Tiffany live in Fullerton, so the day before Thanksgiving, my brother, Admiral, and his friend Don Dockter drove me to Lonnie's for the holiday. Admiral and Don's wives, Marie and Nadine, stayed home to prepare for the big church feed in Indio the next day.

My grandson, Phil, and his family were at Lonnie's, too. Phil had preached nearby on the weekend and would also enjoy the holiday with us.

Tiffany's parents, Greg and Roxanne Hickman, were pastors in Fullerton, and Lonnie was on staff with them. We had Thanksgiving dinner at their house. I stayed with the parents those two nights. It was a private room and "a better bed for Grandma." We had great food and a super time all together.

The day after Thanksgiving, Phil brought me home to Salem by way of the Sequoia National Park. Some of the huge trees were possibly more than 4,000 years old. It was really special to spend those two days with Phil, Kim and the two great-grand ones, Kali and Kennedi, in their luxury van.

Thanks so much, Phil and Kim, for bringing me home.

***

After some months, I had cataracts removed from both eyes. It was a successful operation. This poem tells you my thoughts after the first eye was done. What a discovery!

MORETA: MY STORY

My Eye Is Fixed

My eyesight was wacky, and it was hard to see.
I went for that eye operation.
The doctor was greater than I thought he could be.
He was young, but with real dedication.

My neighbors were there to pilot me home.
I was treated like royalty, with class.
I went out with a smile and a patch on one eye,
And the hope to see better at last.
In just a few days when I looked all around,
I couldn't believe it was so.
Not only the colors and details I saw,
'Twas the other things that shocked me. Oh, no!

When I looked in the mirror and saw what I saw,
What others were seeing all along.
The wrinkles, the splotches, the uglies, oh, my!
I thought I had looked alright, boy, was I wrong!

When I finished my shower, stuck my head out the door,
That wrinkled old face was watching me straight in the eyes.
I finally stepped out and glanced at her once more.
I couldn't believe her look of surprise.

Her body looked worse than mine ever had.
It really was something to see.
I turned my head and looked at her no more.
I was glad it was her, and not me.

I wore my dark glasses everywhere that I went.
I thought I looked better that way.
Then suddenly I realized as I saw through the dark
That others were still seeing me plain as the day.

A new discovery when friends came to my door,
And I hate to confess this is true.
But I could see on your face many wrinkles like mine
And I felt sort of sorry for you.

Chapter 17

That didn't help much when I looked back at myself.
I'm honestly trying to cope.
It's hard to believe I grew old overnight.
And to be young again, I've lost hope.

Moreta Fosner

CHAPTER 18

Nope! Not Yet!

My daughter-in-law, Sandi, was writing memoirs for her boys and had asked me to write about their grandpa, Harry. About the same time, my sister-in-law, Marie, had asked me to write some things about our early family.

Since I had been puny with the flu and was cooped up and couldn't get out, I began writing about my life. That was the beginning of February 2007, and once I started writing my story, I came to a place of no return and had to keep going.

In April of that year, I enrolled in writing classes at the Senior Center in Salem. I could never have made it without those classes. The instructor, LaVerne Miles, was exactly what I needed. She was always helpful to the ones who needed the most help, namely me. The last of the year, she married one of her students, J.C. Winegardner. I thought, *Oh, no! He'll want her to quit teaching and travel.* I was wrong, and we all love her man, Caryl. I'm sure his smile won her over. When he walks into the room with that smile, the whole atmosphere is brighter.

Then after a month or so, my son, Ormel, came and read some of my writings and took me to town to purchase a new computer and printer.

Ormel and Sandi were my greatest encouragers and helpers in writing this book. I called on him many times, day or night, to get me out of a jam when I had troubles with the computer.

I hadn't even wanted to learn the computer, but it had to be. My typewriter had quit working and had gone to the garbage, and I was writing my story with pen and paper. This 85 year old learning to write, going to writing classes every Wednesday and learning the computer — how impossible has that been! I was plain cuckoo to attempt such a thing. For a while, I believed that the computer must be a generational curse. After a rather high learning curve, I gradually began to "get it" just enough to start this book right. Though it was a rough start, I'm sure glad it didn't all have to be written by hand.

CHAPTER 18

Gladly, I give my thanksgiving, love, honor and allegiance to the Father, the Son and the Holy Spirit whom I called upon many times with fasting, prayers and tears.

Hitherto has the Lord helped me. (1 Samuel 7:12)

I haven't given you many "Don'ts" in this book, so let me give you a few now. Don't do as I did in my young, foolish years. Or my older, stupid acts … believe me! Every wrong that I did, every unwise, unholy or unbelievable action that I performed, I have paid for them many times over. Please profit from my mistakes and don't suffer embarrassment for the next 30, 40, 50 years. Search the scriptures … ask your mama, ask your grandmama … we love to give advice! Take it!

So now, with a full year of hibernating and my social life nothing but funerals, potlucks and anniversaries, I am writing the last page of my book, and it feels good to quit for a while.

I have instructed each of my children that if I die before the rapture, please don't make my funeral too much of a celebration. When Pastor Hootman died, the family asked Ormel and Sandi to do the music and requested, "Don't let it be like a funeral. Make it a celebration of his entrance into heaven."

The congregation sang happy choruses and clapped their hands, and that's fine. I want that at my last rites, but, please, have somebody cry just a little! Even if you have to hire mourners.

I've also impressed seriously on each of my kids, "Don't cremate me. I don't want to burn in this life, or the next."

If anybody wants to know, I feel like the old man who was asked, "Have you lived here all your life?"

To which he responded, "Nope! Not yet!"

GOOD CATCH PUBLISHING

www.goodcatchpublishing.com

To contact Moreta
or to order additional copies,
please send an email to
mrcfoz@comcast.net